EXPLORING
RELIGIOUS EDUCATION

Catholic Religious Education
in an Intercultural Europe

Edited by
Patricia Kieran & Anne Hession

VERITAS

First published 2008 by
Veritas Publications
7/8 Lower Abbey Street
Dublin 1
Ireland
Email publications@veritas.ie
Website www.veritas.ie

ISBN 978 1 84730 132 1

10 9 8 7 6 5 4 3 2 1

Extracts from W.B. Yeats' 'The Lake Isle of Innisfree' and 'Among School Children'
appear courtesy of A.P. Watts Literary Agency.

Designed by Vivienne Adu-Boahen
Printed in the Republic of Ireland by ColourBooks Ltd, Dublin

Veritas books are printed on paper made from the wood pulp of managed forests. For every tree
felled, at least one tree is planted, thereby renewing natural resources.

In memory and appreciation of Fiona McSorley

For Anne's two great loves: Donal and beautiful Isabelle

TABLE OF CONTENTS

ABBREVIATIONS

AGCE: Advanced General Certificate in Education

ARE: Adult Religious Education

ARCIC: Anglican-Roman Catholic International Commission

AG: *Ad Gentes*

BJRE: British Journal of Religious Education

CAI: Catechetical Association of Ireland

CCC: *Catechism of the Catholic Church* (John Paul II, 1992)

CCMS: Council for Catholic Maintained Schools

CDF: Congregation for the Doctrine of the Faith

CEC: Scottish Catholic Education Commission

CPD: Continuing Professional Development

CSTTM: *The Catholic School on the Threshold of the Third Millennium* (Congregation for Catholic Education, 1997)

DES: Department of Education and Science

DM: *Dialogue and Mission* (1984)

DMU: Diversity for Mutual Understanding

DP: *Dialogue and Proclamation* (1991)

DV: *Dei Verbum* The Dogmatic Constitution on Divine Revelation (Vatican II, 1965)

DH: *Dignitatis Humanae* Declaration on Religious Freedom (Vatican II, 1965)

GCD: *General Catechetical Directory* (Congregation for the Clergy, 1971)

GDC: *General Directory for Catechesis* (Congregation for the Clergy, 1997)

GIFT: Growing in Faith Together

GS: *Gaudium et spes* The Pastoral Constitution on the Church in the Modern World (Vatican II, 1965)

GE: *Gravissimum Educationis* Declaration on Christian Education (Vatican II, 1965)

ICE: Intercultural Education

JB: Jerusalem Bible

LCS: *Lay Catholics in Schools: Witnesses to Faith* (1982)

LG:. *Lumen Gentium* The Dogmatic Constitution on the Church (Vatican II, 1965)

LTS: Learning and Teaching Scotland, the Scottish Government's advisory body on the curriculum

MM: *Mater et Magistra* Encyclical on Christianity and Social Progress (John XXIII, 1961).

NA: *Nostra Aetate* Declarationon the relation of the Church to Non-Christian Religions (Vatican II, 1965)

NCCA: National Council for Curriculum and Assessment

NI: Northern Ireland

NJB: New Jerusalem Bible

NRSV: New Revised Standard Version

NT: New Testament

OT: Old Testament

OWR: Other World Religions

PCPCU: Pontifical Council for Promoting Christian Unity

PREP: Primary Religious Education Programme

QCA: Qualifications and Curriculum Authority

RCIA: Rite of Christian Initiation of Adults

RDECS: *The Religious Dimension of Education in a Catholic School* (1988)

RE: Religious Education

RSV: Revised Standard Version of the Bible

SACRE: Standing Advisory Council on Religious Education

SCES: Scottish Catholic Education Service

SEED: Scottish Executive Education Department

SRS: *Sollicitudo Rei Socialis* (John Paul II, 1987)

SPCU: Secretariat for Promoting Christian Unity

UR: *Unitatis Redintegratio:* Decree on Ecumenism

VS: *Veritatis Splendor:* The Splendour of Truth (John Paul II, 1993).

ACKNOWLEDGEMENTS

Patricia: In particular I would like to acknowledge Professor Teresa O'Doherty, Dean of Education at Mary Immaculate College, for her continued academic and professional support in this project. Professor Claire Lyons, Head of the Department of Learning, Society, and Religious Education has given constant encouragement and valuable advice. Dr Tony Lyons has always been willing to share his expertise in the history of Education in Ireland. I would like to thank Bishop Michael Smith for his support during my undergraduate and postgraduate studies in Theology and Religious Education. The Research Office at Mary Immaculate College awarded SEED funding which enabled me to spend time researching and writing a chapter and for this I am truly thankful. Mgr Dermot Lane has always been an inspiring guide and along with Dr Joseph Laishley of Heythrop College, University of London, has given impetus to my desire to engage in research in Theology and Religious Education. Gratitude is due to colleagues in Mary Immaculate College who provide an exciting forum for the exchange of ideas especially Dr Eileen Lenihan, Dr Daniel O'Connell, Fr Michael Wall, Dr Paddy Connolly, Professor Eamonn Conway, Dr Jessie Rodgers, Dr Eugene Duffy and Dr Rik Van Nieuwenhoven. I am grateful to Bishop Donal Murray who has consistently nurtured the development of Catholic Religious Education in Ireland. Finally I wish to thank my family who put Religious Education in context on a daily basis.

Anne: I would like to acknowledge and thank my colleague, Dr Raymond Topley, Head of the Department of Religious Studies and Religious Education at St Patrick's College who provided wonderful support, advice and encouragement through out the project. I would also like to thank Dr Joseph McCann CM for his constant support through my undergraduate and postgraduate studies and through all the projects I undertake.

Anne and Patricia wish to acknowledge the continuing love and support of their families:

Martin and Ena Hession; Mary, James, Sarah-Kate and baby James O' Donovan; Catriona, Ger and Grace McNally; Helena and Columba McGarvey; Donal and Isabelle Casey.

Mary (Cregan) Kieran, Anne Mc Carthy, Michael Kieran, Jim Kieran, Margaret Mc Keown, Mary Kieran, Brigid Kieran, John McDonagh and John, Brigid, Patrick, Michael and Meabh Kieran-McDonagh.

We wish to acknowledge and thank our editorial team at Veritas, Caitriona Clarke, Ruth Kennedy and Linda Longmore, for their professional and detailed editorial work. Our final word of thanks goes to a leading light in Catholic Religious Education, Maura Hyland.

Feast of Saint Anne, 26 July 2008.

BIOGRAPHICAL NOTES

Gareth Byrne is Head of the School of Education and lectures in Religious Education at the Mater Dei Institute of Education, a College of Dublin City University. His teaching and research work is focused on Primary and Post-Primary Religious Education and on Faith Development for all age groups. He conducted national research throughout Ireland, North and South, in 2005/6, providing the Irish Catholic Bishops' Conference with a draft National Directory for Catechesis. As well as contributing various articles, he is author of *Religious Education Renewed: An Overview of Developments in Post-Primary Religious Education* (Veritas, 2005) and co-editor with Raymond Topley of *Nurturing Children's Religious Imagination: The Challenge of Primary Religious Education Today* (Veritas, 2004). He is a priest of Dublin diocese and Parish Chaplain in St Gabriel's Parish, Dollymount.

Roisín Coll is a lecturer in Religious Education in the Faculty of Education at the University of Glasgow. Her teaching responsibilities include coordinating or implementing a variety of Religious Education programmes for initial teacher education courses. Her research interests include the faith development of Catholic teachers, the history of Catholic education in Scotland, the professional development of Catholic teachers and faith-school leadership. Her most recent publications include 'Student teachers' perception of their role as Catholic educators' in the *European Journal of Teacher Education* (2007) and 'The struggle for the soul: implications for the identity of Catholic teachers' in the *Australian Journal of Religious Education* (2007). Roisín has been a lay collaborator with the Congregation of the Most Holy Redeemer (The Redemptorists) for nineteen years and is currently Youth-Ministry Coordinator for the London Province.

Robert A. Davis is Head of Department of Religious Education in the University of Glasgow. He has written and broadcast widely on literature, myth and religion, including studies of Richard Wagner and Walter Benjamin. He has taught and written on Catholic education, Religious Education and the philosophy of education. He has also edited two volumes in the Carcanet Collected Works of Robert Graves – *Hebrew Myths* (2005) and *King Jesus* and *My Head! My Head!* (2006). He is currently completing a critical history of the English lullaby and a new intellectual biography of the radical educator Robert Owen for the Continuum Library of Educational Thought.

Patrick M. Devitt is a priest of the Dublin diocese, and Parish Chaplain in St Agatha's. He is a lecturer in Education/ Religious Education at the Mater Dei Institute of Education, Dublin. Former editor of *The Irish Catechist*, the journal of the CAI, 1980–85, he is also an elected member of *L'Equipe Européene de Catéchèse*. He was a member of the Steering Committee for International Consultations on Adult Religious Education, 1995–2005. He is author of *Willingly to School: Religious Education as an Examination Subject* (Veritas, 2000) the first book in the *Into the Classroom* series, which he edited along with Eoin Cassidy.

Fiona Dineen is a primary school teacher in Limerick City. She has recently engaged in post-graduate research in the areas of Music Education and Religious Education. She lectures in Religious Education in Mary Immaculate College, Limerick. Areas of particular interest include sacramental preparation, music in Religious Education and children's liturgy.

Thomas H. Groome is Professor of Theology and Religious Education at Boston College and Director of BC's Institute of Religious Education and Pastoral Ministry. He has written numerous books and articles on the subject of Religious Education. Some of his best known works are *Christian Religious Education* (1980) (Jossey-Bass, 1999), *Sharing Faith* (1991) (Wipf and Stock, 1998), *Educating for Life* (Thomas More, 1998), and *What Makes us Catholic: Eight Gifts for Life* (Harper San Francisco, 2002).

Sharon Haughey is Senior Lecturer in the Department of Religious Studies at Saint Mary's University College, Belfast, where she teaches in the areas of Religious Education and Church History. She is a member of the Irish Episcopal Commission for Catechetics and is secretary of *Le Chéile – A Catholic Ethos Journal*. She has published articles on Special Educational Needs and Bereavement in Schools.

Anne Hession is a lecturer in Religious Education at St Patrick's College, Dublin, a linked college of Dublin City University. Her fields of academic research are in the Religious Education of children and the spirituality of children. She is co-author with Patricia Kieran of *Children, Catholicism and Religious Education* (Veritas, 2005). She is co-editor with Patricia Kieran of *Exploring Theology: Making Sense of the Catholic Tradition* (Veritas, 2007).

Ed Hone is a Redemptorist priest based in Edinburgh, where he is leader of a Mission Development community in St Patrick's parish. The community seeks new and creative approaches to ministry and evangelisation. He has over twenty years pastoral experience working with children, young people and adults. Ed is an Associate Tutor at Glasgow University and lectures part-time on preaching and presentation in Ushaw Seminary, Durham.

Patricia Kieran is a British Foreign and Commonwealth Office Chevening Scholar who has taught Theology and Religious Education in the UK. She currently teaches Religious Education at Mary Immaculate College, University of Limerick. She is co-author with Anne Hession of *Children, Catholicism and Religious Education* (Veritas, 2005) and co-editor with Anne Hession of *Exploring Theology: Making Sense of the Catholic Tradition* (Veritas, 2007). She has published chapters and articles on the subject of Catholic Education, Roman Catholic Modernism, gender and inter-Religious Education. She is currently researching her forthcoming book on *World Religions in Ireland*.

Dermot A. Lane is President of Mater Dei Institute of Education, Dublin City University and a priest of the Dublin diocese serving in the parish of Balally. He is author of numerous works including *The Experience of God: An Invitation to do Theology*, revised and expanded, (Veritas/Paulist Press, 2003) and *Keeping Hope Alive: Stirrings in Christian Theology* (Gill and Macmillan/Paulist Press, 1996/2005) and editor with Breandan Leahy of *Vatican II: Historical and Theological Perspectives*, (Veritas, 2006).

Anne Looney is Chief Executive of the National Council for Curriculum and Assessment, Dublin. A former teacher of Religious Education, she led the development of Religious Education syllabuses for post-primary schools and examinations in Ireland in the 1990s. She has published on curriculum and assessment policy, on religious and civic education and school ethos. She is a member of the editorial board of Irish Educational Studies, and President of the Consortium of Institutions for Development and Research in Education in Europe (CIDREE).

Joseph McCann CM is the former Head of Religious Studies and Religious Education in St Patrick's College, Drumcondra and is currently administering the Management in Community and Voluntary Services Programme in All Hallows College. He is the author of *Church and Organisation: A Theological and Sociological Enquiry* (University of Scranton, 1993), editor of *Religion and Science, Education, Ethics and Public Policy* (St Patrick's College, 2003), and has contributed chapters and articles to religious, educational and administration books and journals. He is co-author, with Fachtna McCarthy, of *Religion and Science – Into the Classroom* (Veritas, 2003) and *Religion and Science – Faith Seeking Understanding* (Veritas, 2006).

Andrew G. McGrady is the Director of Mater Dei Institute of Education, Dublin. He has participated in a number of projects at a national and European level relating to the Catholic school and the religious dimension of education. He is co-editor of the *International Handbook on the Religious, Spiritual and Moral Dimensions of Education* (Springer, 2007) and author of 'The Religious Dimension of Education at the Start of the Third Millennium', in *From Present to Future*, edited by E. Woulfe and J. Cassin (Veritas, 2006).

Maeve Mahon is Diocesan Advisor for Religious Education in Primary Schools in the Diocese of Kildare and Leighlin. She is co-author with Martin Delaney of *Do This in Memory A parish-based sacramental preparation programme for First Eucharist* (Veritas, 2005). Her latest publication, co-authored with Julie Kavanagh, is *A Welcome for your Child: A Guide to Baptism for Parents* (Veritas, 2008).

Amalee Meehan is an experienced teacher, author and researcher. She is on leave from her teaching position with Colaiste Iognaid, Galway, and is currently Faith Development Coordinator with CEIST: Catholic Education Irish Schools Trust. Amalee has completed a Ph.D in Theology and Education at Boston College where her doctoral dissertation focused on 'Thriving or Surviving: Reclaiming Ignatian spirituality as a resource for sustaining teachers today'. Her recent publications include 'Partners in Ministry: The Role of Women in Jesuit Education', *America*, Vol. 198, No. 16, 12 May 2008, and 'Bring Them Home: A Role for Catholic Schools in Ireland Today', *The Furrow*, April 2008.

Vince Murray hails from Co. Down in Northern Ireland. He is Director of Religious Education Programmes at St Angela's College, Sligo, where he is involved in Initial Teacher Education and Continuing Professional Development of post-primary teachers of Religious Education. Arising out of his experiences of teaching Religious Education in Zambia and Birmingham, UK, he is committed to exploring the challenges to and opportunities for Religious Education within contexts characterised by diversity.

Anne M. O'Leary, PBVM, is Assistant Professor of New Testament at St Mary's University, San Antonio, Texas. She is author of *Matthew's Judaization of Mark* (Continuum/T&T Clark, 2006) as well as several articles. She has lectured in the areas of Sacred Scripture and Spirituality, directed retreats and facilitated Ignatian Communal Discernment with groups in several countries – Canada, England, Ghana, Israel, Italy, Pakistan, the Philippines, Turkey, New Zealand and Wales – as well as in her home country, Ireland.

Jane E. Regan is Associate Professor of Theology and Religious Education at Boston College. Her research and teaching focus primarily on adult faith formation. She also serves as a consultant on the local and national levels to the project of effective adult faith formation. She is author of *Gathering Together: First Celebrations of Reconciliation and Eucharist* (Loyola Press, 2004) and *Toward an Adult Church: A Vision of Faith Formation* (Loyola Press, 2002).

David Roberts is a priest of the Diocese of Shrewsbury and is the Episcopal Vicar for Education and Formation. He is the Vice-Chair of the National Board of Religious Inspectors and Advisors and Secretary to the Department for Evangelisation and Catechesis of the Bishops' Conference of England and Wales.

Bert Roebben is Professor of Religious Education at the Institute of Catholic Theology at Dortmund University, Germany. He is currently president of the Dutch Association for Professors of Religious Education, a member of the Board of the Association of Religious Education in the United States and a member of the Board of the International Association for the Study of Youth Ministry in the United Kingdom. His fields of interest are: fundamental practical theology, moral and religious education, inter-religious learning, youth cultures and theology. His latest publications include: *Bewogenheid in beweging. Een visie op de spiritualiteit van een christelijke school* [On the spiritual project of religiously affiliated schools] (Brussels, 2003) and *En Godsdienstpedagogiek van de hoop. Grondlijnen voor religieuze vorming* [On Religious Education and hope] (Leuven, 2007).

Maurice Ryan is a Senior Lecturer in the School of Religious Education at Australian Catholic University, McAuley Campus in Brisbane. His areas of research and teaching interest are the history of Catholic schooling and the theory and practice of Religious Education in Catholic schools. His recent publications include *A Common Search: The History and Forms of Religious Education in Catholic Schools* (Lumino Press, 2007) and the *LearningLinks* series of classroom teaching and learning resources (Lumino Press, 2008).

Peter Schreiner is an educational researcher at the Comenius-Institut in Münster/Germany. This is a Protestant Centre for Research and Development in Education. He is President of the Inter-European Commission on Church and School (ICCS) and moderator of the Coordinating Group for Religion in Education in Europe (CoGREE). He has published widely in the area of Religious Education in Europe.

John Sullivan is Professor of Christian Education in the Theology & Religious Studies department at Liverpool Hope University. He teaches undergraduate and Master's classes and supervises doctoral research in Catholic Studies and in Christian Education. He has many publications (in the UK, Ireland, USA, Australia and Europe) in the area of religion and education, including *Catholic Schools in Contention* (Veritas, 2000), *Catholic Education: Distinctive and Inclusive* (Kluwer Academic Press, 2001), *The Idea of a Christian University* (co-edited, Paternoster, 2005), *Dancing on the Edge: Chaplaincy, Church & Higher Education* (co-edited, Matthew James Publishers, 2007) and more than sixty-five other chapters and articles.

Raymond Topley is Head of the Department of Religious Studies and Religious Education, St Patrick's College, Drumcondra, a college of Dublin City University. His particular interests are in Religious Education methodology and liturgical studies. He is a Fellow of the Lonergan Institute, Boston College and his recent research has focused on the implications of Bernard Lonergan's cognitional theory for Religious Education. His publications include *Nurturing Childrens' Religious Imagination: The Challenge of Primary Religious Education Today* (Veritas, 2004), which was co-edited with Gareth Byrne.

INTRODUCTION

The author and former French politician, André Malraux (1901–1976), suggested that the twenty-first century would be the century of religion. If the first decade of the new millennium is anything to go by he might have been right. In Europe one can discern a slight shift of focus, a change of mood, a hint of renewed interest in the role played by religion in social institutions. Tony Blair recently suggested that 'Religious faith will be of the same significance to the twenty-first century as political ideology was to the twentieth century. In an era of globalisation, there is nothing more important than getting people of different faiths and cultures to understand each other better and live in peace and mutual respect, and to give faith itself its proper place in the future.'[1] Indeed part of the recent emphasis on religion in Europe involves the perception that religion is no longer a private issue. The marriage of religious and political extremism which gave rise to 9/11, the Madrid (2004) and London bombings (2005), as well as other atrocities, has placed religion centre stage, unfortunately for all the wrong reasons. These horiffic acts resulted in the rise of Islamophobia allied to the perception of religion as being inextricably linked to violence, intolerance and hatred. Many concluded that religion contributes to social conflict and potentially inhibits adherents from integrating into society.[2] Indeed it is estimated that religion was 'a contributory cause in more than half of the 115 armed conflicts which occurred between 1989 and 2001'.[3]

In such a climate, European governments began to appreciate that at a political and legislative level they had to take religion seriously. That said, a greater appreciation of religion's role in Europe is not simply a knee-jerk reaction to unprecedented acts of violence. Just as a mixture of religious and political fundamentalism has the potential to motivate believers to engage in horrendous evil and unspeakable violence, religious faith is also capable of promoting the values of respect, justice and compassion. Within Europe, one can see the beginnings of an appreciation of religion as a powerful, social, cultural and indeed political force for good. Inter-faith cooperation and inter-religious dialogue have huge potential to contribute to conflict resolution within Europe. Furthermore, shared conversation between secular and religious groups can lead to open-mindedness and respect. For religious traditions, with their emphasis on shared values, social responsibility and the common good, have something very positive to offer Europe.

Many countries have begun to debate the role of religious and secular worldviews in shaping their societies. For instance religious freedom is one of the fundamental principles underlying the Italian Government's *Charter of Values for Citizenship* (2007). In France, President Sarkozy has shocked many secularists with his repeated emphasis on religion as a significant factor in shaping a society's morals and attitudes. In 2007, in an open letter to all those involved in education, he questioned and some would say undermined, France's ancient secular tradition by suggesting that it was inappropriate to leave religion at the door of the school.[4] In 2008, Tony Blair, a recent convert to Catholicism, launched a Faith Foundation with the aim of promoting inter-religious collaboration and the advancement of faith as an alternative to conflict, in the modern world.[5] The former prime minister currently designs courses at Yale University which seek to promote religion as a force of good as opposed to conflict in the world. Speaking on the eve of the launch of his Foundation, Blair stated: 'In the end, this will be what I dedicate a very large part of my life to'. It must be remembered that not all current or ex-European leaders have placed such emphasis on religion although countries such as Norway, England, Ireland and Switzerland, have engaged in recent debates about the role of religion in society and in particular in their educational systems.

Significant developments indicate that religion and Religious Education are not marginal to social, legislative and educational endeavours at a European level. Indeed new initiatives place Religious Education firmly on the European stage. In 2002, the Council of Europe focused on the religious dimension of Intercultural Education (ICE) and posited that inter-Religious Education might help to contribute a solution to intercultural problems. In 2003, European Education Ministers made ICE, including its religious dimension, a priority for further work. At a conference of the Coordinating Group for Religion in Education in Europe (CoGREE) in November 2005, the EU Commission for Education, Culture and Multilingualism, Jan Figel', spoke of the 'close relationship between education and religious and moral values' as being crucial for the future of Europe. In 2007, the Council of Europe published a reference book for teachers on religious diversity in Europe.[6] Furthermore, in a historic move, the European Commission supported research into religion in education. This emphasis on religion and education at a European level has resulted in an increased number of conferences, publications, networks and research activities focusing on the area of Religious Education. Significant networks such as Teaching Religion in a Multicultural European Society (TRES), the European Community project on Religious Education, Dialogue and Conflict, and The European Network for Religious Education through Contextual Approaches (ENRECA), have initiated large scale research into documenting and improving the teaching of religion across Europe.[7] A further indicator of the increasing profile of Religious Education can be seen in the recently established inaugural chair in Religious Education, in Oxford University.[8]

These are interesting times for religion and, by implication, for everyone involved in education in, for and about religion. This book arises out of an attempt to read 'the signs of the times', as they impact on Catholic Religious Education and as it, in turn, shapes them. With great change comes great challenge. Religious Education is contextual as it is shaped by a specific history and context. One of the major challenges facing European citizens is the challenge of living in an intercultural and inter-religious situation. Bert Roebben observes that 'dialogue with other beliefs takes place, not only in the depth of time (intergenerational), but also in the breath of space (intercultural) and in the perspective of hope for the world (global)'.[9] This book attempts to examine the contours of a contextual Catholic Religious Education that takes this historical time, this specific intercultural European context and these particular challenges seriously. For there is no doubt that the role of religion is being transformed in a society that is characterised by a plurality of religious and non-religious worldviews.

Within the world of Catholic Religious Education there is a renewed sense of the need to return to basics, to classical sources and foundational themes, in order to address the new challenges posed by a plural and intercultural society. In itself, this is unsurprising. A situation of radical religious pluralism, of competing secular and religious worldviews, challenges people to reposition themselves within their new frame of reference. In such a climate, individuals search for a new direction and are often sustained by the classical sources and texts of their own faith tradition, which are meaningful for every generation of believers. This involves neither a disengagement and retreat from the contemporary intercultural context nor a reactionary rejection of new voices and perspectives. It simply means that new horizons offering challenging new questions result in the need to return to one's own faith tradition as a source of guidance and nourishment. This is part of a dialectical process of engagement with the intercultural world and involves a renewal of self which enables respectful, inclusive dialogue to occur.

This book attempts to respond to the pressing need for discernment on how Catholic Religious Education has developed a discourse around inclusion and respect for otherness while simultaneously recognising the distinctive challenges and identity of the Catholic faith tradition. Scripture, tradition and Church teaching are foundations to which Catholics return as they re-source their relationships and self-understanding in a world of pluralism. Classical texts and themes in Religious Education, not all of them dealt with in this book, sustain and nourish the religious educator who struggles with issues of identity, direction and method in an exciting new intercultural environment. Texts such as the *General Directory for Catechesis* (1997), *The Catechism of the Catholic Church* (1992), National Catechetical Directories, key Vatican II constitutions as well as official Church documents on Religious Education, to mention but a few, offer support and guidance.[10] It is beyond the remit of this book to deal with all of these texts however Section Two presents selected foundational documents and texts which offer assistance.

New directions in Catholic Religious Education are manifest in a variety of ways. For example, in Ireland, in the last decade, Catholic Religious Education has witnessed a burst of energy and injection of activity surrounding the definition of what is specifically Catholic about the ethos of a school; the role of all those involved in the school community (the Patron, Trustees, Boards of Management, Teachers, Parents, Children); the generation of a new syllabus for primary schools and guidelines on post-primary syllabi; the establishment of a National Catechetical Office and designated Catechetical Sunday; as well as the generation of a draft national directory for Catechesis.[11] Such a flurry of activity raises the question of whether Ireland's new intercultural and plural context has prompted Catholics into desiring redefinition, reconfiguration and renewal. There is a realisation that Catholic education in general and Religious Education in particular, is not something that happens automatically and that it can not be taken for granted.

In Catholic schools, the encounter with the religious and secular other not only invites recognition and respect for the distinctiveness of the (non-)religious other, it also forces us to re-evaluate and re-appreciate our own religious tradition. Section One of the book acknowledges that issues of origin, tradition and identity are deeply relevant for contemporary Catholic Religious Education in an intercultural context. Indeed a post-modern emphasis on plurality and competing worldviews raises issues of identity and belonging in a striking manner. For Catholic religious educators the plurality of religious and non-religious world views should not be perceived as threats to be avoided, an unknown to be ignored or a context from which they must retreat. On the contrary, the reality of intercultural and inter-religious life in contemporary Europe provides an exciting new context within which Catholic religious educators are invited to engage so that they can reclaim the Catholic faith heritage, witness to the Catholic faith tradition and to relate and translate it anew in this new era. This is a challenging task, as those who are engaged in teaching and learning testify. If Catholic religious educators are unclear about who they are, where they have come from and what their task is, then they are vulnerable to being confused, ineffective and overwhelmed.

The four chapters in Section One of the book outline key issues involved in understanding Catholic education. Chapter One explores a Catholic philosophy of education while chapter two locates Catholic education as lifelong learning in home, school and other learning environments. Chapter three explores the Catechumenate as a paradigm for all catechesis and in chapter four a distinctive Ignatian spirituality of teaching and learning is outlined. Section Two explores key sources of Catholic theology and Religious Education (scripture, tradition and Church teaching), which provide real insight and help in discerning a pathway through the complicated maze of post-modern life. The first chapter in this section focuses on using the Bible, as a normative and foundational source of Christian faith, in teaching Religious Education (chapter five). Furthermore chapters on *The General Directory for Catechesis* (chapter six), *Nostra Aetate* (chapter seven) and Junior and Leaving Certificate Syllabi (chapter eight) help provide direction for contemporary Catholic Education.

The book raises questions about how particular contexts shape and challenge Catholic Religious Education and about how it translates its tradition in ever-changing environments. How can Catholic religious educators educate in a manner which is true to the Catholic tradition while being open to other religious perspectives? There is a tension between continuity and transformation within contemporary Catholic Religious Education which questions the relationship between the Catholic religious tradition, seen as normative and experienced as life-giving for believers, and the many other competing religious and non-religious worldviews. A contextual approach acknowledges that the universal themes and concerns of Catholic Religious Education are shaped, but not entirely defined, by particular contexts. Section three, *Catholic Education as Inclusive Education in the Heart of Europe*, focuses on issues of inter-religious learning and inter-faith dialogue in State and Catholic European schools. Chapter nine presents an overview of the situation of Religious Education in Europe and focuses in particular on three countries (England/Wales, Norway and Switzerland). The following chapter outlines different types of inter-religious learning as well as factors which impede its occurrence in the classroom (chapter ten). Chapter eleven examines the perspective of six world religions on Religious Education (Hinduism, Buddhism, Confucianism, Judaism, Islam and Christianity) while chapter twelve explores the treatment of the 'religious other' in the classroom as well as the banning of religious symbols and clothing in many European state schools. Chapters thirteen to sixteen explore the issues and challenges confronting Religious Educators in Ireland, Northern Ireland, Wales, England and Scotland. Undoubtedly while this book attempts to profile a broader European situation much focus is placed on the Irish and British context for Catholic Religious Education.

The book attempts to integrate theoretical frameworks, which underlie different approaches to Catholic Religious Education, with the lived experience of practitioners. Religious educators are faced with the very specific and challenging task of engaging in cradle to grave faith formation in an intercultural world. Section four attempts to profile some practical situations which educators encounter in homes and parishes as well as primary and post-primary schools, by focusing on key selected themes. While many approaches are grounded in similar theological and epistemological assumptions (chapter seventeen), this book takes a closer look at the areas of early childhood (chapter eighteen), creative prayer (chapter nineteen), sacramental preparation (chapter twenty), and the act of judgement in Religious Education (chapter twenty-one). The challenge of nurturing faith in a climate of dissent (chapter twenty-two) and ongoing debates about the kind of assessment desirable in Religious Education complete this section (chapter twenty-three). The focus here is on presenting best practice for Catholic religious educators.

It is hoped that this book will not just contribute to conversations about Religious Education in an intercultural society but that it will capture something of the energy, commitment and initiatives which characterise Catholic Religious Education in contemporary Europe. The book raises questions about how particular contexts shape and challenge Catholic Religious Education and how it enables its participants to meaningfully communicate and live out the Catholic faith with integrity in ever changing environments. The final section recognises that Religious Education is a vital aspect of a Catholic school both in terms of curricular content and its role within the curriculum (chapter twenty-four). The last chapters explore the important issue of the management of Catholic schools (chapter twenty-five) by locating them in the overall context of the call to faith formation, sacramental initiation (chapter twenty-six) and service to the world.

Notes

1   *The Times*, 29 May 2008.

2   A study of discrimination and racism post-9/11 concluded that 'religion may sometimes be a stronger motivator for discriminatory sentiment and behavior than race or ethnicity'.

        L. Sheridan, 'Discrimination and Racism, Post-September 11', University of Leicester, 2002, http://www.le.ac.uk/ua/pr/press/discriminationandracism.html (accessed 22.06.08).

3   See Oliver McTiernan, *Violence in God's Name*, New York: Orbis, 2003, p. xiii.

4   A Letter to Educators, President Sarkozy, 4 September 2007.

5   *The Times*, 30 May 2008. These words are taken from an interview with Tony Blair at the launch of his Faith Foundation in New York.

6   John Keast (ed.), *Religious Diversity and Intercultural Education: A Reference Book for Schools*, Strasbourg: Council of Europe, 2007.

7   TRES is a trans-national cooperation project in the form of a thematic network funded by the Socrates Programme which started in the autumn of 2005. The TRES launching conference took place in Uppsala, Sweden, in 2006. For further examples of research groups and networks see the Oslo Coalition's project on education for freedom of religion or belief; the European Community Framework 6 project on Religious Education, Dialogue and Conflict involving ten Universities (REDco); The European Network for Religious Education through Contextual Approaches and the International Seminar on Religious Education and Values (ISREV); Co-ordinating Group for Religious Education in Europe (CoGREE); European Association for the Study of Religions (EASR)

8   Professor Terence Copley has been appointed Professor of Educational Studies in Religious Education.

9   Chapter 10.

10   *Catechism of the Catholic Church* (John Paul II, 1992); Documents of Vatican II (1965) including *Dei Verbum*: The Dogmatic Constitution on Divine Revelation; *Gaudium et spes:* The Pastoral Constitution on the Church in the Modern World ; *Lumen Gentium:* The Dogmatic Constitution on the Church; *Unitatis Redintegratio*: The Decree on Ecumenism; *Gravissimum Educationis,* Declaration on Christian Education; *Dignitatis Humanae*, Declaration on Religious Freedom. See also the Rite of Christian Initiation of Adults (RCIA) which was officially declared normative for catechesis in 1972 and *The Religious Dimension of Education in a Catholic School* (1988). For a general text see John Redford (ed.), *Hear, O Islands! Theology and Catechesis in the New Millennium*, Dublin: Veritas, 2002.

11   For example a collaborative trustee body CEIST (Catholic Education – an Irish Schools Trust) came into operation in 2007. *The Catholic School – Imagining the Future* (2002) project gave rise to a national conference and a renewed role for Catholic schools and the *Wellsprings* (2007) project concerns the ethos of Catholic schools. See also Conference of Irish Catholic Bishops, *Draft National Directory for Catechesis*, Maynooth: St Patrick's College, 2005. A state syllabus for Religious Education was introduced into the Junior Certificate cycle in 2000 (first examined in 2003) and the Leaving Certificate Cycle in 2003 (first examined in 2005). An advisory committee to the Irish bishops on their role as patrons of primary schools produced a report in September 2007, entitled *Catholic Ethos in Primary Schools and the Changing Role of the Patron*. This unpublished report engages in an overview of important issues in Catholic primary schools such as governance, leadership, boards of management, principals, classroom, initial teacher training and diocesan support structures. For a recent account of Catholic schools in Ireland see G. Grace and J. O'Keefe (eds), *International Handbook of Catholic Education Challenges for School Systems in the 21st Century*, Vol. 2, New York: Springer, 2007.

SECTION 1

UNDERSTANDING CATHOLIC EDUCATION

CHAPTER 1

PHILOSOPHY OF CATHOLIC EDUCATION

John Sullivan

Catholic education takes place in many different sites. Apart from the school, there is also the home, the parish, youth ministry, college and university, ministerial formation, adult education and other settings. Wherever it takes place, two principal features should accompany and characterise it. Firstly, it should draw upon and exhibit the four main languages that make up the grammar of Christian faith:

- the proclamation of and about Jesus the Christ, the message of the Gospel
- the construction of community or fellowship
- the celebration of worship or liturgy
- the offering of service to those in need, which itself is a form of worship, this time of the image of God in the needy person.

These four languages of faith relate to four aspects of formation for Christians. There is a story and set of concepts to learn; a way of thinking to assimilate and indwell; there is a way of belonging within a community; there is a way of worshipping; and there is a way of behaving. All are necessary. None are complete on their own. Each reinforces the others.

Secondly, Catholic education will emphasise coherence and interconnectedness, both in the curriculum and in the example given by teachers. As it is God's world that we are learning about, and because it is the whole person we are teaching, we have a duty in Catholic education to avoid fragmentation and separation; we should show the connections between the different parts of what we are teaching and between those and the parts of our lives, all of this in an awareness of being in God's presence. Here I limit myself to the school context and to the second of these two essential features. In this chapter I unpack five ways of expressing and understanding the essential interconnectedness of Catholic education:

(1)   the handing on of holy things is very closely linked to the handling of ordinary things

(2)   there is no sharp separation between the sacred and the secular

(3)   we should seek to promote a sacramental perspective on life

(4)   the term 'sublation' usefully brings out aspects of the connection between ordinary and 'holy'

(5)   Catholic schools need a blend of the ministry of witness and the ministry of the Word.

Holy and Ordinary

Let me begin with extracts from two conversations; one which occurred in a school staffroom and one I overheard during a coffee break during an in-service session that I was leading. On my first day working in a north of England Catholic secondary school in 1975 I introduced myself to a colleague as the new Head of Religious Education. In reply I was told by this person that she had 'polished the statues' before I arrived. This short phrase encapsulated for her what the role of a religious educator in the mid-1970s entailed: the preservation of 'holy' things. At the time there was a religious song, performed in a popular style, with the refrain 'keep the rumour going that God is alive.' That was how she saw Religious Education: preserving the holy so that it did not slip out from our memory and keeping alive the thought that God is (still) about the place. I think she saw it as a bit of problem that I was a young, married, lay man, father of two, and very soon to be three, children: somehow this did not quite give off the right vibrations about holiness, the kind of impression I might have given if I had been a professed 'religious', with clothing that set me apart and a lifestyle that separated me from mortgages, sex and children. Needless to say, I saw it as a priority that I disabused her quickly of her view that Religious Education should focus on polishing the statues: this was not how I saw the task at all. Polishing and cleaning is a necessary part of looking after one's home (and other buildings) and is not something to be demeaned as a task; but polishing the statues as a central task for Religious Education conjured up for me something backward-looking – because some of the images being used seemed to me to appeal to a former age – and narrow, because they seemed to treat holiness as removed from everyday life, rather than something that we develop in the midst of it.

Twenty years later, I was leading another in-service day in London for teachers from many different types of school. The theme being explored was how we could promote the spiritual development of pupils in primary and secondary schools. While tidying up during the mid-morning break and as we all had a cup of coffee I couldn't help overhear one teacher say to another: 'There seems to be several people here from Catholic schools. I have never worked in one of these schools. Can you tell me what is different about a Catholic school?' The answer given made me wince. 'Well, we probably give more time to Religious Education than other schools do. Plus, we have Masses at various points throughout the year. But otherwise, really we are just the same as other schools.' Once again, as in the previous conversation about polishing the statues, there was a lack of connection to a bigger picture about education and a narrow focus on what sets Catholics apart in some way. This left the huge bulk of the educational experience being offered untouched by the worldview and lifestyle offered by Catholic Christianity. It implied that, apart from a few special, 'holy' elements, Catholic education was like any other form of education. One wonders why so much trouble is taken and so many sacrifices are made by so many people to pay for, construct and maintain Catholic schools, if all that they provide is some form of 'icing on a cake'; the same cake that is 'baked' anywhere else. The answer given by that teacher revealed that he saw little connection between the 'holy' bits and the rest of the education offered by the school.

Ten years further on, I remain convinced that *the handing on of holy things is inextricably linked to our handling of ordinary things*. That is, the holy is not something cut off from, isolated from, uncontaminated by or opposed by the ordinary ingredients of our lives. Holiness is not about escape, but about a discerning immersion in everyday life. Immersion here means getting stuck into life and accepting its responsibilities; it means being aware of what you are doing, why you are doing it and the effect you are having. At the heart of our faith is the belief that God invites us to respond to the love showered upon us non-stop and to share in the divine life, to be taken-up into the divine set of relationships we call the Trinity. We can say, with Westlife: 'you raise me up.' In the process we will be transformed, not diminished. God wants to embrace all that we are, as special, indeed, unique individuals, with our hopes and drives, our desires, gifts and attachments. Although these might be modified and re-ordered as they are brought together, they are not simply suppressed and left behind. We are to find God above all in the bits and pieces of everyday life, not in remote, specially dedicated, set-apart holy places and events, though these might help us on occasion to be more aware of what God is offering us all the time but less obviously in the normal pattern and practices of our lives. We become holy through the way we see and deal with the ordinary things of life, like hunger, ambition, disappointment, relationships, communication, belonging and decisions, rather than by turning away from them to an other worldly holiness.

Sacred and Secular
Education, in any culture, is about the capacities of human nature, such as energy and emotions, intelligence and memory, conscience and will; it is about how these are developed and oriented, ordered and integrated in service of what is conceived to be the good life. At the heart of Catholic education is the belief that

there is *no sharp separation between the sacred and the secular*. God creates, sustains, redeems and renews everything in our experience. Nothing is beyond God's activity. God is the ultimate environment in which we live and in which we educate. Catholic education is about providing an enriching, relevant, coherent and inviting environment for children and young people to help them to make sense of their *whole lives* in the light of the Catholic traditional way of understanding, appreciating and communicating God's presence to us. In the life of Jesus, in the sacraments and in the working of the curriculum, there is no separation we can make between what is holy and what is ordinary; between what we call sacred and what we call secular. They are intimately related. We do not become holy apart from ordinary living. The great Catholic thinker Thomas Aquinas (c.1225–1274) reminds us that theology is about how *all* things relate to God (since nothing is outside God's creation). Therefore Religious Education in a Catholic school is *not* about polishing the statues; nor is a Catholic education simply about adding to a 'normal' education, a few Masses. This is of course, not to say that the celebration of the Eucharist does not play an important part in clarifying God's love for us, God's call to us, individually and as a community, God's presence and offer of grace to us and God's way of teaching us.

Sacramental Perspective

One very common way of characterising a Catholic approach to education is to say that it aims to promote a *sacramental perspective* among students. A sacramental perspective views the world as a whole, as the theatre of God's grace. It does not restrict God's operation to special moments in church, to holy places or activities. Instead it acknowledges that God can be encountered anywhere, anytime. Thus, God could be experienced, not only in celebrating the Eucharist, in Religious Education, in moments of prayer, in special pilgrimage centres, in the reading of Holy Scripture, but also on mountain tops, in forests, along riversides, in music, poetry, art and literature, in relationships, in times of trouble, pain, stress and illness, as well as in the diverse variety of positive experiences, the 'high' moments of life. Catholic education should strive to invite students to see God's presence in all these aspects of their experience. It cannot guarantee that students will come to see the world like this, and it certainly cannot force them to do so, but it can witness to them what it is like, the difference it can make to see the world this way. Every subject in the curriculum has the potential, though some more easily than others, to allow us to see some feature of the world as a way into appreciating at least part of God's nature, purpose, call and presence. Of course, if the teacher does not perceive the world in this way, as a place where God is present and available everywhere and in all circumstances, s/he cannot mediate this capacity to students. This will be evident less in what is said than in how the teacher 'sees' and conveys that 'seeing'.

Sublation

One term that hints at how, in the context of Catholic education, the holy is encountered in the ordinary, how the sacred and secular meet and how the sacramental perspective might be understood is *sublation*.[1] To sublate something is to take it up and to include it, integrating it in a higher unity. For example, a painting sublates paint. It uses the raw materials of paint and does something creative with it, so that it becomes something with more meaning than simply a collection of substances with colour. Similarly a symphony sublates instruments: it goes beyond a separate collection of trumpets, violins, cellos, piano and so on and makes of them a unity; it organises them into a larger system. Instead of chaos and noise, we hear a piece of music where the parts are co-ordinated, so that they work together to make something whole. We might say that adolescence sublates childhood. It takes it up to a different stage, goes beyond it, but never completely leaves it behind. Another example is that desire sublates instinct: where instinct is unconscious, automatic and is thus not fully free, desire builds on instinct, rather than contradicts it, but makes it conscious and modifies it into something we can influence and re-direct. We might say that Einstein sublates Newton, in the sense that he takes Newtonian science but deploys it in a more complex and sophisticated system. Thus, although Newton is no longer the last word in science, his findings are still included, though scientists have gone beyond them. For Christians, what has traditionally been called the New Testament sublates the Old Testament, in that the Old Testament's insights into God's relationship with God's people remain, but are now included into a new level of appreciation of God's ways. When something is sublated its normal functioning is not suppressed or interfered with, but it is used in such a way that it serves a higher purpose than could have been thought of at its own level. We speak in a similar way of grace building upon nature, harnessing its capacities for purposes beyond nature's own, unaided powers.

In the context of Catholic education we can claim that vocation sublates professionalism. That is, all the skills and tasks required by any professional teacher will be required by a teacher seeking to offer a Catholic education. There are many aspects to these tasks. They include designing a curriculum, planning a lesson, laying out a classroom, deploying learning resources, setting tasks that promote learning, managing time and keeping good order. They also include ensuring that all students participate, promoting equal opportunities, displaying fair treatment, the use of technology in support of learning, consistent and appropriate assessment of students' work, reporting progress to parents and others and collaborating with colleagues. Vocation sublates these professional tasks in the way it views them as a whole and in the way it directs them. It connects them all to a bigger picture of who we are and what we are about. The work is not simply carried out as a way of earning a living, or pursuing an interest; it is also a way of serving the world, of contributing to the common good, of improving the condition of human beings, of developing myself as a teacher and it can be a way of relating to God and exercising our discipleship. To put this in another way, when vocation sublates professionalism, we do not so much do different things as teachers, as tell ourselves a different story about who we are, who our students are, what we are doing and why. Catholic educators are conscious that they teach people who, like them, are made in the image and likeness of God, who belong to the body of Christ, temples of the Holy Spirit, who have an eternal destiny.

To take a very practical example of how the ordinary can be a vehicle for the holy and of how an everyday capacity can be sublated so that it carries a higher level of significance, let us take the gift of speech. The mission of a Catholic school will be expressed probably most obviously in how we talk to one another. The use of the tongue is double-edged: with it we can encourage, instruct, praise, inspire, enlighten and delight others; however, we must also admit that in speaking we can depress, confuse, deceive, terrify, embarrass and demoralise too. As Plato stated in *Gorgias*, 'speech is a great power, which achieves the most divine works by means of the smallest and least visible forms; for it can even put a stop to fear, remove grief, create joy, and increase pity.' Therefore we must watch the way we talk, remembering we are always in the presence of God.

Ministry of Witness and Word
It follows from the above analysis that, for the effective functioning of Catholic education, two things are needed. First, there must be a *ministry of witness*. This will be shown in how the ordinary things in school are handled. This will largely be implicit: in welcoming and warm relationships; in an encouraging tone; in a positive and non-punitive ethos; in fostering patterns of behaviour that display and bring out the best side of people; in personal example that models what it preaches; in the quality of gentle but growth-inducing pastoral care; in the willing and generous support for students with difficulties; in the vibrant quality of community life. Everybody, without exception, has an important part to play in this implicit witness. Without this implicit witness, the careful handling of ordinary things, a Catholic school, no matter how orthodox its teaching is in religious terms, cannot convey the faith adequately. Without this, it invites accusations of hypocrisy and inhumanity; it renders its religious faith incredible. However, remaining at the level of the implicit – though essential and necessary – is insufficient on its own.

Secondly, there must be a *ministry of the Word*. This will point out how the catholic is framed, guided and inspired by the Catholic. This requires making explicit what underpins the implicit day-to-day life of the school: naming the source of grace; telling the Christian 'story'; formal religious teaching; liturgy and worship. It is more important to be able to experience the warmth of the sun than to be able to give a scientific account of it; an understanding of science can enhance our capacity to respond appropriately to the sun's rays. Humanity as a whole is endangered if it fails to appreciate how it depends upon and relates to the sun. Similarly, it is more important in a Catholic school to live the ministry of witness in the careful handling of ordinary things than to be able to articulate the ministry of the Word; but it is better for both to be addressed. While not everybody may be able to exercise what I have called the ministry of the Word, alerting people to how the ordinary and the holy are intertwined, there does need to be a critical mass of people who can do so. Even those who cannot, either through choice or through lacking the necessary Catholic 'literacy', exercise this second ministry, still have a part to play in that valid insights, questions and criticisms can come from the questioning, wavering, alienated, peripheral members of the community. Catholic educators should be open to and responsive in the face of such challenges if their schools are to reduce the gap between current reality and the ideal for which they strive.

If Catholic schools address these five ways of understanding interconnectedness and link them to the four languages of faith described in my opening paragraph, they will be developing a Catholic philosophy of education, one that does justice to the whole body of teachers and learners as a whole, to the wholeness of the curriculum, to the connections between learning and life and above all to the need to attend to the presence of God all around us.

Note

1   My understanding of 'sublation' owes much to and draws heavily upon Sebastian Moore, 'Getting the Fall Right', *The Downside Review*, Vol. 116, No. 404, 1998, pp. 213–222, although I have deployed the term in ways he may not have intended. I have also been influenced by my reading of Bernard Lonergan's *Method in Theology*, London: Darton, Longman & Todd, 1972.

Further Reading

Bunge, Marcia (ed.), *The Child in Christian Thought*, Grand Rapids: Eerdmans, 2001.

Byrnes, James, *John Paul II & Educating for Life*, New York: Peter Lang, 2002.

Groome, Thomas, *Educating for Life*, Allen, Texas: Thomas More Press, 1998.

Jacobs, Richard, *The Grammar of Catholic Schooling*, Washington, DC: National Catholic Educational Association, 1997.

Kieran, Patricia and Hession, Anne, *Children, Catholicism & Religious Education*, Dublin: Veritas, 2005.

Sullivan, John, *Catholic Schools in Contention*, Dublin: Veritas, 2000.

—— *Catholic Education: Distinctive and Inclusive*, Dordrecht, Kluwer: Academic Press, 2001.

—— 'From Formation to the Frontiers: the Dialectic of Christian Education', in *Journal of Education & Christian Belief*, Vol. 7, No. 1, 2003, pp. 7–21.

CHAPTER 2

LIFELONG FAITH DEVELOPMENT IN THE HOME, PARISH AND OTHER EDUCATIONAL ENVIRONMENTS

Gareth Byrne

On the first Sunday of Lent in our parish this year, the congregation, young and not so young, having been blessed on Ash Wednesday, gathered together to hear once more the story of Noah's Ark (Gen 7–8) and then Jesus' call to repent and believe the Good News of God's everlasting love for us (Mk 1:14). The children receiving their first Eucharist in May were present with their parents or guardians, invited to celebrate another moment of parish sacramental preparation with their faith community. We were conscious too that seventeen adults from parishes in our diocese were, on that day, being called to set out, during Lent, on their final preparation for Baptism, Confirmation and Eucharist. We would live Lent in joy, anticipating the Easter Vigil, when we would celebrate new life for all in Christ.

During the ninety days of Lent and Eastertide in Catholic homes, parishes and educational environments, the community is in festival. Everyone has something to do: prayer, fasting and practical action in Lent; celebration, holidays, visiting family and friends at Easter time. Everyone has a role to play. Everyone has something to learn, as first the community turns back to God, then lives through Holy Week with Christ, and finally celebrates his resurrection from the dead, transforming our understanding of life and love. By the time we arrive at Pentecost, and the celebration of the birth of the Church through the power of the Holy Spirit, many children and adults will have been baptised, celebrated their first Eucharist and/or their Confirmation. All those who have been invited to journey with them will have lived through a period of retreat, reflection and renewal. So it will continue throughout their lives. Each year the Christian community recommits itself, during Lent and Easter, to the Lord and to one another. In this chapter the question of lifelong faith development is addressed from within the Christian perspective, a perspective that recognises the journey that all people take in life and seeks to be in open dialogue with all people of faith and with those who are searching for meaning outside a faith context.

We Never Stop Learning

> When did you stop learning?
> I haven't.
> When will you stop learning?
> I never will!

How true it is, we never stop learning. We never stop learning about ourselves, about others, about our world, and about God. As we engage with life, our religious faith develops too. We are challenged to grow into adults who have reflected on their faith through all the joys and sorrows of life. The rainbow in the sky reminds us that, no matter what rain is falling in our lives, God loves us. We are on a journey: the journey of life; the journey of faith. We are always growing into or out of relationship with God and with each other. There is no standing still. New learning awaits us around every corner. New religious experiences, new ways of seeing life, a more personal connection with Jesus; everything is possible with God, if we have eyes to see and ears to hear what is taking place all around us.

The Christian person is, in fact, only beginning to learn. The expectation of the followers of Christ is that, in him, they can learn and grow every day of their lives. Like Jesus, they are committed to being open, caring and engaging people who are prepared to welcome whatever circumstances they encounter in life as gift and opportunity. Not always easy, perhaps. Not always what any of us would choose. But life is a gift for the Christian and the experience of life provides them with opportunities to engage with all of reality. The deep-down questions we find ourselves asking are to be celebrated and reflected on courageously. They challenge and change who we are and who we are becoming throughout our lives. Such questions are ultimately religious questions. The Christian person recognises them as an invitation to realise their need for and trust in God; they awaken in them the possibility that they can truly love and encourage others at the deepest level. Beginning with the Christian community and moving out beyond it Christians see the need to care and be of service to each other:

- Witnessing in everyday ways to the transforming presence of Christ.
- Supporting each other in worship and prayer before God.
- Reaching out to the poor and those in any need, placing justice, peace and reconciliation at the centre of the Christian way of life.
- Building together a vibrant parish community, living already the coming Kingdom of God.[1]

Partnership between Home, Parish and Educational Environment

At home, in the parish and wherever the Christian community reflects in an educational setting, there is an invitation to live with each other, to minister to each other, to love each other. Teaching and learning is a lifelong activity that is not confined to school. It finds its natural place in all that happens in the home and in the parish as well as within the school and other educational environments. Ongoing faith development takes place informally day-by-day, wherever Christians live, gather, pray and reach out practically to their friends and neighbours. This kind of informal teaching and learning is often not recognised or planned for but passes on strong messages to all as to what is believed, what is significant, what is valued within the particular family or community.

At a more formal level, faith development is an invitation to all Christians to become involved not only in learning about their faith and acquiring religious skills, but also to deepen their personal commitment within a faith community and grow into mature Christians. They are to be responsible for their own faithfulness, capable of supporting others and willing to offer leadership in faith when asked.

With regard to *children and young people*, it is clear that home, parish and school strive to be places of formal teaching and learning, as well as centres of love, celebration, friendship, participation and belonging. They can each contribute to faith development, each supporting the other in a collaborative and dynamic partnership. Parents are the first and natural catechists of their children. Family rituals such as prayers at mealtime or when going to bed, visiting an elderly relation or someone who is ill, as well as chats about the place of God in family life, what is right and wrong and why, contribute enormously to the faith formation of the young person. Participating in the children's choir and attending the Sunday Family Mass will be helpful for the child in coming to understand the invitation the parish community offers them to belong within its care.2 For young people belonging to the parish's youth initiative, folk group, or prayer group, may be helpful in encouraging them to know and live their faith. Learning about the meaning of religion in school and its significance in the life of believers, as well as participating in charity events, liturgy, prayer moments and retreats, all contribute to the faith journey of young people. Although it is not always the case, partnership between home, parish and the Catholic school should be at its most visible in the way in which all three contribute together to the sacramental preparation of children.

For *young adults* the invitation is to make one's own the gift of faith; that which has been shared and passed on by others. This time in life, when major choices are being made, is a time, too, to grasp and understand the meaning of faith and the impact it can have on life. Young adults are the group that have withdrawn more than any other to the edge of the institutional Church and indeed to the margins of other aspects of culture and society. Some have built-up negative stereotypes about 'religious' people while others find themselves confused about life itself. Some returning to practise their religion are quickly disillusioned by the human failings of the faith community. Others, having had a positive experience in parish, school or college, are open to an invitation to belong, meeting with or setting-up a young adult faith group of one kind or another.[3] Very often these young adults need assistance to move from the faith they learned as children to a personal appropriation of faith as adults. This is often a time, too, to forgive the inadequacies of those who sought to pass on faith to them and the shortcomings of the teaching methods they may have employed.

As *adults* there are a variety of ways by which to avail ourselves of opportunities for faith development in the community of the Church. *The Rite of Christian Initiation of Adults* exists in order to assist adults who wish to be Baptised, Confirmed and receive the Eucharist within the Catholic Church. For those already committed to the Church the Parish Priest and Parish Pastoral Council, working with energetic parishioners, will try to facilitate parish structures, perhaps together with other local parishes and the diocese, offering ongoing faith education.[4] For Christians who are less connected with the faith-life of the Church, new evangelisation programmes have been developed to help reconnect them with their faith community and encourage them to contribute to its growth. Colleges specialising in theological studies will often provide a variety of opportunities for pastoral education and training, sometimes in conjunction with parishes. Retreat houses offer a wide selection of possibilities for adult reflection, prayer and spiritual direction. The purpose of all these efforts is to encourage the adult population to own and develop their faith, to minister to each other, and to find ways of sharing their faith with younger generations. Adult faith development will always begin by taking into account the experience of the participants and the ways in which adults learn. Young adults, parents, single people, priests and religious, the elderly, as well as those training for lay ministry, all deserve specific attention. The disadvantaged in society, the Travelling People, migrants and other newcomers, people with special needs, and those living with illness will all have particular needs in this regard.[5] The home, the parish and a variety of educational environments can be sources of religious faith development for adults as much as for children and young people. The material set out in the Irish Republic's new Leaving Certificate Religious Education Syllabus, for example, is a good starting point for adults who have missed out on the opportunity now being given to young people to study religion and grapple with faith at a significant level before leaving school. The textbooks and teacher resources provide much for adult reflection.[6] We are all teaching and learning together.

A Lifelong Effort, Full of Surprises

The Christian journey is a lifelong pilgrimage, an intersecting of each person's and each faith community's story with the story of Jesus and the story of his followers down through the ages. It is a journey of faith lived trusting in God. It is a way of life rooted in the hope Jesus Christ brings to the world. It is love lived in this time and place, guided and challenged by the Holy Spirit.

Faith development, then, should be seen as an ongoing pursuit. The Christian person is willing to put a lifelong effort into this task and always expects to be surprised by what can be learned. They trust that they will be supported not only by God but by family and friends, parish and neighbours. Education in faith will better equip them to read and understand and live life to the full.

In summary, there are many ways in which to learn how to draw close to Christ. Individuals, supported by the Christian community, may seek, for example, to:

- Find ways of creating space in life for Jesus
- Learn different forms of prayer
- Contribute to parish music ministry
- Train for liturgical ministry
- Act on behalf of those in need, especially the poor
- Work for justice in the community
- Build up the faith community
- Volunteer for responsibility within a parish group
- Investigate the basic elements of faith
- Take a theology course
- Consult a spiritual director.

Working together with like-minded individuals, more can be achieved. This is not to suggest that providing continuing faith development opportunities at home, in the parish, at school, or within other settings, is an easily achieved goal. Everyone has to live with inadequacies and prejudices, their own and those of others. Noah and his community had to learn how to begin all over again. When members of a faith community are building each other up, when access is clearly open to all, and when the welcome is deeply felt, what a joy it is to behold. When there is a sense that the Christian community is very precious, what hope is created for all those involved! When there is outreach beyond the community, offering to be of service to others and to society, then Christians, following in the footsteps of Christ, have power, in his name, to forgive, heal, strengthen, liberate and renew:

Go therefore and teach all nations, baptising them in the name of the
Father and of the Son and of the Holy Spirit, and lo, I am with you to
the ends of the earth. (Mt 28:19-20)

It is not arrogant to believe that you are gifted by God for we are all gifts of God
to our world, to our loved ones, and, yes, to ourselves. We are not perfect, any of
us, but it is not inappropriate to feel called, to be in some small way available to
others, to help them own and engage with their faith and, then, grow in that
faith. We are called to listen carefully to each other. We are invited to learn and
learn again, and continue learning all our lives. Then we may become teachers
too, inspiring others as we live and learn:

> Jesus doesn't want us to live in a cocoon. He sends us forth. He sends us
> out to be instruments of peace in the world of war. To be instruments of
> love in the world where there is so often hate or indifference. That
> doesn't mean sending us off to a far country, but sending us off in a new
> way in our family, in our school, place of work or parish … Holiness is
> not hiding oneself and saying prayers. Holiness is becoming like Jesus
> and taking our place in the world to reveal that God is mercy; God is
> love, God has come to bring us together and wants us to be people filled
> with hope, and also with joy. 'I say these things to you', says Jesus, 'so that
> your joy might be full and my joy might be within you.' (Jn 15).[7]

Notes

1   See Benedict XVI, *Deus Caritas Est: God is Love,* Dublin: Veritas, 2006, pp. 20–25.

2   See G. Byrne, 'Children's Religious Education: Challenge and Gift', in R. Topley and G. Byrne
     (eds), *Nurturing Children's Religious Imagination: The Challenge of Primary Religious Education Today,*
     Dublin: Veritas, 2004, pp. 237–251.

3   See J.C. Cusick, and K.F. DeVries, *The Basic Guide to Young Adult Ministry,* Maryknoll/New York:
     Orbis, 2001.

4   See J. Doherty, O. Crilly, F. Dolaghan and P. Curran, *Think Big, Act Small: Working at Collaborative
     Ministry through Parish Pastoral Councils,* Dublin: Veritas, 2005.

5   See Irish Catholic Bishops' Conference, *National Directory for Catechesis* (forthcoming).

6   See M. De Barra (ed.), *Faith Seeking Understanding Series,* Dublin: Veritas, 2004/6, a series of school
     textbooks; E.G. Cassidy and P.M. Devitt (eds), *Into the Classroom* Series, Dublin: Veritas, 2000/5,
     a series of eleven teacher/parent support books.

7   J. Vanier, *Encountering the Other,* Dublin: Veritas, 2005, pp. 45–47.

Further Reading

Benedict XVI, *Deus Caritas Est: God is Love*, Dublin: Veritas, 2006.

Cassidy, E.G. and Devitt, P.M. (eds), *Into the Classroom* Series, Dublin: Veritas, 2000/5.

Cusick, J.C. and DeVries, K.F., *The Basic Guide to Young Adult Ministry*, Maryknoll/New York: Orbis, 2001.

De Barra, M. (ed.), *Faith Seeking Understanding* Series, Dublin: Veritas, 2004/6.

Doherty, J., Crilly, O., Dolaghan, F. and Curran, P., *Think Big, Act Small: Working at Collaborative Ministry through Parish Pastoral Councils*, Dublin: Veritas, 2005.

Groome, T.H., *What Makes Us Catholic: Eight Gifts for Life*, San Francisco: HarperCollins, 2003.

Irish Catholic Bishops' Conference, *National Directory for Catechesis* (forthcoming).

Topley, R. and Byrne, G. (eds), *Nurturing Children's Religious Imagination: The Challenge of Primary Religious Education Today*, Dublin: Veritas, 2004.

Vanier, J., *Encountering the Other*, Dublin: Veritas, 2005.

CHAPTER 3

CATECHUMENATE AS 'INSPIRATION FOR ALL CATECHESIS'

Jane E. Regan

Where can we begin to describe the nature of catechesis that might be appropriate for the Church today? How do we weave together the reality of contemporary culture, the demands of a post-modern worldview, and the genuine searching by those both within and outside the Church for a sustaining spirituality? What are the models or approaches that we might consider as we engage in the ever present task of proclaiming the Gospel for our own time and place? These are the questions that all religious educators are called to address as they give shape to the work of catechesis into the future.

There are a variety of points of entry into this area of inquiry, many of which are examined in other chapters in this collection. For this chapter, we turn to one of the core insights set out in the *General Directory for Catechesis*, which was promulgated in 1997.[1] This document is designed to bring together the best theological and pastoral principles that 'are capable of better orienting and coordinating the pastoral activity of the ministry of the word, and concretely, catechesis' (GDC 9). One principle that has generated a good deal of discussion and that warrants further consideration makes a clear connection between the general nature and aim of catechesis and the dynamics that underpin the catechumenate. After discussing the objects and tasks of catechesis in Chapter III, the writers of the GDC suggest that the baptismal catechumenate can serve as an important point of reference for how we approach catechesis. While acknowledging that there are significant differences between pre-baptismal and post-baptismal catechesis, the document's authors propose that that the catechumenate can nevertheless serve as model or inspiration for all catechesis.

What were the writers of the GDC imagining when they said that the catechumenate is the 'model of [the Church's] catechising activity' or a 'source of inspiration for ... catechesis' (GDC 90–91)? What vision of catechesis and the catechumenate directed their thinking and gave meaning to this statement? A careful read of the document itself brings into focus two themes that run throughout the Directory and have particular import for this discussion:

- the fundamental connection between catechesis and evangelisation; and
- the emphasis on the centrality of adult faith formation to the whole catechetical enterprise.

Incorporating insights from earlier Church documents on catechesis, the writers of the GDC situate catechesis within the mission of the Church and describe it as one of the 'moments – a very remarkable one – in the whole process of evangelisation' (GDC 63). As a ministry of the Word, catechesis is a participation in the fundamental task of proclaiming the Good News of Jesus Christ through words and deeds, that is, it is a participation in the work of evangelisation.[1]

The term 'evangelisation' has not generally been part of Roman Catholic conversations in the past. Although used in key places in the documents from Vatican Council II – in defining the task of the Church, describing the role of the laity, and discussing the work of bishops and priests, for example – the concept of evangelisation really became part of the discussion of the nature of catechesis in the middle of the 1970s with the apostolic exhortations on evangelisation and catechesis.[2] In these documents, evangelisation means 'bringing the Good News into all the strata of humanity, and through its influence, transforming humanity from within and making it new' (EN 18). This is presented as the fundamental work of the Church; it exists in order to evangelise (EN 14).

We are called to be an evangelising Church, to be evangelising parishes. It is at the heart of our corporate identity and of our work as Christians. Evangelisation as an ecclesial action is not simply a series of activities or programmes; it is not something to put on the parish's list of committees and activities. At its heart, evangelisation has to do with how the parish lives and makes all of its decisions. As the idea has developed across Church documents over the last thirty years and is reflected in the GDC, evangelisation is as much about who we are as what we do. In this context, it might be helpful to think not only of the noun 'evangelisation' but of the descriptor 'evangelising' as well. When we speak of evangelisation, there is the temptation to set it out as another activity the parish does – catechesis, liturgy, education, pastoral care, evangelisation. Or to see it as the responsibility of a single committee – the Evangelisation Committee, similar to the other committees a parish might have, such as the Social Committee, the School Committee, or the Finance Committee.

Using 'evangelising' to strengthen the commitment that who we are as Church – our mission and identity – is rooted in engaging in all activities through the lens of evangelisation. To speak of 'evangelising pastoral care,' for example, reminds us that as we visit the sick, as we care for the bereaved or lonely, as we counsel the lost or confused, we do all of these activities in a way that recognises the close connection between human life and the liberating word of Jesus Christ. We do all of these activities so as to proclaim the Gospel in word and action and thus further the Reign of God. And so we can speak of evangelising youth ministry, evangelising liturgy, and even evangelising Finance Committee.

This first core theme from the GDC – the fundamental connection between evangelisation and catechesis – sets the framework for the second theme: the emphasis on the centrality of adult formation to the catechetical enterprise. Looking at the work of catechesis through the lens of evangelisation makes meaningful statements that have been appearing in catechetical documents since the first General Directory for Catechesis in 1971[3]: 'catechesis of adults, since it deals with persons who are capable of an adherence that is fully responsible, must be considered the chief form of catechesis. All the other forms, which are indeed always necessary, are in some way oriented to it' (GCD 1971, 20).

If we understand that, as people engaged in Religious Education, we are called to form an evangelising Church, then it follows that the focus has to be on adult faith formation. This is understood not in an exclusive way but in a radical way. The idea is not to set aside or ignore the catechesis of children and youth, but to set that activity within a broader context. It is the members of the adult community that have primary responsibility for living their faith in such a way that the Good News of Jesus is brought into all strata of human life. Making this connection between evangelisation and adult faith formation, one of the documents on adult catechesis includes this statement:

> In summary, in order for the Good News of the Kingdom to penetrate all the various layers of the human family, it is crucial that every Christian play an active part in the coming of the Kingdom … All of this naturally requires adults to play a primary role. Hence it is not only legitimate, but necessary to acknowledge that a fully Christian community can only exist when a systematic catechesis of all its members takes place and when an effective and well-developed catechesis of adults is regarded as the central task in the catechetical enterprise.[4]

To grow in capacity, to be an evangelising Church, adults must be deeply rooted in their faith, committed to giving expression to it in their daily lives, and able to talk about it when the opportunities arise.

With this image of the task of catechesis in mind, one that is rooted in evangelisation and oriented toward adults, we can return to the question: what does it mean to say that the catechumenate is the inspiration for all catechesis? Put another way: *How does the catechumenate contribute to a vision of catechesis that enhances the evangelising nature of the faith community and strengthens the lived faith of all the members, particularly the adults?*

To begin, we can look to the Rite of *Christian Initiation of Adults*[5] for a description of the catechumenate and its component parts. In RCIA 75 we find this description of the catechumenate: 'an extended period during which the candidates are given suitable pastoral formation and guidance, aimed at training them in the Christian life.' This section then includes a list of four elements of such formation: suitable catechesis, community context, suitable liturgical rites, and participation in the mission of the Church. A careful look at each of these elements provides us with some sense of the insights and inspiration that the catechumenate can offer catechesis.

Suitable Catechesis
This catechesis is described as 'gradual and complete in its coverage, accommodated to the liturgical year, and solidly supported by celebrations of the word.' One can easily see that this would be a great starting place for describing any form of catechesis. In light of this description, what insight does this element of the catechumenate provide all catechesis?

1. All catechesis is complete and systematic. The scope and sequence charts that accompany many Religious Education textbook series provide good starting points. They set out an overview of how the various elements of the Christian story and the Church's teaching are present across the year levels. But, again, this is just a starting point. Returning to the earlier discussion of the centrality of adult formation, we recognise that the depth of the Christian tradition can be most fully expressed by adults who have, as the GDC says, ' a right and a duty to bring to maturity the seed of faith sown in them by God' (173). So the question of how catechesis is complete and systematic needs to be raised in terms of the adult community as well as children and youth.

2. The goal for all catechesis is first and foremost a relationship with Jesus Christ. The study of scripture, the explanation of Catholic doctrine, the review of Church history, the consideration of core principles of morality: all of these are important to the degree to which they disclose the reality of God's love for us expressed, in Jesus Christ. Whether we are engaging children or adults, this becomes the criterion for deciding what to present and how we present it: does this provide an opportunity for participants to reflect upon and deepen their relationship with Jesus?

3. All catechesis is oriented to the liturgical year. The dominance of the schooling model of Religious Education has given pride of place to the

academic calendar in how we plan and schedule catechesis. A look to the catechumenate for inspiration reminds us that it is the ebb and flow of the liturgical year that shapes the rhythm and themes of catechesis. This does not mean ignoring the realities of school holidays and summer vacation, but it does call us to increase our awareness of the essence of each liturgical season in our planning and to give attention to those holydays that often fall outside the school calendar – Pentecost and Ascension, for example.

Community Context

In addition to suitable catechesis, three other characteristics are mentioned as a means by which the faith of the catechumens are 'brought to maturity.' Key to these is the community context within which the catechumenate takes place. One of the hallmarks of the RCIA both as it is described in the document and as it comes to expression in various parishes, is the involvement of numerous members of the faith community. Sponsors and godparents, catechists and liturgists: all come together to support the catechumens and to deepen their own faith as well. The catechumenate makes clear: catechesis is not effectively done alone or in isolation from the faith community.

4. Catechesis takes place in and through the community. Since it is understood as a moment in the process of evangelisation, catechesis, like evangelisation, is an ecclesial activity. As an ecclesial action, catechesis takes place in the context of the Christian community and at the same time shapes and defines that community. In planning and implementing catechesis at all levels – from children to elders, the connection between specific elements of the catechetical enterprise and the life of the parish, the community of faith, needs to be highlighted. By recognising these mutual connections, each gathering of catechist and learners as well as the wider community are supported as all strive to grow in faith and strengthen their relationship with Jesus Christ and one another.

5. All catechesis is marked by a spirit of hospitality. The community context of the task of catechesis reminds us of the indispensable nature of hospitality. In thinking of hospitality, our first thoughts can simply be about providing refreshments and comfortable space. Undoubtedly these are important. Yet the Christian notion of hospitality goes beyond these to include a spirit of invitation and welcome to those who are different from us, those who are 'other.' With the catechumenate as our inspiration, we need to regularly ask: How do we receive, hear, and respond to the stranger, the person whose beliefs differ from ours, or the one whose understanding of Church teaching challenges our own?

6. Catechesis is journey and the parish community is an important location for the journey. There is movement inherent in the RCIA – from time of inquiry and pre-catechumenate, to catechumenate, to period of purification and one's status as an elect, to initiation and, finally, entry into mystagogy as a neophyte. And for the Christian, this is only the beginning of a lifelong journey of faith. The parish community serves as an important place where that journey can be sustained and nurtured for each of us. As religious educators, seeing ourselves in the role of supporting people in their journey is important, as is the recognition that a particular parish or programme may be just one location where a person grows in faith and may be just one stop along the way.

Suitable Liturgical Rites

The rich interplay of ritual and reflection effectively marks the movement of the catechumen from entry into the process to initiation. Particularly when the rites are celebrated at Sunday liturgy, they highlight the intimate connection between the experience of the catechumens and the full Christian community. This is especially true during Lent when the three scrutinies and the presentations of the Creed and the Lord's Prayer bring to mind for the catechumens and for the whole community the place of repentance, purification, and prayer at the heart of our Lenten practices. What implications might this dimension of the catechumenate have for catechesis?

7. All catechesis is in some way connected to the Sunday assembly. When we gather for Sunday Eucharist our identity as Christians and as members of our parish community is strengthened. We remember and we celebrate our common beliefs and commitments. These same beliefs and commitments are at the heart of catechesis. In many contexts, when catechesis takes place during the week or through the school, that connection is not as clear as it could be. As we engage in planning and implementing various programmes ranging from adults to children, it is important to highlight the relationship between catechesis and liturgy.

8. Through catechesis we learn how to pray, we learn the importance of prayer, and we experience prayer. Learning the prayers of the Catholic tradition, particularly those that are part of Sunday liturgy, and learning the place of prayer in the life of the Christian are key elements of any curriculum. Equally important is providing opportunities for prayer as an integral part of each catechetical session. The richness of our prayer traditions is best learned by doing; intentionally weaving a variety of prayer forms into our gatherings at every level is key. Consider these: guided meditation, prayers of intercession, centering prayer, Liturgy of the Hours, the rosary, and the responsorial psalms.

Toward Participation in the Mission of the Church

As the catechumens grow in their understanding of the Gospel and the call of bringing their Christian faith to life, they also become increasingly aware of the evangelising nature of the Church and the role that they are called to play in bringing the Good News into every strata of humanity. Having received the gift of faith in their own lives, they are invited to pass that on to others through the witness of their Christian living and through actions for charity and justice. How might we accomplish this in catechesis?

9. Effective catechesis draws on the formative role of actions for charity and justice. In a way similar to the prior discussion of prayer, through catechesis we not only learn about the Church's mission and see that actions for charity and justice are essential to the Gospel. Catechesis can provide opportunities for people of all ages to engage in works of service and then to reflect on those experiences in light of the Gospel and their own lives as believers.

10. Catechesis is a moment of evangelisation. As religious educators, the connection between evangelisation and catechesis needs to permeate all of our work. If we could take a snapshot of the process of planning and implementing effective catechesis, in the foreground would be all the details – people of all ages, specific programmes, curriculum, speakers, books, catechists, facilitators, etc. And in the background, as the horizon against which we do all of our work, is the task of 'bringing the Good News into all the strata of humanity, and through its influence, transforming humanity from within and making it new' (EN 18). Contributing to the formation of an evangelising people is our primary task as religious educators.

In reviewing these ten proposed themes which view catechumenate as inspiration for all catechesis, religious educators might understandably be overwhelmed. There does seem to be a lot to keep track of! Three final presuppositions that I believe are key to the catechumenate are important to remember: first, any particular catechetical event is, like the catechumenate itself, just a beginning. We don't do everything at once; these are themes that are introduced through various experiences of catechesis. Second, the catechumenate enters the participants into a lifelong apprenticeship to Jesus Christ; catechesis is the on-going formation of this apprenticeship. Recognising the lifelong nature of catechesis gives religious educators the confidence to believe that people will experience all the various dimensions of the Christian tradition over time. And finally, throughout the catechumenate everyone – candidates, catechists, presiders, and faith community – pray for and count on the presence of the Spirit as source of guidance and inspiration. Let's be sure to do the same each time we engage in catechesis.

Documents cited

Congregation for the Clergy, *General Catechetical Directory* (GCD), 1971.

Congregation for the Clergy, *General Directory for Catechesis* (GDC),1998.

International Council for Catechesis, *Adult Catechesis in the Christian Community: Some Principles and Guidelines, with Discussion Guide* (ACCC), 1992.

John Paul II, *On Catechesis in Our Time (Catechesi Tradendae)* (CT), 1979.

Paul VI, *On Evangelisation in the Modern World (Evangelii Nuntiandi)* (EN),1975.

United States Catholic Conference, *Rite of Christian Initiation of Adults*, 1988.

Further Reading

Groome, Thomas and Corso, Michael (eds), *Empowering Catechetical Leaders*, Washington DC: National Catholic Education Association, 1998.

Horan, Michael P. and Regan, Jane E., *Good News in New Forms: A Companion to the General Directory for Catechesis*, Washington, DC: National Conference of Catechetical Leaders, 1998.

Horrel, Harold and Groome, Thomas (eds), *Hopes and Horizons of Religious Education*, New York: Paulist Press, 2002.

CHAPTER 4

A SPIRITUALITY OF TEACHING AND LEARNING

Amalee Meehan

Teicht do Róim,
Mór gaído, becc torbai;
In rí chon-daigi hi foss,
Mani-mbeara latt, ní fogbai

To go to Rome,
Much labour, little profit;
The king you seek here,
Unless you bring him with you – you will not find.
(Old Irish Rann, 8th–11th century)

The title of this piece invites the question: what do we mean by spirituality, especially in the context of teaching and learning? There are many different definitions of spirituality; for some, it is interchangeable with faith, others pose it over and against religion. Although spirituality is frequently expressed through religious faith and practices, it reflects the much deeper existential question of the human condition. It is indigenous to who we are as human beings. Moreover, spirituality can enhance teaching and learning. When teachers and learners draw upon their own spiritual depths and engage on a spiritual level, the experience transcends hoops and hurdles and becomes resonant with the mysteries of life and of the soul.

Spirituality can generally be defined as the search for and expression of that which is life-giving and connects with the larger whole. This definition emerges from reflection upon the work of writers such as Parker Palmer, James Fowler, John J. Shea, and Una Agnew. Spirituality starts as the search for authentic self and moves out to connect with what is larger than the self. Our spirituality shapes our relationship with ourselves, with other people, and with whatever transcendent or higher power of which we conceive.

Spirituality is intimate to each of us. It reflects our deepest values and what we hold dear. To some degree, we bring our spirituality into our personal and professional lives, including our work as teachers. It is expressed in the just and loving ways we live. It is directed toward what we value as real and true – when I connect with my real self I find a depth within which does not belong to me but to which I belong – a depth theologians call the Spirit dwelling within me.

Whatever its focus may be, and whether it is religious or not, spirituality is not something 'other than' the human, or 'transcending' the human, it is not tacked on to the human condition, like the tail wagging the dog. Spirituality is an integral part of our human development because the need for meaning and to be part of a larger whole is inherently human. Further, spirituality calls us to live into the wholeness of who we are even as it invites us to relate to some meaningful larger whole or larger reality.

The Spirituality of Teachers

We expect a lot from our teachers. We expect teachers to be expert in their disciplines, to build and maintain trusting, loving relationships, to create a safe environment for students where real learning is promoted, and to recognise and cater for the needs of every individual student. We also require teachers to coax the best out of every student and to guide each one to a love of learning, personal growth and social responsibility. Yet little thought is given as to where teachers will find the resources to meet these expectations. At the same time, teachers, like all other people, are trying to make sense of their lives and of the yearning and searching that is characteristic of the spiritual dimension of being human. Indeed sometimes teachers experience burn-out when they cannot respond to these spiritual yearnings.

Nonetheless, teaching, like many other professions can be extraordinarily fulfilling and life-giving, especially if lived as part of a spiritual calling or vocation (Latin 'vocatus' meaning called). Parker Palmer warns that when we give something we do not possess, it is a false and dangerous gift. To live full, authentic lives, we must learn to embrace opposites, to live in a creative tension between our limitations and our potential. Otherwise, high demands can quickly exhaust our resources. Intentional spirituality can help to build up and replenish these resources, particularly by helping teachers discern if, through teaching, they have found a place where the talent and joy of their deepest selves meets the world's great need for education.

There is a resounding ring of truth to the statement that the quality of a school is only as good as the quality of its teachers. But what keeps teachers alive and enthusiastic within the profession? What keeps good teachers in the classroom?

It was Plato's contention that people will care for, and do well at, work they love. Tapping into the spiritual root of teaching can keep teachers enthusiastic and fresh in practice, even after many years. Once we realise that teaching is a spiritual activity, we recognise that our starting point must be the teacher in the classroom. Rather than teaching subjects or students, we primarily teach who we are – from within – from the standpoint of our own integrity and identity. Spirituality can help address the question 'Who am I?' which leads inevitably to the equally important question 'Whose am I?' for there is no selfhood outside of relationship.

In order to teach in a manner that is energising and enlivening, it is important to understand that the outcome does not depend solely on the teacher. Teaching and learning are part of ongoing everyday living – a continuous cycle of growth and re-growth, different for every individual on the journey we call life.

The Spirituality of Learners
The spirituality of learning is about what W.B. Yeats describes as 'hearing in the deep heart's core'.[1] It is important that what we teach resonates in the hearts and souls of our students and connects with what really matters to them. Real learning takes place when the subject matter is linked with the everyday lives of the learners. Regardless of the subject at hand, from the characters and dynamics of *Macbeth* to the events that precipitated the First World War, we can ask 'What of this do you see in yourself and in your own life?' The aim and end product of good teaching involves the penetration of the spirit of the person and not just the mind. Teachers challenge each learner to reach whatever potential they have at this stage in their lives. This involves affirming the learner while simultaneously asking them to challenge and expand their minds, hearts and hands. In so doing good pedagogy engages the soul.

As teachers we are constantly confronted with the question of how to teach well and learn with and from our students. How do we grow as persons and enable our classroom communities to grow in spirituality and learning alongside us? One great pedagogy that honours the spirituality of teaching and learning is the pedagogy of discovery. Through the *Eureka* moment our spirits connect with the great and timeless spirit of re-discovered knowledge. For instance, over my years of teaching, I have noticed that for the most part, young people love colour – colourful clothes, classrooms, diagrams, and crystals! In order to wrestle with the concept of Brownian motion, my Junior Cert Science students filled a set of beakers with cold water, collected some tiny concentrated (and hence very dark) crystals,[2] and slowly inserted them, one by one, into the beakers. As the solid dissolved, they could see exquisite strands of colour moving randomly through the water until the formerly colourless liquid was a rich shade of purple. As they repeated the procedure, they discovered that each time, a different pattern emerged in the water. Thus, they came to understand that the movement of the crystal particles in the water was random. Like the disciples on the road to Emmaus, the students came to see for themselves.

In order to honour the spirituality of learners, and indeed their own spirituality, teachers have to strike a balance and use their power as 'power with' rather than power over or against. 'Power with' means conserving from the past and creating for a new future. It is a way of being with students, as pilgrims together. Learning is spiritual when it helps us to enter into trusting relationships, with ourselves, with others, with God. In this way we can also enter into true communion with all of God's people.

Spiritual Engagement – The Ignatian Tradition
So far, we have discussed an understanding of spirituality and how that relates to both teachers and learners. The conversation now turns to how teachers can go about caring for their own souls while engaging the souls of their students. There are many spiritual traditions and charisms we can draw from to address this challenge, but spirituality based on the life and teaching of Ignatius of Loyola (1491–1556) otherwise known as the Ignatian tradition, is a particularly life-giving one. Ignatian spirituality was part and parcel of the ministry of education from the first days of the Society of Jesus.

Superior General of the Society, Peter-Hans Kolvenbach, interprets Ignatian vision as 'a positive vision of humanity, summoned to freedom and summoned to take up the burden of *returning the world to God*.'[3] Fr. Kolvenbach speaks of the need for discernment as a means of discovering God's will, and the place of reflection and judgment in good pedagogy. Although its achievement is demanding and time-consuming, the result of this fusion of the spiritual and the pedagogical is deeply contemporary.

Key in Ignatian spirituality is the students' own reflection and discernment – coming to see for themselves, being agents rather than dependents in their own learning – looking at 'data' and drawing from their own experience to understand it, make judgements, and come to their own decisions. This can be applied to all aspects of life and learning. Furthermore, the Ignatian approach emphasises the role of the teacher as a central player in the educational process.

An authentic personal relationship between teacher and student is a crucial factor in this approach. How the teacher conceives of learning, engages students in the quest for truth, as well as the teacher's own integrity and expectations, are seen to have a significant effect on student growth.

According to Ignatian spirituality, my lesson on Brownian motion would not end when the student comes to understand the scientific concept. Rather, it raises an opportunity for critical reflection and discernment. Ignatian spirituality asks students to reflect on where they see themselves in the lesson – how does it belong to them and how does it belong to the world they know? This might involve asking students what springs to mind when they witness the random movement of particles, if the collision between the particles reminds them of any phenomena from their own worlds, or what analogy they can draw between their own lives and the process that results in a small dark solid transforming a large body of water into a richly shaded and harmonious liquid of gorgeous colour.

Ignatian spirituality has many blessings and benefits to offer both teaching and learning. It guides people towards the process of discernment by helping them to recognise what lifts them up and what brings them down, what seems to give them life and what seems to drain life from them. It enables them to trace and take note of the patterns of these movements in their lives. It frames education as a ministry to help souls, as a profoundly meaningful and mutually rewarding service just as it was to the early Jesuits.

Ignatian spirituality has always been a gift. Today's post-modern climate offers an opportunity to unwrap that gift in new and creative ways. We cannot assume that teachers in any school, regardless of the tradition or affiliation of that school, express their spirituality in organised religion. The Jesuit, Michael Amaladoss, asserts that Ignatian spirituality provides a method for accommodating the culturally and religiously diverse contexts that teachers live and work in.[4] This is because God's action is not limited to what God does in Jesus, in other words Ignatian spirituality is not Christo-monistic. Amaladoss concludes that encounter with other cultures is good for Ignatian spirituality and vice versa. The religious experience of Ignatius left him with a great respect for the experiences of every individual and this openness to religious experience is the touchstone for all Jesuit spirituality.

Ignatian spirituality has a very positive view of the whole created order. For Ignatius, God is in all things, and the world is our home. Jesuit spirituality extends to every category of person, no matter who they are or what religious beliefs they hold or abandon. It holds every created thing as sacred. This gives us a lot to think about as teachers and learners in a world of war, famine, and planetary destruction.

Becoming Intentionally Spiritual in Teaching and Learning
The spirituality of teaching and learning can be fostered by various school-based experiences. These might include the experience of leaving home, even

temporarily – perhaps for a retreat or school exchange, and encounter with a perspective radically different to one's own. Reaching out to those in need, what the early Jesuits called 'helping souls', is another foundational block of Ignatian spirituality. Here again the social implications are vast and appeal across religious and cultural boundaries. For instance, service programmes that build on our natural human self-sacrificing impulses can enlarge our horizons and awaken our spiritual impulses. Such experiences can lead to critical reflection on how one's own values and beliefs are formed and changed. This type of experience provokes examination of self, background and values. Community formation is a central task in constructing an intentionally spiritual environment so that people can still seek a relationship with God and affirm the transcendent dimension of humanity even if they are distant from or distrust the institutional Church.

Another factor that can contribute to lifting up the spiritual dimensions of teaching and learning is a positive encounter with a guide, mentor or wisdom figure. Therefore, spiritual mentoring is an important element in schools. Conversation that engages memory, imagination and critical reason allows us to pay attention to the conditions in which we find ourselves, assess how we came to be where we are, and reflect on the possible paths ahead. This is one way of creating a compass to guide us as we move into the future.

We need to create time to pause, reflect, and assess; and we need to learn the value of silence. Silence, paradoxically can be busy or peaceful. Busy silence is the silence that surrounds us as we study, write, mark papers or prepare classes, However interior silence, the type of silence we intentionally seek out for our inner selves helps us to tune into the ebb and flow, the longing and loneliness of the restless spirit. It opens us to our heart's deepest desires. Another important element of this process is the development and practice of a consciousness of connection. Contemporary society steeps us in the virtues of individualism, making us vulnerable to assuming we have autonomy and control, when we do not. Moving beyond this individualism may involve asking 'why' questions, as well as those of 'what' and 'how'. Finally, we can attend to the character and use of language, by choosing images and language that uncover and name, rather than obscure and manipulate, the realties of the world in which we live.

School communities can sponsor appropriate and ongoing lifelong development in spirituality by taking ongoing adult development in spirituality seriously. However, spirituality is not solely a developmental matter. Human beings are gifted at birth with the yearning that is intrinsic to spiritual growth. The restless heart, aching for connection with the larger whole, is part of the human condition. Healthy spirituality is a pattern of being in relation to self, to others and to God. It is about knowing the King within.

Conclusion

Teachers can change lives forever. Perhaps it is because our lives as teachers also continue to be changed forever by our students that we stay in teaching. In the final stanza of the poem 'Among School Children',[5] Yeats rejects the sort of education that excludes any part of existence; instead he finds that life gains purpose and meaning by moving towards ever-greater wholeness and largeness.

> Labour is blossoming or dancing where
> The body is not bruised to pleasure soul,
> Nor beauty born out of its own despair,
> Nor blear-eyed wisdom out of midnight oil.
>
> O chestnut tree, great-rooted blossomer,
> Are you the leaf, the blossom or the bole?
> O body swayed to music, O brightening glance,
> How can we know the dancer from the dance?

As a member of the Irish Senate, Yeats found that the school visits he conducted inspired various and sometimes conflicting ideas of education. His fear was that no possible life could fulfill the dreams of the schoolchildren he met, or even their teachers' hopes, but ultimately concluded that education should be a dance (revealing the unity of humankind, moving towards union with God). This transcendent destiny gives our lives meaning, value and significance that we begin to realise here and now through our relationships. It influences the way we approach life, the way we relate to others and, the way we teach and learn.

As teachers we enter the profession with a myriad of hopes and dreams. The successes and disappointments we experience can change who we are as persons and how we envision life. Nobody leaves their spiritual self in the car park or enters the workplace as a body without spirit. How we see ourselves and, how we deal with the ebb and flow of daily living are part and parcel of how we conduct our classrooms. We are in our very essence spiritual beings. We dream, hope, imagine, remember, create, grieve and do so much more that bespeaks the spiritual nature of humanity. Our spirituality affects how we connect, appreciate or turn away from life itself. It is part of the human condition to try to make sense of our lives and to connect with something larger than ourselves. How we do this individually and collectively and the broad stroke answers we come up with makes a difference to how we look at life, and how, as teachers, we live our lives inside and outside the classroom.

Notes

1 'The Lake Isle of Innisfree' in W.B. Yeats, *The Poems*, ed. Daniel Albright, London: Everyman/J.M. Dent, 1994.

2 I use crystals of Potassium Permanganate ($KMnO_4$). These crystals are so concentrated that they appear almost black, so the rich purple colour that the students 'create' makes quite an impression!

3 Peter-Hans Kolvenbach, in *Men of God: Men for Others*, interview by Renzo Giacomelli, United Kingdom: St Paul Publications, 1990, p. 96.

4 Michael Amaladoss, 'Inculturation and Ignatian Spirituality', *Ignatian Spirituality and Mission, The Way Supplement*, No. 79, Spring 1994.

5 'Among School Children', in Yeats, op. cit., p. 263.

Further Reading

Durka, Gloria, *The Joy of Being a Catechist – from Watering to Blossoming*, New York: Resurrection Press, 1995.

Glazer, Stephen, *The Heart of Learning: Spirituality in Education*, New York: Jeremy P. Tarcher/Putnam, 1999.

Groome, Thomas H., *Educating for Life*, Texas: Thomas Moore, 1998.

Palmer, Parker, *The Courage To Teach*, San Francisco: Jossey-Bass Publishers, 1998.

SECTION 2

READING FOUNDATIONAL DOCUMENTS AND TEXTS

SECTION 2

CHAPTER 5

CREATIVE USE OF THE BIBLE
IN RELIGIOUS EDUCATION

Anne O'Leary

With the help of the Holy Spirit who dwells in us,
look after that precious thing given in trust.

(1 Tim 1:14 NJB)[1]

Christians believe that the creativity of the cosmos, the world, and each living thing is a reflection of the Great Creator, God. Within the grand scale of created things 'humanity alone is called to assist God. Humankind is called to co-create' (Hildegard of Bingin).[2] The creative use of the Bible in Religious Education is one such exercise in co-creativity, not least because it holds the account of and transmits that 'precious thing given in trust' that the author of 1 Timothy speaks about (cf. 1:14). The role of the religious educator in creatively using the sacred text is to facilitate greater connectivity between the divine and human realms. The role of the student is to investigate the Sacred Story, which is laden with meaning and to apply its religious wisdom to life.[3]

The dimension of intelligence that manifests itself as imagination is what is most called upon in undertaking any creative project. When a religious educator can share that sense of his or her awe of God and faith-matters in *play-full*, *prayer-full* and *practical* ways, something 'precious' happens.

The creative use of the Bible in Religious Education works best when a lesson is planned as a dialectical process. In a good lesson, both the religious educator and the students can be formed and nurtured by the Word, Jesus Christ. Both can participate happily, albeit in different capacities, in the business of 'creating heaven on earth' or, in biblical diction, bringing about the Kingdom and Reign of God. Both can be busy about what the ancients imagined the purpose of religion to be – the enterprise of re-linking (Lt., *religare*) the natural world to the supernatural one.

In keeping with the theme of re-linking, the approach in this chapter is based on the principle of integration. The chapter will suggest ways in which the Bible can be used creatively in Religious Education, by linking it with all seven areas of the Irish 1999 curriculum – Language, Social Environmental and Scientific Education (SESE), Social, Personal and Health Education (SPHE), Arts Education, Mathematics, Physical Education (PE) and Religious Education (RE).[4] The methods outlined below must, of course, be adapted to match the age and stage of development of the students. For any of the methods suggested, the Religious Education teacher can invite other teachers to participate in the lessons, especially those with special expertise in the particular discipline(s) with which Religious Education is being linked.

The Christian Bible

The Christian Bible is made up of two parts: the first and larger part consists of the forty-six books of the Hebrew Bible ('Old Testament') which tells us much about the God of the Israelites; the second and smaller part consists of the twenty-seven books of the New Testament (NT), which tells us much about Jesus of Nazareth. The books of the Old Testament (OT) are divided by genre into four categories – Torah/Pentateuch ('the Five Books of the Law of Moses'), History, Wisdom and the Prophets. Thirty-nine of these books are also found in the sacred scriptures of Judaism which is called 'The Hebrew Bible'. The other seven are called 'Deutero-canonical books' ('secondary but sacred'– namely, Tobit, Judith, Wisdom, Sirach, Baruch, One and Two Maccabees) because they were composed in Greek and added to the first collection of books composed in Hebrew (c.third century BCE). It is common today to refer to all the books in the OT as the 'Hebrew Bible' as it keeps to the fore the debt that Christianity owes to Judaism.

The Hebrew Bible provides a record of the Israelites' experience of God's involvement with them in the geographical and spiritual journeys that they made throughout their history. The books of the NT are divided by genre into three categories – Gospels (Matthew, Mark, Luke-Acts, John), Letters or Epistles, and one Apocalyptic book (Revelation). It provides a record of how God becomes involved in the history of the world in an utterly new way through the incarnation that happens when God becomes flesh in Jesus (Jn 1:14). The NT records Jesus' pre-existence with God since the beginning of time and how at a point in history he is born of Mary in Bethlehem through the power of God's Holy Spirit (c. 4 CE). It records how, in his life, death, and resurrection, he reveals himself to be the Messiah whom the people called 'the Christ' ('Anointed'), 'the Son of God' and 'Saviour of the world', and it records that, subsequent to the resurrection, he promises that his spiritual presence will be with those who believe in him and in the community that forms the Church (Gk., *ekklesia*).

The entire Bible provides a testimony of faith that continues to be normative and authoritative for Christians of every generation. It is, therefore, a foundational text without which the subject of Religious Education cannot be adequately taught.

Creative Methodologies

1. Linking the Bible with Language: *Learning the Story*
A fundamental purpose in using the Bible in Religious Education is to teach the Great Story of God in the history of the salvation of humankind and the cosmos by means of teaching some of the many short(er) stories found in its different books. Here are four suggestions for the creative use of the Bible in learning the Story.

Creating one's own *Bible Reader* or *Class Bible* is a way of introducing the Bible stories gradually and at the appropriate level of the students in order to better prepare them to come to know and love the canonical Bible. Begin by telling the stories and having the students re-tell them ('oral tradition'). Follow this by having the students write or type paraphrases of the stories ('scribal work'). Collect these accounts ('collection'). Through discussion, select what OT and NT stories will be put in the *Bible Reader* or *Class Bible Edition* (which is akin to determining the 'canon'). Edit the version of each story that has been selected ('redaction'). Finally, have the students write the final edition of the stories using calligraphy on hand-made paper or by typing them in an old-style script on computer to which can be added other appropriate computer-generated effects. Place these in a scrapbook or bind them between covers ('codex'). If one wishes to be able to add stories over a period of time, placing them in a ring binder may be a good option.

This is one creative way of teaching the students the formation process that was involved in the creation of the Bible. Bible stories can be read from this edition during the school year, and it may be kept by the teacher as a sample *Bible Reader* or *Class Bible* for students of a similar age or stage in subsequent years.

Bi-lingual or multi-lingual students, and English as an Additional Language (EAL) students, may complete this project in full or in part in another language. The work of recording and translating biblical texts into the languages of the world has been done ever since the Hebrew Bible was translated into Greek *(Septuagint)* c. 300–200 BCE. At that time, Greek had become the spoken language of many of the Jews living outside of Israel and so the change ensured that the stories could continue to be told and remembered.

A very popular method of learning language and communication skills in the United States is through the method of *Spelling Bees* or spelling competitions among students. These competitions occur at local-school, regional and national levels. For the creative use of the Bible in Religious Education, teachers can create their own *Bible Spelling Bee* list; that is, a list of words taken from a Bible story or stories that they wish the students to learn to spell, to understand and also to incorporate when they re-tell the story or write their version of it. If the teacher selects key words from a story, the students may be asked to indicate the story in which a key word or cluster of key words is found (e.g. 'tax collector', 'sycamore tree', 'welcome', etc. as found in the story of Zacchaeus, Lk 19:1-10). Competitions may be organised within a class, or between classes of a year group, and/or throughout the particular cycle of a school (e.g. Junior, Senior). A variant on the above exercise could be the playing of *Bible Scrabble* where the students, using a regular scrabble board, may make words from the *Spelling Bee* list that the teacher has created.

Finally, another creative way of linking language study and the Bible is to select 'riddles' from it, and to ask the students to discuss these and explore their meaning. These 'riddles' can be short pithy statements or long(er) parables. They belong to the genre of wisdom sayings in the Bible. Consider the following samples: Jesus said that, 'Many who are first will be last, and the last will be first' (Mt 19:30); or '[The Kingdom] It is like a mustard seed that someone took and sowed in the garden; it grew and became a tree, and the birds of the air made nests in its branches' (Lk 13:17 pars.). Part of the riddle involves knowing that mustard seeds do not grow to be trees but small shrubs (Mt 10:39; Jn 4:13; 6:35). A class can compile a collection of their favourite *Bible Riddles* over a period of time and, perhaps, memorise some of them.

2. Linking the Bible with Social Environmental and Scientific Education (SESE): *Inside-Out*

The study of the natural, human, social and cultural dimensions of the peoples of the Bible contributes also to learning about and understanding 'the world behind the text'. Here are three suggestions for the creative use of the Bible in learning about the historical and scientific world of communities mentioned in the Bible and their relationship with God. This exercise also focuses on the geography of the Bible lands, in particular, that of Israel (Hb. 'land of God').

One such creative way is to create a *Cosmic Story Time-Line* with 'markers' and key details for each of the major epochs or stages in the creation of the cosmos and planet earth. This can be linked with the seven stages or days outlined in the first Creation account in the Bible (cf. Gen 1:1-2:4). It helps if the *Time-Line* can be plotted on the floor of a room so that students can 'walk' from epoch to epoch.

Create a *Bible/Salvation Story Time-Line* of the major religious and historical events in the life of the Israelites as they became a Covenant People up to and including the time of Jesus who wrought the New Covenant. Setting the second *Time-Line* along side the first (or a 'marker' for it) can help the students to see, often with radical amazement, the expanse of time from the beginning of creation to the birth of Jesus, the Son of God, into history.

Another interesting exercise for students can be the study of a selection of biblical texts about cosmology, and in particular, the sun, moon and stars and the God who created the heavens and the earth (cf. Gen 1:1-2:4; 37; Ps 148). This study can be linked to what we now know about the planets through more recent scientific discoveries. A field trip to a planetarium, or perhaps more realistically, a virtual on-line tour of a planetarium would be an ideal element to link with this exercise. Also an outdoor prayer service thanking God for the wonders of the cosmos using some of the key biblical texts cited above would link the majesty of the universe with the students' experience of it.

A third exercise might involve the creation of a *Bible Cultures* Index. This index would focus on aspects of some or all of the main Bible Cultures including: Egyptian; Assyrian and Babylonian; Canaanite; Greek; Roman; Samaritan and especially Jewish culture. This would involve studying select biblical texts and using resource tools such Bible Dictionaries to find out about aspects such as the language, dress, cuisine, occupations, social, political and religious customs, roles of men and women, categories of outcasts, and the geography of where they lived and worshipped. This can help students to enter into both 'the world behind the text' that is, the real world of the relevant period of the OT and/or NT, and 'the world within the text', that is, the world as recorded by the author of the particular book(s). The students could then be asked to compare the culture(s) studied with their own culture(s) and to solicit the similarities and differences between them.

Finally, a teacher can introduce students to eco-spirituality by studying biblical texts that have to do with creation and ecology and by doing a project about the animals, minerals and precious stones, and vegetables that are mentioned in the Bible. Students can be asked to look up references that the teacher selects from a Bible Concordance. This can be complemented by finding pictures from the world of nature which can be found in picture Bible Dictionaries (cf. Gen 7:7-9; Ex 24:10; 28:18; Mt 6:25-34; Lk 15:4-7).

A teacher may also have students create a windowbox or outdoor Bible/Prayer Garden. In reading related biblical texts, students can come to appreciate that everything is created by God and that everything exists to give God glory (cf. Dan 3:57). By sowing and nurturing seeds that will bring life and beauty to the school and/or local environment, students are continuing to fulfil the great mandate that the Risen Jesus gave to his first disciples: 'Go into all the world and proclaim the good news to the whole creation' (Mk 16:15, NRS; cf. Rom 8:23; Gal 5:22).[5]

3. Linking the Bible with the Religious Environment: *Building Faith, Building Family*

We live in what many biblical scholars call 'the world in front of the text'. Like all generations before us who heard or read Bible stories, we are called to use them positively to build faith and family. This includes the biological family, the school family and the ecclesial family or Church: 'God's purpose through Scripture within the Church, is to shape us as people, to bring us into conformity with Christ'.[6] Here are three suggestions of how this can happen.

It has long been customary for parents to read Bible stories at bedtime to children. Older family members or guardians can support this practice if they have their own personal Bibles and are seen to prayerfully read passages that are of help in reviewing the gift of each day at its close. Teachers can guide parents in recommending good resources that can be used at home – such as daily guides to the Bible, Bible story books, liturgical calendars, bedroom posters with scripture quotations, or biblically inspired symbols.

Bible stories can be incorporated regularly in the life of the school community. For example, a short section can be read at assemblies or as part of the schools' daily prayer-over-the intercom or placed on the school's website. Suitable Bible posters and quotations can adorn the sacred-space(s) where the change of the liturgical seasons and special days are creatively marked – for example, the opening/closing of the school year, retreat days, feast days, times of bereavement or particular gratitude, etc.

As students prepare for the Sacraments of Initiation, religious educators ordinarily teach them about related Bible stories that help make them more meaningful. When planning and rehearsing for these or any other liturgies, a teacher can avail of the opportunity to teach students something about the function of the ministry of the Word and the role of lectors in the liturgical life of the Church.

4. Linking the Bible with Social, Personal and Health Education (SPHE): *Me and You Together, Building a Better World*

One of the aims of Religious Education is to foster the relationship of each student with God, with others, with themselves and with the whole of creation. It is about fostering 'right relationships' as a way of helping to bring about the Kingdom/Reign of God upon earth. The aim of SPHE is 'to foster the personal development, health and well-being of the child, and to help him/her create and maintain supportive relationships and become an active and responsible citizen in society'.[7] Here are two suggestions of how the use of the Bible in Religious Education links well with SPHE.

The creation of *Bible Buddies* is a way of linking both of the above aims. *Bible Buddies* involves getting an older person (perhaps grandparent, sibling, student(s) of another culture/faith tradition) to meet with a student or group of students at a regular time over a set period of time (e.g. once a week) to read and share selected Bible stories. As well as learning about the Bible, it can help to build supportive inter-generational, inter-cultural and inter-faith/religious relationships.

Another way of having a *Bible Buddy* is to select a biblical character to befriend (it can be God, Jesus, an angel, or any other biblical person). After reading the Bible story/stories in which this character appears, each student writes a response to this character or an imaginary dialogue between herself/himself and the character in a journal/on a blog. The teacher sets the reading programme for the students and gives feedback periodically. This is an exercise in theological reflection, the chief purpose of which is to foster self-reflection and to deepen a student's relationship with God such that s/he can begin to find the sacred in all of life's experiences. The poet, Gerard Manley Hopkins, assures all faith-seekers that they will not be disappointed if they look at life with expectant eyes 'for Christ plays in ten thousand places'.[8]

Teachers can also introduce students, from a very young age, to the idea of 'doing justice in the way of Jesus' through the creative use of NT stories. An excellent educator will help students explore ways in which the principles of justice that Jesus promotes may be applied today. The nature of the application will vary with the nature of the class group but at all levels the aim of the applied element is to foster generosity, self-sacrifice and prayer-inspired action. These gifts, in turn, often bear fruit in some form of volunteerism toward the creation of a more ethical community.

5. Linking the Bible with Arts Education: *Seeing is Believing*
It has long been recognised that 'the Bible evokes art and inspires artistic interpretation, which in turn *redescribes* its primary text'.[9] The Bible is often most creatively used when the methodologies used in visual arts, music and drama are called into play. Here are some suggestions on how to creatively link the Bible with Arts education.

Many of the great biblical narratives have been painted or sculpted by great artists through the ages – such as Michelangelo (1475–1564) and Leonardo da Vinci (1452–1519). Artists understand more than most that the soul speaks in images. Copies of such great art can be used to teach these bible stories to students. Upon seeing such art, or upon hearing/reading the stories of the Bible, students of all stages and talents can present their responses through drawing, painting, creating collages or pottery. Such 'training in perceptual skills is comparable to training in literacy'[10] and can be very effective as part of the meaning-making process ('hermeneutic of interpretation') which is at the heart of Religious Education.

The use of drama, mime, music, and song or a combination of these can also prove wonderfully effective in the teaching of the Bible in Religious Education. Many of the Bible's narratives are relayed in dramatic forms that have often been used as the basis of musical compositions, dramas, operas, and musicals down the ages. Creative use of these – for example: the use of drama editions of the Bible; the composition and production (or viewing on DVD) of select Bible stories adapted as dramas, operas or musicals; the use of some of the great religious music of the ages, can bring much of the biblical world and meaning to life for the students.

Music forms a great part of life and worship of the people of the OT and NT. It can be a wonderful exercise to study the biblical stories that give accounts of how the ancients expressed their feelings toward God in music and song at the temple during the annual feasts (cf. Pss 140–150). It can be effective to follow such a study by teaching students music for worship and biblical songs or hymns which, in turn, can be used for (para-)liturgical occasions at the school or local church (cf. Eph 5:19; Col. 3:16; Jam 5:13; Rev 15:3).

6. Linking the Bible with Mathematics: *Adding it All Up*
If mathematics helps students 'to think and communicate quantitatively and spatially, and solve problems'[11] then these skills can contribute to a better understanding of much that is recorded in the Bible and, concomitantly, be further honed by the application to same. Let us explore two creative ways in which the use of the Bible and mathematics can be integrated.

A teacher can creatively explore the Bible with students by comparing the use of numbers in biblical times with the present time by examining topics such as the use of calendars, dates of feast days and key events, people's ages, currencies, games, and measurements. Creating charts to record findings of such numbers, or cardboard replicas of buildings – such as the Temple in Jerusalem or a domestic house at the time of Jesus – can be ways of coming to understand better the worlds of the patriarchs, kings, prophets and priests, and most especially, Jesus, and comparing these to our own.

Certain biblical numbers such as three, seven, twelve, forty, fifty and a thousand, have religious meanings. A study of texts where these occur can be a way of introducing students to number symbolism in the Bible. A list of the texts in which these numbers are used can be found in a Bible Concordance or by doing a search using bible software. For senior students, the use of numbers in structuring biblical books, whole or in part (e.g. Gospel of Matthew), is a way of introducing students to the theology of inspiration, that is, the way God, the Ultimate Author, chose and inspired gifted people to write these accounts for posterity. Most Bible Commentaries and Study Bibles provide an analysis of the structure of the book(s) you may wish to study.

A creative way to summarise the findings of a biblical story can be to create 'religious equations'. For example, in response to reading the story of the Good Samaritan (Luke 10; cf. James 2:17–18), a teacher might offer the following two equations and get the students to assess which 'adds up' and which does not:

1. Holiness + Helpfulness = builds the Kingdom/Reign of God (cf. Lk 10:33-35, 36-37)
2. Holiness − Helpfulness = fails to build the Kingdom/Reign of God (cf. Lk 10:30-32)

Of course, the cryptic nature of the equations offered must reflect the stage of development of the students. Equally, the students may create their own 'religious equations' in response a biblical story.

7. Linking the Bible with Physical Education (PE): *A Prize Worth Running After!*
In teaching students about 'the precious thing given in trust' (1 Tim 1:14), namely the Bible, one is ultimately saying that the Truth it contains is worth 'running after'. Paul reminds us of this: 'Do you not know that in a race the runners all compete ... run in such a way that you may win it. Athletes ... do it to receive a perishable wreath, but we [the disciples of Jesus, do it to receive] an imperishable one' (1 Cor 9:24, NRS). The Truth, which is the prize, can be summed up in one sentence: 'God is love, and whoever remains in love remains in God and God in him [her]' (1 Jn 4:16 NJB). The disciples knew that the sending of God's son, Jesus, was the greatest sign of God's love. Today, as in Jesus' time, his disciples 'run' in order to win the prize of knowing God's love as revealed in Jesus Christ through the power of the Holy Spirit.

Here is a final suggestion about the creative use of the Bible in Religious Education. A teacher can use creative dance as a response to many biblical texts which invite its hearers/readers to praise God for all things, including the gifts of the human body and movement (cf. Ps 68:4). It can be used as a medium to reflect on the many ways in which Divinity dances into our lives asking us if we would like to join in the dance of life (cf. Zeph 3:17). As a way of reflecting on the uniqueness of each person in God's eyes, students can be invited to dance 'into who they are and toward who they are called to be' as they respond to the music of different tempos. Using biblical hymns, or suitable instrumental music pieces (perhaps, from different parts of the world), a teacher can teach or facilitate a group of students to design a liturgical dance movement which can be used at special liturgies or para-liturgies at the school or local church as an exercise in the worship of the Lord of the Dance, Jesus Christ. Today, as in Jesus' time, his disciples are willing 'to move everything' in their lives in order to become anchored in him (cf. Mk 1:16-20 pars.).

Conclusion

To engage in the creative and faith-full use of the Bible in Religious Education is to be about the business of looking after something very precious that has been given to us in trust. It is to be about the business of co-creating with God. It is to be about the business of linking heaven and earth. Anyone who engages seriously is drawn to learn the Great Story inside-out such that it moves her/him to teach others the importance of participating in the building of faith and family (in all its expressions). Using the Bible in Religious Education also has a corporate 'we' dimension. It about 'us': me and you together, seeking to build a better world. It is about 'seeing and believing' that, somehow, it all does 'add up'; and that, ultimately, the 'precious thing' is a prize worth 'running after'. It is a prize worth the trouble of 'moving everything on earth' because of the assurance of the reward of attaining 'everything in heaven'.

The greatest resource in the creative use of the Bible in Religious Education is the teacher. The educator's happy task is to up-skill herself/himself in the creative use of the Bible in Religious Education, and then to do so in the classroom, continually learning through reflection upon the experience. The potential of such an approach finds echoes in the words of the poet C.P. Sisson: 'What we vividly imagine, ardently desire, enthusiastically act upon, must come to pass'.[12] Let us vividly imagine a (new) generation of religious educators who will, with creativity and enthusiasm, use the Bible with young people so that the process enables them and those they are educating to 'Be Good News'[13] for our moment of history in the cosmic story of salvation (cf. Eph 3:16–20).

Notes

1   New Jerusalem Bible.

2   Cited in Julie Cannato, *Radical Amazement: Contemplative Lessons from Black Holes, Super Novas and Other Wonders of the Universe*, Notra Dame: Sorin Books, 2006, p. 80.

3   See *Dei Verbum*, 6:24, cited in Austin Flannery, ed., *Vatican II Documents*, New York: Costello Publishing Company, 1975.

4   The method of integration that will be presented below is based mostly on the 1999 Primary

School Curriculum of the Department of Education and Science, Ireland. However, the model may be adapted to suit the creative use of the Bible in classes at second level education and other learning environments.

5   New Revised Standard Version.

6   John Colwell, 'The Church as an Ethical Community', in Paul Ballard and Stephen R. Holms, *The Bible in Pastoral Practice: Readings in the Place and Function of Scripture in the Church*, London: Darton, Longman & Todd, 2006, pp. 296–304, especially, p. 215.

7   Primary School Curriculum. See n. 4 above.

8   The Windhover.

9   Gail Ricciuti, 'The Bible and the Arts', in Paul Ballard and Stephen R. Holmes, op. cit., p. 298.

10   Jo Milgrom, *Handmaid Midrash: Workshops in Visual Theology*, Philadelphia: The Jewish Publication Society, 1992, p. 5.

11   Primary School Curriculum; see n. 3 above.

12   C.P. Sisson, *Winged Thoughts from the Heart: A Traveller's Journey*, New Zealand: Total Press, 1990, p. 1.

13   This phrase was inspired by the title of the new Draft National Directory for Catechesis, *Be Good News*, commissioned by the Irish Catholic Bishops in 2005.

Bible Tools

Biblical Dramas. For 4–12 Yr Olds. Alive-O Religious Education Programme for Primary School, Dublin: Veritas, 2007.

BibleWorks 7 Bible Software, www.bibleworks.com (accessed 10.08.08).

Logos Bible Software 2007, www.logos.com (accessed 10.08.08).

Michael Perry (ed.), *The Comprehensive Dramatised Bible*, London: HarperCollins, 2004.

Further Reading

Be Good News, Draft National Directory for Catechesis, Maynooth: St Patrick's College, 2005.

Cannato, Julie, *Radical Amazement: Contemplative Lessons from Black Holes, Super Novas and Other Wonders of the Universe*, Notra Dame: Sorin Books, 2006.

Conference of Irish Catholic Bishops, *Draft National Directory for Catechesis*, Maynooth: St Patrick's College, 2005.

Flannery, Austin (ed.), *Vatican II Documents*, New York: Costello Publishing Company, 1975.

Milgrom, Jo, *Handmade Midrash: Workshops in Visual Theology*, Philadelphia: The Jewish Publication Society, 1992.

Primary School Curriculum of the Department of Education and Science, Ireland, www.education.ie.

Ricciuti, Gail, 'The Bible and the Arts', in Paul Ballard and Stephen R. Holms, *The Bible in Pastoral Practice: Readings in the Place and Function of Scripture in the Church*, London: Darton, Longman & Todd, 2006, pp. 296–304.

Sisson, C .P., *Winged Thoughts from the Heart: A Traveller's Journey*, New Zealand: Total Press, 1990.

CHAPTER 6

GUIDING PRINCIPLES FROM THE GENERAL DIRECTORY FOR CATECHESIS

Thomas H. Groome

The modern catechetical movement is often dated from the emergence of the 'Munich Method' around the beginning of the twentieth century. This was the first notable attempt to draw upon the still-young science of pedagogy to enhance the Church's catechetical ministry. Initiated within the archdiocese of Munich, it was a significant departure from the then reigning question/answer memorisation of the national catechisms; it strongly encouraged active participation by students in a teaching/learning dynamic and that they correlate instruction in faith with their everyday lives.

In the intervening one hundred years or so, many movements and authors have contributed to what we now identify as 'contemporary catechesis.' Much ground has been gained toward effective ways to educate and nurture people in life-giving and responsible Christian faith. There would be many ways to draw together a summary of what now might be called 'guiding principles' as we move forward. However, I propose that the *General Directory for Catechesis* (hereafter GDC) does this for us and with the authority of a document from the magisterium for the universal Catholic church.

Issued on August 15, 1997 by the Congregation for the Clergy, the Vatican agency entrusted with oversight of the Church's catechetical ministry – the GDC replaces even as it builds upon the *General Catechetical Directory* of 1971. It opens with a resounding affirmation of Vatican II as 'the great catechism of modern times' (no. 3), and then celebrates that 'the catechetical renewal developed in the Church over the past decades continues to bear very welcome fruit,' listing its significant achievements (no. 24).

The GDC has five sequential parts that focus on the *nature* and *purposes* of catechesis, its *content*, its *pedagogy*, its participants, and its *context* in the particular Church and culture. I will review each part to highlight its guiding principles, sometimes echoing other sections that amplify the same point. Of course, my listing of the principles is partial, in both senses of the term – limited and perspectival. This is why the whole document is really worth reading.

Overview and Guiding Principles
The very title of Part I – 'Catechesis in the Church's Mission of Evangelisation' – summarises the understanding of the *nature* of catechesis reflected throughout. It describes evangelisation as 'the process by which the Church, moved by the Holy Spirit, proclaims and spreads the Gospel throughout the entire world' (no. 48). Here catechesis is the deepening function within that evangelising umbrella. 'Catechesis, distinct from the primary proclamation of the Gospel, promotes and matures initial conversion, educates the convert in the faith, and incorporates him [or her] into the Christian community' (no. 61).

As such, catechesis is to be 'a school of faith, an initiation and apprenticeship in the entire Christian life' (no. 30). Such apprenticeship in Christian faith is ongoing, requiring 'permanent catechesis' – a phrase repeated throughout. Indeed, 'Adhering to Jesus Christ sets in motion a process of continuing conversion, which lasts for the whole of life' (no. 56). Principle: *catechesis should inform, form, and transform people in Christian faith by schooling them in its wisdom, nurturing their identity, and embarking them upon lifelong conversion.*

The *purposes* of catechesis are stated variously but all are shaped by the core conviction that lived discipleship of Jesus Christ is the defining intent. So, catechesis must 'put people in communion and intimacy with Jesus Christ (no. 80), and 'apprentice' them to Jesus (an oft-repeated term), presenting 'Christian faith as the following of his person,' (no. 41), which requires 'full and sincere adherence to his person and the decision to walk in his footsteps' (no. 53). Further, this apprenticeship can be effected only by incorporating people into Christian community (no. 65–68 and passim). Principle: *The defining purpose of catechesis is that people become Christian disciples, as in living 'the way' of Jesus, in and through Christian community.*

Following on, Christian discipleship is not simply for one's own sake nor is the Church an end in itself. The core of Jesus' preaching was 'the Kingdom of God, as the urgent and definitive intervention of God in history' (no. 34). So, the ultimate purpose of catechesis is to build up this 'Kingdom of justice, love and peace' that was 'so central to the preaching of Jesus' (no. 102). As 'catechist of the Kingdom of God' (no. 163) – what a lovely title – Jesus preached and lived a 'message of liberation'; through his paschal mystery, Christ effected a 'radical liberation' in human history. Now his disciples are called to 'a preferential option for the poor' and to help bring about true liberation for all (no. 103–105). Principle: *Catechesis should promote the social responsibilities of Christian faith, empowering people to do God's will 'on earth as it is in heaven.'*

Part II, entitled 'The Gospel Message,' offers 'norms and criteria' for what should be taught as the 'content of the Gospel message' (no. 92, 93). A vital point in this section and echoed throughout is the GDC's holistic sense of Christian faith. So, when realised in people's lives, Christian faith has 'cognitive, experiential, [and] behavioural' aspects (no. 35); it engages people's minds, emotions, and wills; it permeates how we make meaning out of life, the quality of all our relationships, and the ethic by which we live (no. 16). Later, it echoes the traditional tripod of Christian faith as *lex credendi, lex orandi,* and *lex vivendi* – what Christians believe, how to pray and worship, and the morals and values by which to live (no. 122).

This point has great catechetical significance. The Council of Trent (1545–1563) clearly favoured a 'cognitive belief' understanding of Christian faith, understandable in the context of the time when so many beliefs were being challenged. Immediately thereafter the Church's primary catechesis became the question/answer summary of its beliefs. Vatican II, however, retrieved a much more holistic sense of Christian faith; and the GDC follows its lead. Of course, knowledge of the faith is vitally important (e.g. no. 85), but Christian faith requires 'integral formation rather than mere information' (no. 29), so that 'the entire person, at his [her] deepest levels, feels enriched by the word of God' (no. 67). As such, 'formation for the Christian life … comprises but surpasses mere instruction' (no. 68). Principle: *catechesis should engage and educate in faith people's heads, hearts, and hands, their beliefs, their spirituality, and their ethic of life.*

The overall guideline for the content of catechesis is 'the word of God contained in Sacred Tradition and in Sacred Scripture' and as 'given an authentic interpretation' by the Church's Magisterium (no. 95, 96). Earlier, the GDC expressed concern that in the aftermath of Vatican II, catechesis tended to become too Scriptural, neglecting 'the Church's long experience and reflection' congealed in its Tradition (no. 30). Now, while reiterating that 'Sacred Scripture should have a pre-eminent position' (no. 127), the GDC calls for thorough education in both scripture and tradition. It elaborates that the 'seven foundation stones' of catechesis are 'the three phases in the narration of the history of salvation' – the Old Testament, New Testament, and era of the Church – and then the Creed, Sacraments, Morality, and Prayer (no. 130). Principle: *Catechesis must teach the whole Story and Vision of Christian faith.*

Since the working criterion to monitor the doctrinal content taught is the *Catechism of the Catholic Church;* the GDC refers to the *Catechism* repeatedly as 'the doctrinal point of reference for all catechesis' (no. 93, 121, etc.). The *Catechism,* 'structured around the four pillars which sustain the transmission of the faith (the Creed, the Sacraments, the Decalogue, the Our Father)' (no. 122), provides 'a sure and authentic reference text for teaching Catholic doctrine' (no. 121). Principle: *catechists must represent Catholic Christian faith in conformity with the Catechism.*

Part III, entitled 'The Pedagogy of the Faith' proposes a rather amazing general principle by way of methodology, namely that all approaches to catechesis should reflect 'the divine pedagogy' – how God reveals Godself to humankind. In gist, God communicates divine revelation in a deeply human mode, through what the document earlier called 'the fundamental experiences of peoples' lives' (no. 133). I elaborate this methodology below because it is a crucial point of the whole document; for now, enough to say that God's revelation always comes 'according to the mode of the receiver.'

Jesus likewise used such a learner-centered pedagogy, beginning with people's ordinary lives (see the parables) in order to teach great Gospel truths and bring them to lived faith. While catechesis is 'forever the work of the Holy Spirit,' its human agents should employ approaches consonant with 'the school of Jesus the Teacher' (no. 138) by engaging the experiences of those being taught. Principle: *catechetical methods must first consider those being taught to engage their lives and touch their souls.*

From Part IV, entitled 'Those to be Catechised,' I highlight three guiding principles, though indeed there are more. First, and echoing the recommended pedagogy, catechesis must always be crafted to appeal in 'diverse life situations' and adapt 'the Christian message and the pedagogy of the faith' (no. 165) according to age, capacity, background, culture, and so on. In sum, the GDC here and throughout strongly favours inculturation because the Incarnation calls for no less (no. 169); because God in Jesus took on a particular culture, the Gospel must become as native to every time and place. Of course, inculturation must take 'as its necessary and eminent guide' 'the rule of faith', 'illuminated by the Magisterium of the Church and further investigated by theology' (no. 202). Furthermore, in every culture catechesis must discern and build upon 'what has an authentic Gospel value' and likewise oppose 'what bears the mark of sin' (no. 204). Principle: *every catechetical context has seeds and weeds for the Gospel; be alert for both.*

Second, Part IV reiterates a theme throughout the document, that every Christian and Christian community needs 'permanent catechesis'. Beginning with a normative emphasis on adults, it outlines catechesis from infancy to old age, and raises consciousness about catechesis for people with special needs (e.g. the disabled, marginalised). Principle: *catechesis must shift from being child-centred to include all Christians and the whole Christian community.*

Third, here as elsewhere, I love the central emphasis placed on the role of the family in catechesis; 'nothing replaces family catechesis' (no. 178). Yet, instead of putting a didactic role upon parents, the GDC wisely emphasises the ethos of the home. Understanding the family as 'the primary agent of an *incarnate* transmission of faith; (no. 207), its function is to provide a 'positive and receptive environment' and the 'explicit experience and practice of the faith' (no. 178). Family catechesis is 'a Christian education more witnessed than taught, more occasional than systematic, more on-going than structured into periods' (no. 255).

Elaborating around the image of 'domestic church' – revived by Vatican II – the family catechises effectively by reflecting within its life 'the different aspects and functions of the life of the entire Church' (no. 225). In its own way, each family is to share its faith around the word of God, join in prayer and worship within the home, give witness to Christian faith and service to those in need. Principle: *empower parents – with resources, training, networking, programming – to be proactive and primary in the faith formation of their children through the ethos and lifestyle of the home.*

Part V. 'Catechesis in the Particular Church' repeats many of the principles already outlined. As 'catechesis is a responsibility of the entire Christian community' and 'of every member of the community' (no. 220), it outlines the catechetical responsibilities of bishops, priests, parents, educators – everyone has a crucial function in catechesis. Catechesis simply must be communal; 'the Christian community is the origin, locus and goal of catechesis' (no. 254). By community it means 'the family, parish, Catholic schools, Christian associations and movements, and basic ecclesial communities' (no. 253).

Following on, everything about the life of each community should be a source of catechesis for its members and for the community as a whole (no. 221). In fact, every Christian person and minister should have what I call a 'catechetical consciousness,' being intentional to catechise well with every opportunity. Even for Catholic schools, the GDC calls for a shift 'from school as institution to school as community.' Again, the crucial issue is school environment; it should be 'an atmosphere animated by a spirit of liberty and charity' that by its very ethos helps 'to orientate the whole of human culture to the message of salvation' (no. 259). Principle: *The whole life of each Christian community – parish, family, school or programme – should be reviewed for what it teaches and every aspect of each should be crafted so as to maximise its catechetical potential.*

That each Christian person and community must catechise does not at all diminish the need for designated catechists for parishes and schools and that they be thoroughly prepared, spiritually, theologically, and pedagogically. The Church, local and universal, should encourage the 'vocation of catechist,' and give those so called both 'basic training and continuing formation'; catechesis 'is placed at risk if it does not rely on truly competent and trained personnel' (no. 233 and 234). This in turn calls for institutes, colleges, and programs to provide such thorough preparation of catechists and catechetical leaders (no. 250). Principle:

The human agents of catechesis — through whom the Holy Spirit works — must be thoroughly prepared in theology, pedagogy and their own spiritual formation.

Regarding Pedagogy
Though Part III of the GDC focuses on 'the pedagogy of faith,' this is a frequent theme throughout. Since our teaching approach significantly determines what gets done as catechesis, I will dwell at greater length on the pedagogical principles offered by the GDC. In summary: the GDC strongly favours a pedagogy

- that engages people as active participants in the teaching/learning dynamic;
- that draws upon their own life experiences to teach faithfully the scriptures and traditions of Christian faith;
- that enables people to correlate and integrate their own lives and Christian faith into a lived and living faith.

Principle: *Catechesis should be an active and participative process.* A distinguishing feature of contemporary catechesis has been to shift away from a passive mode of instruction as reception and memorisation toward people actively participating in the dynamic through learning from experience and conversation, by reflection and sharing faith together, and by recognising for themselves what it means for their lives. The GDC canonises this paradigm shift in pedagogy.

For example, catechesis should 'promote active participation among those to be catechised' (no. 145), and encourage 'a sense of dialogue and sharing' (no. 159) within the teaching/learning community. Following on, 'in the catechetical process' every participant 'must be an active subject, conscious and co-responsible, and not merely a silent and passive recipient' (no. 167). The rationale for this is both anthropological and theological: 'the active participation of all the catechised in their formative process is completely in harmony, not only with genuine human communication, but specifically with the economy of Revelation and salvation' (no. 157). As noted earlier, God communicates with us 'according to the mode of the receiver'; catechists should do likewise.

Integral to people's active participation, the GDC highlights the role of critical reason in the affairs of faith. It is needed for reflection on human experience, for understanding the faith tradition, and for making it one's own. Instead of blind faith, the GDC urges a 'right understanding of the faith' so that 'the truths to be believed are in conformity with the demands of reason.' It notes that such critical understanding is needed 'to overcome certain forms of fundamentalism as well as subjective and arbitrary interpretations' (no. 175).

The GDC sees a place for memorisation in catechesis – especially 'of the major formulae and texts of the Bible, of dogma, of the liturgy, as well as the commonly known prayers of Christian tradition' but 'such formulae should be proposed as syntheses after a process of explanation' (no. 154). In other words, memorisation should be subsequent to a participative pedagogy, a capstone rather than the foundation.

Principle: *Catechesis should engage people's experiences in teaching the scriptures and traditions of Christian faith.* The past fifty years has been marked by a debate often framed as being between an experiential or a kerygmatic approach to catechesis – whether to emphasise people's experiences or the content of the faith tradition – with a biblical emphasis. In effect, the GDC says 'do both,' urging catechists to engage people's lived experiences as a locus of God's self-disclosure and then to faithfully echo into their lives the word of God as mediated through Scripture and Tradition. (Note: the Greek *katechein* means 'to echo.')

That God reveals Godself in a normative and definitive way through the Bible and Christian Tradition has long been a foundational conviction of Catholicism. We pushed back against the Protestant reformers (Luther, Calvin, etc.) and their cry of '*scriptura sola*' to insist that the Holy Spirit continues to unfold divine revelation and guides the Church to teach it faithfully through time-tested Christian Tradition. As noted earlier, the GDC calls for a balance that duly honours both Scripture and tradition.

Why then should catechesis engage people's lived experiences, encouraging them to reflect upon their lives in order to 'learn' their faith? First, in order to bring 'life' and 'faith' together as 'lived faith' people need to pay attention to 'life' – to what they know from experience, to what is 'going on' in their lives, and to how they might appropriate Christian faith to their every day. The GDC summarises with a bold statement: 'this formation must be closely related to praxis; one must start with praxis to be able to arrive at praxis' (no. 245).

Then, the GDC affirms throughout that God continues to make Godself known in the existential lives of people, using 'human events and words to communicate' (no. 38). Pedagogically, then, 'every dimension of the faith, like the faith itself as a whole, must be rooted in human experience and not remain a mere adjunct of the human person' (no. 87). For the truth is that 'experience promotes the intelligibility of the Christian message'; 'experience is a necessary medium for exploring and assimilating the truths which constitute the objective content of Revelation' (no. 152). Catechesis is most effective if it presents every aspect of the faith tradition 'to refer clearly to the fundamental experiences of people's lives' (no. 133).

Principle: *Catechesis should enable people to integrate their lives and their Christian faith into lived faith.* Following on from the previous principle, the document throughout recommends a pedagogy that correlates life and faith. For example: 'on the one hand, [catechesis] assists the person to open to the religious dimension of life, while on the other, it proposes the Gospel' (no. 147); 'interpreting and illuminating experience with the data of faith is a constant task of catechetical pedagogy'; the key task is to mediate 'a correct ... correlation and interaction between profound human experiences and the revealed message' (no. 153).

Further, 'the relationship between the Christian message and human experience is not a simple methodological question. It springs from the very end of catechesis which seeks to put the human person in communion with God (no. 116). It is by 'correlating faith and life' (no. 207) that 'catechesis ... bridges the gap between belief and life, between the Christian message and the cultural context' (no. 205). Earlier when describing 'the pedagogy of God,' the GDC speaks of 'making one's own' the 'wisdom' of faith and a personal relationship with God (no. 139); such personal appropriation is possible only as people come to see for themselves what their faith means for their lives.

A nuance I would add here is that I don't think 'correlate' is a strong enough term – at least in English – for what the document intends to say; I prefer the term 'integrate.' It is by integrating life and faith – bringing their lives to their faith and their faith to their lives – that people come to be formed in Christian identity and to live as disciples of Jesus. As reflected throughout, the GDC proposes such lived and vibrant faith – discipleship – as the primary purpose of Catholic Christian catechesis.

Some Reservations
Let me emphasise: there are other guiding principles for contemporary catechesis that can be raised up from the GDC. The reader is encouraged to read it for him/herself. Nor do I intend to canonise it as the 'last word' and a perfect document. On the contrary, I have some reservations about it as well. For example, I wonder about the wisdom of placing catechesis entirely within the context of evangelisation, as a kind of sub activity.

Now, the GDC clearly favours Pope John Paul II's proposal of 'a new evangelisation.' By contrast with the 'old,' the new does not emphasise 'bringing them in' – converts into the Church – as much as 'bringing Christians out' into the world with lived and joyful witness to their faith. The GDC also makes clear that the whole Church is itself ever in need of evangelisation. Though evangelisation retains 'an accent on missionary character' (no. 33), this is not the proselytising of previous eras. In fact, catechesis must 'assume an ecumenical dimension everywhere' (no. 197), helping to overcome all forms of religious prejudice and ignorance toward other religious traditions (no. 198), and 'in particular to overcome every form of anti-semitism' (no. 199).

Who knows, maybe the sense of being evangelisers and missionaries again will give those of us in old inculturated faith traditions that 'fire in the belly' we need to catechise effectively – with enthusiasm and excitement about our faith. Yet, the effective history of the word 'evangelisation' strongly implies converting other people – rather than ourselves; so I wonder if it will be effective as the umbrella for all catechesis, and especially in traditional Christian cultures. Which brings me to a second reservation.

I wonder about the GDC's insistence that 'the model for all catechesis is the baptismal catechumenate' (no. 59). The document seems to imagine only through this lens, never recognising that though a rich perspective, it is a limited one. Consequently it tries to fit – nay squeeze – every aspect and kind of catechesis within the paradigm of the catechumenate and specifically the Rite of Christian Initiation of Adults.

Now, it is true that one can 'map' the emergence of adult converts into Christian identity as a catechumenal dynamic – ever gradual and Christocentric – from first interest in the Gospel, to conversion, to profession of faith, to lifelong journey into holiness of life (no. 56). Or, stated in RCIA terms, adult converts should move from the pre-catechumenate, to the catechumenate, to purification and illumination, to mystagogy (no. 88). However, is this the most useful way for parents, for example, to understand their catechetical function in the lives of their children? Might it not be more helpful for them to focus on providing a home ethos suffused with Christian values and to share their faith with their children at every teachable moment. It seems contrived to imagine parents processing their children through the stages and rites of the catechumenate.

I thoroughly appreciate the RCIA and am fully convinced of its pastoral effectiveness. Likewise, the Rite of Christian Initiation of Children, with appropriate adaptation, can be very effective to initiate older children who have not been nurtured in the faith. The GDC itself hits the mark when it says that 'the catechumenate truly and properly belongs' to 'non-baptised adults' (no. 172). Beyond that, to force all catechesis into a catechumenal mode seems too much of a stretch to me.

Lastly, even though the GDC cautions catechists to 'speak a language suited' to the participants (no. 208), its own language – at least in the English translation –

is egregiously insensitive to gender inclusivity. We can surely do better than telling women that they are 'to grow towards the maturity of a free son' (no. 139), or 'to become the perfect Man' (no. 142). This fine document deserved a better rendering.

My critiques notwithstanding, I reiterate that the GDC is a real service to the catechetical mission of the Church and the challenges this central ministry faces in our times. It both helps to hold ground already gained and will open up new horizons in many different contexts.

CHAPTER 7

NOSTRA AETATE AND RELIGIOUS EDUCATION

Dermot A. Lane

In a recent autobiography entitled *The Mighty and the Almighty* (2006), Madeleine Albright, Secretary of State during the second term of Bill Clinton's presidency of the US, regretted that she did not take more interest in religion because of its influence on international affairs, especially in the Middle East. Nicholas Sarkozy, President of France, in the autumn of 2007, sent a letter to teachers suggesting that religion should be taught in all schools, in spite of the strict separation of Church and State in that country. A January 2007 issue of *The Economist* suggests that religion will be a major influence on politics in the twenty-first century.

In spite of the surge of secularisation in the twentieth century, religion has not gone away. To the contrary, religion has made a comeback, even though it must be admitted that this return of religion is fraught with ambiguity. Talk about a 'clash of civilisations' and a 'war on terror' captures some of the emerging ambiguity surrounding the rise of religion. Slogans like these do little to advance an authentic understanding of the religions of the world. Whether we like it or not, religion has the potential to effect great moral and spiritual good in the world. On the other hand, religion also has the capacity to create political conflict and violence as can be seen in the Middle East, Iraq and Afghanistan.

Within this new context, Religious Education has an important role to play in promoting a balanced understanding of individual religions as well as fostering a spirit of mutual respect and understanding among all religions. This new role for Religious Education is increasingly significant in a multicultural and global world. It is important, therefore, for Religious Education, especially Catholic Religious Education, to know where to begin within this new context. Religious Education must ask key questions such as: 'what are the theological foundations inspiring dialogue among the religions?'; 'what are the marks of an authentic dialogue between religions?' and 'what are the implications of this dialogue for Religious Education in the twenty-first century?' The purpose of this article is to outline a brief response to each of these questions.

A Catholic Theology of Inter-Religious Dialogue

For the construction of a Catholic Theology of inter-religious dialogue, a good place to start is the *Declaration on the Relation of the Church to Non-Christian Religions* issued at the second Vatican Council in 1965 and known as *Nostra Aetate* (hereafter abbreviated as *NA*). The history of the genesis and many redactions of this *Declaration* need not detain us here.[1] Instead a summary of the content and subsequent developments will be sufficient for the purposes of this article.

It is enough to note that the original plan at Vatican II was a document on the Jews, and it was only towards the end of the Council in 1964 that it was decided to include the other religions in such a document. *NA* was approved in October 1965, with 2,313 in favour, and 88 against. *NA* has been dubbed 'the Declaration that almost didn't happen',[2] 'a miracle that it was ever passed',[3] and the document which 'revolutionised the Catholic Church's attitude to Jews and Judaism'.[4]

To make a long story short, a document finally entitled a *Declaration on the Relation of the Church to Non-Christian Religions* was issued in October 1965. This document, composed of forty-one sentences, is structured around five articles. While it is the shortest document of the Council, it may be the longest in influence.

Article One declares that humanity forms one community: all come from the same stock created by God and all share the same common destiny.

Article Two notes that throughout history there is found a certain awareness of a hidden power and even recognition of a supreme being. Religions in general seek to answer the big questions of life.

In particular, Hinduism explores the divine mystery and seeks release from the trials of life by ascetical practices, meditation and recourse to God. Buddhism testifies to the essential inadequacy of life in a changing world, and therefore promotes liberation and illumination. This same article goes on to point out that the 'Church rejects nothing of what is true and holy in these religions' and that these religions 'often reflect a ray of that truth which enlightens all'. The article concludes by urging Catholics to 'acknowledge ... the spiritual and moral truths' in other religions.

Article Three points out that 'the Church has ... a high regard for Muslims. They worship God ... who is one, living and subsistent, merciful and almighty, Creator of Heaven and Earth who has spoken to humanity'. They 'submit themselves ... to the decrees of God and they link their faith to Abraham, and they venerate Jesus as a prophet'; they honour Mary, the Virgin Mother; they await the Day of Judgement and the reward of God following the Resurrection of the Dead. This article also acknowledges that there have been controversies over the centuries between Christians and Muslims, urges mutual understanding, and invites Christians and Muslims to promote together peace, liberty, social justice and moral values.

Article Four, the longest, addresses the relationship between the Church and Judaism:

- It recalls the 'spiritual ties which link the people of the New Covenant to the stock of Abraham'.
- It 'acknowledges that in God's plan of salvation, the beginning of its (Christian) faith and election are to be found in the patriarchs, Moses and the Prophets'.
- It says that 'the pillars on which the Church stands, namely the Apostles, are Jewish, as were many of the early disciples'.
- It states that the Jews remain very dear to God since 'God does not take back the gifts He bestowed or the choice He made'.
- It encourages mutual understanding and appreciation through 'biblical and theological enquiry'.
- It notes that 'neither all Jews indiscriminately … nor Jews today, can be charged with crimes committed during "the Passion of Christ"'.
- It points out that 'Jews should not be spoken of as rejected or accursed as if this follows from Holy Scripture'.
- It concludes by stating the Church 'deplores all hatred, persecution, displays of anti-Semitism levelled … against the Jews'.

Article Five concludes by saying 'the Church reproves as foreign to the mind of Christ any discrimination or harassment on the basis of race, colour or religion' and appeals to Christians 'to conduct themselves well among the gentiles'(1 Pet 2:12) and 'to be at peace with all'.

In addition to this *Declaration*, other documents of the Council also deal with the religions of the world, and these are important for understanding and interpreting the full import of *NA*. These documents can be summarised as follows:

The Dogmatic Constitution on the Church, known as Lumen Gentium (November 1964), in article 16 declares that those who have not accepted the Gospel are nonetheless related to the people of God 'in various ways'. There are, first of all, the Jews and then come Muslims who hold to the faith of Abraham and adore the one God. A third group are those who 'in shadows and images seek the unknown God'. Then come those who do not know Christ but who seek God with a sincere heart and follow the dictates of their conscience. Lastly, there are those who, though they do not know God yet, seek to lead a good life and are 'not without grace'. All of these groups, in one way or another have the possibility of attaining salvation through the grace of God. 'Whatever is of good or truth among them is considered to be a preparation for the Gospel' and is given by the God who enlightens all. The claim that the Salvation of God is possible for these different groups raises the question: how is God's Salvation communicated to these different groups?

The beginnings of an answer to this question are given in the Pastoral Constitution on *the Church in the Modern World*, known as *Gaudium et Spes* (December 1965), which points out that 'the Spirit offers to all the possibility of being made partners, in a way known only to God, in the Paschal Mystery' (a.22). In the *Decree on the Church's Missionary Activity*, known as *Ad Gentes* (December 1965), the Council picks up on the theme of the Spirit and says that the Spirit was at work in the world before Christ (a.7) and that the Spirit 'calls all ... to Christ and arouses ... the submission of Faith by the Seed of the Word and the preaching of the Gospel' (a.15). This same *Decree* also talks about 'elements of Truth and Grace ... found among people which are, as it were, a secret presence of God' (a.9) and it also recognises 'those Seeds of the Word which lie hidden' among other religions (a.11).

Looking back at NA in 1965 it must be said that it represented, at that time, 'a watershed in the development of a theology of religions':[5]

1. This was the first time that the Catholic Church reached out positivelyto other non-Christian religions, and this stands out in stark contrast to the traditional representation of religions prior to Vatican II.
2. This was the first time also that the Church had spoken out against thepersecution of the Jews and the presence of anti-Semitism.
3. This was the first time that the Church had opened up the way for dialogue between Christianity and Judaism on the grounds that God does not take back his gifts, and that the Jews, in the past or in the present, cannot be held responsible for the death of Christ.

The reception of NA has been positive, and this can be seen from the following documents of the Church which support the new relationship between Jews and Catholics:

1. In 1974 'Guidelines and Suggestions for implementing the Conciliar Declaration *Nostra Aetate*, Article 4' were promulgated by the Vatican Commission for Religious Relations with Jews.

2. In 1985 'Notes on the Correct Way to Present Jews and Judaism in Preaching and Catechesis in the Roman Catholic Church' were issued by the same Congregation.

3. In 1998 a document entitled 'We Remember: A Reflection on the Shoah' was released by the same congregation.

4. In 2001, the Pontifical Biblical Commission produced a substantial document on *The Jewish People and their Sacred Scriptures in the Christian Bible.*

In addition to these documents on Judaism, mention must also be made of the following documents which deal with the relationship of the Church to other religions:

1. *Dialogue and Proclamation: Reflections and Orientations on Inter-Religious Dialogue and the Proclamation of the Gospel of Jesus Christ,* issued jointly by the Pontifical Council for Inter-Religious Dialogue and the Congregation for the Evangelisation of People, in 1991 to commemorate the twenty-fifth anniversary of *NA.* This document is regarded as the clearest and most important expression of the Church's teaching on inter-religious dialogue.

2. 'Christianity and the World Religions', published by the International Theological Commission in 1997.

3. *Dominus Jesus: On the Unicity and Salvific Universality of Jesus Christ and the Church,* issued in the year 2000 by the Congregation for the Doctrine of the Faith. This document articulates the uniqueness of the Christ-event in the context of other religions and the uniqueness of the Church in the context of ecumenism.

To these documents there must be added the substantial body of writing by John Paul II in support of inter-religious dialogue, especially his encyclicals on the Holy Spirit (*Dominum et Vivificantem,* 1986) and on the Missions (*Redemptoris Missio,* 1990). Instead of detailing this body of substantial literature we will refer briefly to some of the prophetic gestures by John Paul II towards other religions.[6]

In 1986 there was the ground-breaking gathering in Assisi of leaders from other religions with the express purpose of 'being together to pray' for peace, as distinct from praying together. It was a prophetic event that captured the religious imagination of many.

In 2000, the striking image of John Paul II inserting a prayer for forgiveness into a crack in the Western Wall in Jerusalem was captured dramatically by the visual media.

In 2002, a second gathering of the leaders from other religions in Assisi, by way of response to the events of 9/11, took place.

On his election as Bishop of Rome, Benedict XVI pledged to continue the commitment of his predecessor to ecumenism and inter-religious dialogue. On September 12, 2006, the controversial Regensburg Lecture took place which caused offence among many Muslims. On September 17, however, Benedict apologised for offending Muslims, stating: 'I am deeply sorry for the reactions in some countries to a few passages in my address at the University of Regensburg'. In November 2006, Benedict made a journey to Turkey, visited Istanbul's Blue Mosque, during which he gave a 'reflection' and made a gesture of reverence by turning towards Mecca within the Mosque.

In October 2007, 138 Muslim scholars issued 'An Open letter and call from Muslim Leaders' to Benedict XVI and other Christian leaders. This open letter has helped to intensify dialogue between Muslims and Christians around the world, including a series of meetings between Muslim leaders and Vatican officials throughout 2008.

The point emerging from this review of *NA* since the Council is that the Catholic Church has been active in spear-heading inter-religious dialogue. An important body of literature and praxis is available that should inform the commitment and conviction of Religious Educators to inter-religious dialogue as something integral to Catholic Religious Education.

Theological Foundations of Inter-Religious Dialogue
As we have seen, an outline of the foundations of inter-religious dialogue was drawn up at Vatican II in *NA* and other documents. This outline, however, was not developed in any systematic way at the Council; it was advanced in the post-conciliar period by many of the Church documents reviewed above and by the work of Catholic theologians.

By way of introduction to the foundations of inter-religious dialogue, it needs to be noted that *NA* explicitly commends Christians to enter into dialogue with other religions:

> The Church, therefore, urges its sons and daughters to enter with prudence and charity into discussions and collaboration with members of other religions (*NA*, a.2).

The seeds of inter-religious dialogue sown at Vatican II may be summarised as follows:

- All are called by God's grace to Salvation (*LG*, a.13)
- The Spirit offers to all the possibility of being partners in the Paschal Mystery (*GS*, a.2)
- The Spirit of God was active in other religions before Christ and, by implication, after Christ (*AG*, a.4 and *GS*, a.41)
- The seeds of the Word are hidden in other religious traditions (*AG*, a.11 and a.15)
- 'Elements of truth and grace' can be found in other religions (*AG*, a.9)
- The 'Church rejects nothing of what is good and true' in other religions (*NA*, a.2)
- Christians should seek out 'the spiritual and moral truths found among non-Christians' (*NA*, a.2)
- Other religions 'often reflect a ray of that truth which enlightens all' (*NA*, a.2).

From this teaching of Vatican II we will focus on the foundations of the action of the Spirit of God, the seeds of the Word of God, the universality of God's Grace, the uniqueness of the Christ-event, and the unity of the human race.

Dialogue and Proclamation points out: 'the foundation of the Church's commitment to dialogue is not merely anthropological, but primarily theological. God ... has offered and continues to offer salvation to humankind'.[7] The God of Christianity is a God of dialogue and that dialogue came to a point of perfection and fullness in the Incarnation of God in Jesus.

An important foundation for inter-religious dialogue, implicit at Vatican II and developed explicitly by John Paul II, is the universal presence and action of the Spirit of God in the members of other religions. For example, in the Encyclical Letter on the *Permanent Validity of the Church's Missionary Mandate*, known as *Redemptoris Missio*, John Paul II says that the presence and actions of the Spirit 'affect not only individuals, but also society and history, peoples, cultures and religions' (a.28). This action of the Spirit, however, 'is not to be separated from his particular activity within the body of Christ, the Church to whom he gives life and whom he impels to proclaim Christ' (a.29). This emphasis on the universal action of the Spirit is regarded by many as the enduring contribution of John Paul II to inter-religious dialogue. It is interesting to note that when he came to justify the gathering of the other religions in Assisi in 1986 he appealed theologically to the universal presence of the Spirit as the source of all prayer.

It is this action of the Spirit that sows the seeds of the Word of God in other religions. Thus the *Decree on the Church's Missionary Activity* encourages those involved in mission to 'uncover with gladness and respect those seeds of the Word which lie hidden' in other religions (AG, a.11). This reference to the seeds of the Word of God is a retrieval of the doctrine of the seeds of the Word of God emphasised by the early fathers of the Church. In particular Justin Martyr in the second century talks about the seeds of the Word of God scattered throughout the world (*spermatikos logos*) and it is those seeds of the Word that are gathered up, crystalised, and personally made flesh in Jesus of Nazareth. The particular incarnation of the eternal Word of God in Jesus as outlined in the prologue of John's Gospel alludes to the seeds of the eternal Word scattered in Hellenistic philosophy and the history of Judaism. This universal action of the Word of God in creation and history, before and after the Christ-event, must not be separated from the particular incarnation and revelation of the Word in Jesus.[8]

A third theological foundation for inter-religious dialogue can be found in the statement by Vatican II that 'all are called to belong to the new people of God ... and all (are) called by God's grace to salvation' (*LG*, a.13). The universality of God's saving grace and will is stated clearly in the New Testament: 'God ... desires all to be saved and to come to the knowledge of the truth' (1 Tim 2:4). This doctrine of the universality of God's saving Grace in the world has been developed most persuasively by Karl Rahner.

All human beings, according to Rahner, are graced by God from the dawn of time. For Rahner this means that every human being has been gifted with a particular disposition and calling to communion with God. This orientation towards God must be freely accepted by the individual in terms of a faith response which is itself a gift from God.[9]

The ultimate foundation for inter-religious dialogue from a Christian point of view is the uniqueness and universality of the Christ-event. There are, of course, many dimensions to the uniqueness and universality of the Christ-event: revelation, redemption, and the *praxis* of Jesus.

In terms of revelation, Jesus completed and perfected revelation through 'his words and works, signs and miracles, but above all his death and glorious resurrection from the dead, and finally His sending of the Holy Spirit of Truth' (*Dogmatic Constitution on Divine Revelation*,1965, a.4). Jesus as the Christ is the fullest revelation of God to humanity and of humanity to humanity in history (*GS*, a.22). As the revelation of humanity to humanity, Christ 'restores to the children of Adam that likeness to God which had been disfigured ever since the first sin' (*GS*, a.22). Christ 'is the goal of human history, the focal point of the desires of history and civilisation, the centre of humanity, the joy of all hearts, and the fulfilment of all aspirations' (*GS*, a.45, see also *GS*, a.10 and a.22). In Christ we discover who God really is, who we are as human beings, and the opening up of a new vision for the future of the world.

In terms of redemption, the historical death and resurrection of Christ unites Him with every human being, and in doing so prefigures the future of humanity and the destiny of the world: 'in Christ, light is thrown on the mystery of suffering and death ... destroying death by His death' and offering new life through the gift of the Spirit (GS, a.22). On the cross, Christ dies out of love in solidarity with humanity and through the resurrection he anticipates the future glory of the world. For the Christian, the shape of the future is cruciform, the colour of that future is one of 'a bright darkness' wherein brightness emerges out of the darkness of the cross, and the rhythm of that future in the present is paschal in pattern.

In terms of the *praxis* of Jesus, it is noteworthy that the historical Jesus practises inter-religious dialogue in his day. Though sent to the house of Israel, Jesus engages in dialogue with the Samaritan woman at the well (Jn 4: 1-6), heals the daughter of the Canaanite woman in the district of Tyre and Sidon (Mt 15:21-28), and reaches out to the good thief on the cross. There are other instances in the Gospels of Jesus reaching out to the non-Jewish population (Mt 8:5-13; Mk 5:1-20; Mk 7:24-30; Mk 7:31-37; Lk 17:11-19). To follow in the footsteps of Jesus Christ requires that Christians be hospitable to all, especially the religious 'other'.

It is important, however, not to isolate the Christ-event in its particularity from the rest of history. Instead, the Christ-event should be seen as directly linked to the action of the Spirit and the presence of Word in history before and after the Incarnation. Further, the Christ-event is the high-point, perfection and fullest expression of the universal action of the Spirit and the presence of the Word in creation and history in the past and in the present 'until He comes again'.

There are a number of other foundations for inter-religious dialogue that can only be noted in passing here. These include the existence of 'spiritual and moral truths' in other religions (NA, a.2), the recognition that other religions 'often reflect a ray of that truth which enlightens all' (NA, a.2), and the unity of the human family which comes from the same stock and shares a common destiny (NA, a.1). The latter, namely the unity of the human race, is an increasingly important foundation for inter-religious dialogue in the light of globalisation, the migration of peoples, and the ecological threat to the integrity of creation. These new challenges make inter-religious dialogue all the more important and urgent in the twenty-first century.

Marks of Authentic Inter-Religious Dialogue

In the light of these theological foundations for inter-religious dialogue, it is important to have some sense of the qualities, attitudes and characteristics that should accompany dialogue with other religions. It needs to be stated that dialogue is no longer some kind of optional extra for Catholic educators. Rather, in the light of Vatican II and the post-conciliar developments, an essential part of what it means to be a Catholic in the twenty-first century is to be in respectful dialogue with other religions.

Two major documents, published in the early 1990s, capture some dimensions of authentic inter-religious dialogue. In December 1990, John Paul II issued his encyclical *Redemptoris Missio* that gave priority to proclamation as proper to the missionary activity of the Church (a.34). In that encyclical, John Paul II was concerned that the missionary activity of the Church might be replaced by inter-religious dialogue (a.4). Yet, he also recognised that inter-religious dialogue has an important part to play in the missionary life of the Church: 'Inter-religious dialogue is a part of the Church's evangelising mission' and, as such, is not in conflict with the proclamation of the Gospel. Moreover, 'these two elements must maintain both their intimate connection and their distinctiveness' (a.55). The reason why inter-religious dialogue is important to the Church is because 'the Spirit's presence and activity affect not only individuals, but also society and history, peoples, cultures and religions' (a.28).

In May 1991, *Dialogue and Proclamation* was published. This document is regarded by many as the most important statement of the Church on the nature of inter-religious dialogue, and has significant things to say about the nature of that dialogue. This document, building on NA, and other documents of the Council, encourages Catholics to become involved in dialogue at all levels. It lists these levels in terms of the dialogue of life, action, theological exchange and religious experience (a.42). *Dialogue and Proclamation* explicitly acknowledges that dialogue can lead to a deepening and even modification of one's Christian faith 'because the way Christians sometimes understand their religion and practise may be in need of purification' (a.32).

Dialogue and Proclamation outlines various dispositions required for participants in inter-religious dialogue. These include openness (a.47), receptivity (a.47 and a.48), and a 'readiness to allow oneself to be transformed by the encounter' (a.47). Further, the 'Christian must be prepared to learn and to receive from and through others the positive values of their traditions' (a.49). In addition, *Dialogue and Proclamation* says that 'sincere dialogue implies, on the one hand, the mutual acceptance of differences, or even contradictions and, on the other hand, respect for the free decision of persons taken according to the dictates of their conscience' (a.41).

In brief, *Dialogue and Proclamation* points out that 'Far from weakening their own faith, true dialogue will deepen it'. This document also stresses that through inter-religious dialogue Catholics 'will become increasingly aware of their Christian identity and perceive more clearly the distinctive elements of the Christian message'. Further, through dialogue their 'faith will gain new dimensions as they discover the active presence of the Mystery of Christ beyond the visible boundaries of the Church' (a.50).

It should be clear from this summary of *Dialogue and Proclamation* that Catholic theology, and especially Catholic Religious Education, encourages dialogue and acknowledges that one's own faith expressions and practises may be challenged, purified and deepened by inter-religious dialogue. Further, *Dialogue and Proclamation* teaches that theological differences between religions are not, and should not be, perceived as an obstacle to dialogue. Instead, theological differences among participants who are engaged in genuine dialogue are sources of reciprocal learning and understanding.

It must be emphasised that engaging in dialogue with other religions is not about watering down one's own faith convictions or the convictions of others to the lowest common denominator. Instead, inter-religious dialogue is about respectfully engaging differences in a way that can often enrich one's own faith and religious self-understanding. The deeper and more mature one's own faith is, the greater the possibility that there will be theological enrichment arising out of the dialogue.

For the Christian it is ultimately one's commitment to the person of Christ, the Word made flesh and Saviour of the world, that carries with it a commitment to dialogue with others. The words of the Canadian theologian Douglas Hall, capture the implications of what commitment to Christ means for the Christian in the twenty-first century:

> I can say, without any doubt at all, that I am far more open to Jews and Muslims and Sikhs and Humanists, and all kinds of other human beings, including self-declared atheists, because of Jesus than I should ever have been apart from Him.[10]

Implications of *Nostra Aetate* for Religious Education
In the light of the teaching of *Nostra Aetate* and the post-conciliar period, it should be clear that inter-religious dialogue is not some kind of optional extra within Religious Education. Instead, inter-Religious Education is an essential element within Catholic Religious Education today. Of course, it is by no means the only element. In truth, inter-religious dialogue within Religious Education presupposes

a level of theological maturity within one's own Christian faith which is of course one of the primary aims of Religious Education.

In promoting inter-religious dialogue, Religious Education will go beyond the approach of simply communicating detached information about other religions. Religious Education will resist going down the road of Religious Studies or the phenomenology of religion. Instead, Religious Education will seek to promote an authentic encounter of mutual engagement and understanding of the other with a view to opening up the possibility of deepening one's own faith and the faith of the other. Religious Education, therefore, will refuse to reduce other religions to one and the same reality as oneself.

Further, Religious Education that promotes inter-religious dialogue will recognise that a maturity of Christian faith is required among participants and that the deeper one's own Christian commitment is within dialogue, the more enriching the encounter will be and the outcomes of that encounter.[11] Genuine inter-religious dialogue presupposes faith among those around the table, a particularity of faith rooted in a specific tradition. Christianity only exists as embedded in a particular tradition and community and the same principle applies to other religions of the world.

Through dialogue, Religious Education will seek to safeguard the right of Christians and other religions to be different in their faith commitment. This means, in effect, that Religious Education will respect the irreducibility of the other to more of the same. In this way, Religious Education will go out of its way to take difference seriously, to value otherness, and to welcome diversity as a source of richness. Within this perspective, Religious Education will see the 'Religious other' not as a threat but as a gift to be welcomed, not as an outsider but as a companion on the journey of faith, not as a rival but as a partner in promoting the values of the Reign of God in the world.

Further, Religious Education will also seek to avoid temptations towards fundamentalism in its own self-understanding, relativism in its relationship with other religions, and syncretism within dialogue. Fundamentalism is based on a literal interpretation of sacred texts and an opposition to all other points of view which thereby forecloses on dialogue. Relativism sees all religions as equally valid and refuses to accept that particular truth is available in any of them. And syncretism selects in an arbitrary manner different doctrines and practices from all religions.

In contrast to these temptations, Religious Education will also promote a dialogue among religions, in which 'Christians and others are invited to deepen their religious commitment, to respond with increasing sincerity to God's personal call and gracious self-gift which, as our faith tells us, passes through the mediation of Jesus Christ and the work of the Holy Spirit'.[12] A Catholic Religious Education will recognise that while dialogue and proclamation are separate and distinct, they are also complementary and interconnected. Within this larger context, Religious Education will recognise that part of the agenda of inter-religious dialogue is 'the deeper conversion of all towards God' and that therefore given this aim, inter-religious dialogue 'possesses its own validity'.[13] An underlying objective of inter-religious dialogue within Religious Education is to promote, advance and deepen one's understanding of the absolute mystery that is God. In searching out the many and various ways in which God has spoken in our world, Christians will privilege the Christ-event, in its many layers, as the key to understanding the action of the Spirit and the Word of God in history.

This revelation of God in Christ, however, does not exhaust the incomprehensible mystery that is God. The reality of God is more than we can fully understand or imagine. God remains beyond all we can ever know. The God revealed in Christ (Deus revelatus) remains the God who is hidden (Deus absconditus). This basic theological principle is summed up in Augustine's dictum that if you have fully understood, it is no longer God you are talking about (Deus semper maior). It is the basic Christian insight that drives inter-religious dialogue in its search for the Spirit and Word of God in history and culture.

To sum up the thrust of this chapter we can say: To be Christian is to be inter-religious in terms of having a positive but critically informed relationship with the believers of other faiths. This flows from the teaching of Vatican II and the fact that we now live in a multicultural and globalised world characterised by religious pluralism. A basic requirement of living as a Christian is learning about other religions. The role of Religious Education is to enable this to happen, not its primary role but certainly an increasingly important role. Inter-religious dialogue is one of the inescapable challenges facing Religious Education in the twenty-first century. Dialogue with religious difference, otherness and pluralism is no longer an option; instead it is at the centre of Catholic Religious Education.

Notes

1   See, for example, Alberto Melloni, 'Nostra Aetate and the Discovery of the Sacrament of Otherness', in The Catholic Church and the Jewish People: Recent Reflections from Rome, Philip A. Cunningham, Norbert J. Hofmann and Joseph Sievers (eds), New York: Fordham University Press, 2007, pp. 129–151 and George Tavard, 'Nostra Aetate: Forty Years Later', Jews and Catholics Together: Celebrating the Legacy of Nostra Aetate, ed. by Michael Attridge, Ottawa: Novalis, 2007, pp. 13–47; Dermot A. Lane, 'Nostra Aetate, Forty Years On', Doctrine and Life, January 2006, pp. 4–9 and p. 21; Dermot A. Lane, 'Nostra Aetate: Encountering Other Religions, enriching the theological

imagination', *Vatican II Facing the Future: Historical and Theological Perspectives*, Dublin: Veritas, 2006, pp. 202–236.

2   L. Nemer, *New Catholic Encyclopaedia*, Revised Edition, 2003, p. 686.

3   F. Koenig, 'It Must be the Holy Spirit', *The Tablet*, 21 December 2006, p. 6.

4   Neville Lamdan, 'Introduction', *Nostra Aetate: Origins, Promulgation, Impact on Jewish-Catholic Relations*, Münster: Lit Verlag, 2007, p. 1.

5   Michael Barnes, *Theology and Dialogue*, Cambridge: Cambridge University Press, 2002, p. 31.

6   An account of John Paul II's teaching on this subject can be found in *Inter-Religious Dialogue: The Official Teaching of the Catholic Church from the Second Vatican Council to John-Paul II*, edited by Francesco Gioia, Boston: Pauline Books and Media, 2006, pp. 253–1112.

7   *Dialogue and Proclamation*, a.38.

8   For a fuller development of this see Dermot A. Lane, *The Reality of Jesus: An Essay in Christology*, Dublin: Veritas/New York : Paulist Press, 1975/1995, pp. 95–97.

9   See Karl Rahner, *Foundations of Christian Faith: Introduction to the Idea of Christianity*, New York: Crossroad Publishing Company, 1978, pp. 116–133.

10   Douglas J. Hall, *Why Christian? For Those on the Edge of Faith*, Minneapolis: Fortress Press, 1998, pp. 33–34.

11   Insofar as inter-religious dialogue pre-supposes an already existing and mature faith, it is debateable whether the Primary School Curriculum is the appropriate place to introduce inter-religious dialogue. Without some formation in one particular faith tradition, it is difficult to see how the encounter and engagement and dialogue with the other faith traditions would make much sense. The indiscriminate introduction of children at a tender age to a wide variety of religions seems questionable from an educational and theological point of view. The presentation of religions ab externo could have the effect of obstructing or inhibiting an internal understanding not only of one particular faith tradition but also of other religions. Further, it could reduce the need for ongoing dialogue among religions at a later stage. It is important to realise that Religious Education is more than an exercise in sharing information about the other, and it is more than just sociology of religions. Just as an education in other languages and cultures pre-supposes a fluency in one language and one culture, so also an appreciation of one religion would seem to be required in order to foster an understanding of other religions. There is no such thing as religion in general: religions exist only as embodied in particular traditions. Equally there is no such thing as a view of religion from nowhere: one must begin somewhere. On the other hand, it would be important that the Primary School Curriculum would introduce openness to the other, a respect for pupils of other faiths and no faith, and an appreciation of cultural and religious differences. Further, Primary School Religious Education could and should introduce pupils to awareness and an appreciation of what the three great mono-theistic religions hold in common as well as the significant differences that obtain among the children of Abraham.

12   *Dialogue and Proclamation*, a.40.

13   *Dialogue and Proclamation*, a.41.

CHAPTER 8

THE JUNIOR AND LEAVING CERTIFICATE SYLLABI: BACKGROUND, ISSUES AND CHALLENGES

Vince Murray

Ireland has changed considerably in the last number of decades. This change presents both challenges and opportunities for Religious Education. Now that Ireland has moved into the post-Celtic tiger era, commentators are beginning to assess the legacy of the economic boom and the changing nature of Irish society. The biggest innovation within post-primary Religious Education in Ireland in the last decade has been its introduction as a State examination subject at Junior and Leaving Certificate Level.

Two Major Challenges Facing Contemporary Post-Primary Religious Education in Ireland
Since the 1980s, the Republic of Ireland has undergone a period of enormous economic, social, cultural and religious transition. The so-called 'Celtic Tiger' brought unprecedented economic growth and, as a consequence, large numbers of foreign nationals came to live and work in Ireland. There has also been a steady increase in the number of people seeking refugee status in Ireland. This has led to the Republic of Ireland being categorised in general discourse as increasingly intercultural and inter-faith. While Ireland has always been religiously diverse, this diversity has traditionally been analysed in terms of Protestant and Catholic relationships rather than in terms of relationships between Christianity and other world faiths. However newspaper headlines such as, 'The battle continues for the divided hearts and minds of Irish Muslims'[1] signal a change in the religious topography in Ireland. Ireland is not insulated from contemporary, global, cultural, political, and religious issues and is moving beyond identifying itself mainly in relation to Britain, the US and the European Union. The first challenge facing post-primary Religious Education in Ireland emerges from diverse religious and international contexts. The 2006 census[2] shows that nearly 420,000 (ten percent) persons who were usual residents of the State in April 2006 indicated that they had a nationality other than Irish. The corresponding figure in 2002 was 224,000 (5.8 per cent). In this context the challenge for Religious Education in Ireland is to contribute to the creation of an inclusive, non-sectarian society which values and engages with religious diversity.

Recent research[3] shows a steady decline in Catholic Church mass attendance and changes in religious belief and practice. Eoin Cassidy writes that,

> the evidence points to a decline in the moral authority of the Church, a loss of confidence in the Catholic Church and a decline in religious observance. But despite these changes the Irish remain a deeply religious people with a healthy sense of what is best in the culture of modernity.[4]

This view is consistent with the view of Oliver Brennan who, in characterising contemporary Irish culture as belonging to Late Modernity or Post-Modernity, sees some hope for the Christian Church within it.

> I believe that the search for wholeness and for a meaningful spirituality, which is evident among increasing numbers of contemporary youth, is at least open to, and offers the possibility of, dialogue with the Christian story in its institutionalised, symbolic expression.[5]

While the first challenge and opportunity for post-primary Religious Education in Ireland concerned the need for an adequate response to the recent increase in religious diversity in Irish society, the second challenge and opportunity for post-primary Religious Education is centred on an internal challenge to Catholic Religious Education as a means of developing faith in, and commitment to, the Catholic Christian Tradition. There is an increasing body of evidence to support the view that many young Irish people are finding current forms of Religious Education, which tend to focus on sacramental socialisation, in other words, on preparing Catholics to become members of a practicing Catholic community, increasingly irrelevant to their lives and concerns. While belief in God and some spiritual practice remains, regular mass attendance and conformity to official Church teaching on issues such as sexual morality is rapidly diminishing.[6] Thus the second challenge to Religious Education is to develop approaches that engage young people with the Catholic Christian tradition in ways that are relevant to their life-questions and that foster individual and communal, spiritual and moral development. These two challenges are complementary rather than mutually exclusive and the State examination syllabus for Religious Education can make a significant contribution in responding to both.

The Junior and Leaving Certificate Religious Education Syllabus

In the year 2000, the Junior Certificate Religious Education Syllabus was first taught in selected schools in Ireland before being made available to all schools. By 2007, 24,601 students sat the Junior Certificate at the end of their third year of the post-primary programme but only 535 students from approved schools sat the Leaving Certificate at the end of their five-to-six year post-primary education.[7] Prior to the National Council for Curriculum and Assessment's (NCCA) initiative in developing, implementing and examining Religious Education as a state subject at Junior Certificate, responsibility for Religious Education was seen as exclusively belonging to the Christian Churches and particularly to the Roman Catholic Church which managed the vast majority of post-primary schools. For example, in a discussion paper for the Course Committee for Religious Education, the NCCA, as part of its planning for an examination syllabus, questioned whether it should be 'common' or 'denominational' and suggested that the design of the new syllabus might need to consider the rights of students who are withdrawn from Religious Education to 'a spiritual/moral/ethical education'.[8] However, when the syllabi were published the opening section on 'Religious Education in the Curriculum: an Educational Rationale' outlined general aims for education from the 1995 White Paper. The aims listed include:

- To foster an understanding and critical appreciation of the values – moral, spiritual, religious, social and cultural – which have been distinctive in shaping Irish society and which have traditionally been accorded respect in society.
- To nurture a sense of personal identity, self esteem and awareness of one's particular abilities, aptitudes and limitations, combined with respect for the rights and beliefs of others.
- To create tolerant, caring and politically aware members of society.
- To ensure that Ireland's young people acquire a keen awareness of their national and European heritage and identity, coupled with a global awareness and a respect and care for the environment.[9]

While stressing the role of Christianity as part of Ireland's 'rich cultural heritage' this document adds:

> However, effective functioning in an increasingly complex culture demands that people have an understanding of a variety of religious traditions encountered not just in Ireland but in Europe and in the wider world.[10]

These religious traditions are enshrined in the five aims of Religious Education which are:

1. To foster an awareness that the human search for meaning is common to all peoples, of all ages and at all times.
2. To explore how this search for meaning has found, and continues to find, expression in religion.

3. To identify how understandings of God, religious traditions, and in particular the Christian tradition, have contributed to the culture in which we live and continue to have an impact on personal life-style, interpersonal relationships between individuals and their communities and contexts.

4. To appreciate the richness of religious traditions and to acknowledge the non-religious interpretation of life.

5. To contribute to the spiritual and moral development of the student.[11]

Assessment at Junior and Leaving Certificate consists of a final written paper and journal work, and is 'based on the objectives relating to knowledge, understanding, skills and attitudes within each section of the course.'[12] However, the Guidelines continue significantly,

> While students will draw on their own experience in an examination, their personal faith commitment and/or affiliation to a particular religious grouping will not be subject to assessment for national certification.[13]

The structure of each syllabus contains compulsory and optional sections which allow for a choice between Christianity and world religions in addition to sections with a thematic approach.

Reactions to the Introduction of Religious Education as an Examinable Subject
In Ireland the response to the introduction of Religious Education as an examinable subject was mixed and led to extensive debate in educational and religious circles. In the Catholic community this took place primarily in *The Furrow*, a popular monthly Catholic journal. In one article, Thomas Deenihan claimed that, 'the proposed syllabus has been given a broad welcome by the teacher unions, the diocesan advisors for Religious Education, the religion teachers' associations and the voluntary schools' national management bodies.'[14] The Catechetical Commission of the Irish Episcopal Conference welcomed the introduction of a State examination syllabus as 'a challenge and an opportunity'.[15] However Deenihan opposed the substitution of Religious Instruction by Religious Education, as he viewed these as involving two very different and distinct activities. For him Religious Instruction is by definition denominational and catechetical in its aims whereas Religious Education is non-denominational and secular. He asserted:

> The position of religious instruction has been eroded by allowing it to be combined with a non-denominational examinable syllabus for Religious Education that will most certainly change in the future.[16]

Originally, but for different reasons, Anne Looney of the NCCA, the organisation which was responsible for introducing the syllabus, supported 'a creative divorce' between catechesis and Religious Education with the latter emphasising a more scholarly, critical approach to the study of religion in schools and the former emphasising formative catechesis taking place within the home and family.[17]

Still others, mostly influenced by the thinking of Thomas Groome,[18] go beyond the either/or thinking of formation versus information to argue that these are not mutually exclusive but they are actually necessary for each other. In 'Religious Education and Catechesis; no divorce, for the children's sake' Groome argues in favour of the examination syllabus and faith formation using a pedagogy which redresses the 'debilitating dichotomy left by the Enlightenment era between critical reason and faith formation'[19] by recreating an educational symbiosis between knowing and being. He argues that:

> We should teach a religious tradition, whether our own or another, in ways that honour it as a source of great spiritual wisdom, enabling people not simply to learn *about it* but to learn *from it* for their lives, to allow the information to shape their formation.[20]

The pedagogy which can 'do both' Religious Education and catechesis, he argues, is called *shared praxis* which is 'a shared (Christian or Buddhist or Jewish etc.) teaching dynamic that critically correlates 'life' with 'religious tradition' enabling people *to bring their lives to faith and faith to their lives*.[21]

Furthermore, Dan O'Connell, in an article entitled 'Religious Education and the Public Sphere' suggests that 'Religious Education needs to become more mindful of the public dimension of Christian faith and educate deliberately to help participants find ways to bring their faith into the public sphere'.[22] In recommending shared praxis as a way to achieve this, he urges the necessity of thorough analysis by the participants not only of their own 'place' in society but also of the structures, values and meaning around which society organises itself to ensure that what they bring from the Christian tradition into the public sphere goes beyond the 'shallow and superficial'. In this he concurs wtih Oliver Brennan's insight that:

> The narrow understanding of the aim of Religious Education which confines it to that of nurturing faith is no longer viable. The exploration of the wider meaning of Religious Education can contribute to the establishment of right relationships among peoples within nations and between the nations of the world themselves.[23]

Anne Holton also argues for the introduction of the syllabus to increase the status of the subject in school, to give students more motivation and to renew teachers' sense of professionalism. When she asserts, 'our aim is faith formation' she sees no dichotomy between this and Religious Education as an examinable subject. She justifies this approach by claiming that human beings are by nature spiritual and that all humans are open to the transcendence of God. Furthermore the syllabus, which is intended for those belonging to different religions as well as none, recognises this great truth. Thus 'to refrain from faith formation or spiritual development is to be *untrue to the very nature of the human being*.[24]

Interestingly, when the Leaving Certificate Guidelines for Teachers were published as the final official document from the Department of Education and Science (DES), an essay by Thomas Groome entitled, 'Shared Praxis – A way towards educating for spiritual wisdom',[25] was included along with guidelines on using critical questioning in Religious Education and teaching for diversity. This suggests an attempt by the DES to take a position on the current debate on the nature, context and aim of Religious Education in Ireland and perhaps suggests a more integrating synthesis than the original 'divorce' between informative and formative approaches.

Many of the contributions to this debate seem to rest on the underlying assumption that the students taking the syllabus will emerge from some type of Catholic background. The 'other', if now inside the State, is still outside the classroom. Thus, the Catholic Bishops have issued guidelines for the teaching of the examination syllabus to Catholic pupils[26] and the Religion Teachers' Association claims that they helped the bishops 'formulate guidelines for the implementation of the NCCA Syllabus in Catholic Secondary Schools'.[27] However, in these guidelines there is absolutely no reference to teaching the syllabus to students from other faith traditions within Catholic schools. The tension between the Church and the State's responsibility for Religious Education seems to be ongoing. This is evidenced by the exclusion of Catholic Diocesan Advisers for Religious Education from teacher in-service days[28] as well as some Diocesan Advisers discouraging schools from adopting the syllabus.

The above provides a glimpse of the academic debate over the introduction of Religious Education as a state examination subject in Ireland. However, within schools the issues take on a different hue. From extensive Teaching Practice visits to schools and post-Teaching Practice seminars with student teachers, I have heard much praise for the new syllabus because it increases students' motivation in the subject to achieve points in the State Examination. I have also witnessed a small amount of extremely sharp criticism of Religious Education as an examination subject because it takes away from faith formation and replaces it with learning religious facts. One teacher exclaimed angrily, 'I did not become a Religious Education teacher to do this!' However, in all my discussions with current teachers of Religious Education, I have yet to meet one who claims that it is possible to prepare students to achieve high grades in Religious Education at a state examination and simultaneously nurture their faith in a meaningful manner. It would appear that for these teachers shared praxis is fine in theory but the praxis does not work out in practice.

Responding to the Challenges

Perhaps one reason for this inability to integrate the informative and formative/ transformative aspects of Religious Education lies in the popular perception that a teacher's ability to teach a subject area is judged primarily according to the examination results which their students achieve. This is a long way from the moral, spiritual, religious, social and cultural aims of education in the 1995 White Paper. One requirement of the DES which might help to bridge the gap between vision and reality would be that each school, in its whole school planning, be required to draw up a policy and implementation strategy for the aims of education as outlined in the White Paper. Each subject discipline, including Religious Education, would have the opportunity to contribute to this policy and its implementation. One of the foundational principles of this process would be that the school as public institution, with public funding, should participate in the public sphere, a principle clearly articulated in the educational rationale for the new Religious Education syllabus. As a model for creating 'tolerant, caring and politically aware members of society'[29] the process of drawing up the Religious Education contribution would be a participative democratic one, involving all interested and involved parents, faith communities and the students themselves. Some of the issues to be resolved could include:

- The school's decision regarding the adoption or otherwise of the examination syllabus and the rationale behind this decision
- The Religious Education department's educational approaches towards education for religious diversity in the classroom and in the wider society
- The relationship between the schools 'particular religious ethos' and the NCCA's educational rationale for Religious Education.

In relation to achieving a symbiosis of knowing and being within Religious Education as an examination subject, the types of questions in the assessment process are crucial. From an initial analysis of the written examinations and project work at Junior and Leaving Certificate levels, it appears that the written examination only asks for subject-specific academic knowledge, understanding and skills, while the project work requires all of the above plus the type of self-analysis and reflection characteristic of the *shared praxis* approach. I suggest that all elements of the examination (written and project) should require that ability to integrate academic and personal learning if learning in Religious Education at examination level is to transcend the information versus formation dichotomy.

Conclusion

I wish to conclude by sharing some relevant insights from my own practice of Religious Education. Each year I facilitate a week of inter-faith and ecumenical encounters in Belfast between student teachers of Religious Education from the Republic of Ireland and individuals and communities from diverse Christian and other faith traditions. The students also get to experience the work of ecumenical Christian groups working for reconciliation in Northern Ireland. As well as completing an academic essay arising from these encounters, students are invited to articulate their own personal and professional learning as a result of involvement in this educational process. Several themes and outcomes have been repeated in the student feedback over a period of years. These include:

- Personal encounter with the wisdom gleaned from a range of spiritual traditions has led students to question and recommit themselves to their own spiritual development within their inherited faith tradition
- As professional teachers they have come to see the fundamental importance of educating for tolerance and understanding within Religious Education
- The quality of the students' written coursework has improved due to the increase in the students' awareness of the complex religious issues fostered in interfaith dialogue.

One student concluded her essay entitled, 'Can peace and reconciliation be found amidst pain in Northern Ireland?' by reflecting on Christian understandings of reconciliation and by interviewing those working for it:

> I have to say that if it were not for my own experience, I would not have written this essay. I most likely would have very little interest in peace issues at all. But experience has led me into this situation. I have been in many a peace rally, I have been one of the children who stood and spelt out the letters, S.T.O.P., stop terror, oppression and pain. I cannot blot out those memories. However, I can eliminate my bitterness and be more optimistic and although this essay has taken me a very long time to compose it has helped me realise that peace and reconciliation are possible. And I am not saying this for the sake of conclusion purposes, I am saying it because I mean it, I hope for it.

My firm conclusion is that academic scholarship, supported by the Junior and Leaving Certificate Syllabi in Religious Education, as well as faith development which engages with religious traditions and social action in the public sphere, are best achieved together because each needs the other to flourish.

Notes

1   Gerry Gregg, *Sunday Independent*, 24 December 2006.

2   Central Statistics Office, *Census 2006 – Principal Demographic Results*, Dublin: Stationery Office, 2007.

3   Eoin G. Cassidy (ed.), *Measuring Ireland: Discerning Values and Beliefs*. Dublin: Veritas, 2002. In a Red C Poll published in *The Examiner* in 2008, weekly mass attendance was 45%.

4   E. Cassidy, 'Modernity and Religion in Ireland: 1980-2000' in E.G. Cassidy (ed.), *Measuring Ireland: Discerning Values and Beliefs*, p. 41.

5   Oliver Brennan, 'The Cultural Context for Religious Education Today' in E. Brennan (ed.). *Critical Issues in Religious Education*, Dublin: Veritas, 2005.

6   Michael Breen, 'Different from their Elders and Betters: Age Cohort Differences in the Irish data of the European Values Study (EVS) 1999' in E.G. Cassidy (ed.), *Measuring Ireland: Discerning Values and Beliefs*, pp. 94–106.

7   Department of Education and Science website (accessed 09.07.07).

8   The National Council for Curriculum and Assessment, Course Committee for Religious Education (Post-Primary) Discussion Paper, 1994, pp. 3–4.

9   Department of Education and Science, *Junior Certificate Religious Education Syllabus*, Dublin: The Stationery Office, no date, p. 5.

10   Ibid, p. 3.

11   Ibid, p. 5.

12   Ibid, p. 45.

13   Ibid, p. 45.

14   Thomas Deenihan, 'Religious Education and Religious Instruction: An Alternative Viewpoint', in *The Furrow*, Vol. 53, No. 2, February 2002, pp. 75–83.

15   Ibid, p. 75.

16   See Micheál de Barra, 'Religious Education and Catechesis: The View from the Middle Ground', *The Furrow*, Vol. 53, No. 2 , May 2002 , pp. 292–301. This article contains a reply to de Barra from T. Deenehan, pp. 298ff.

17   Anne Looney, 'Testing Times? A New Challenge for Religious Education' in *Doctrine and Life*, September 2000, p. 389.

18   Thomas Groome, *Christian Religious Education; sharing our story and vision*, San Francisco: Harper and Row, 1980.

19   Thomas Groome, 'Religious Education: no divorce for the children's sake', in *The Furrow*, Vol. 53, No. 11, November 2002, p. 589.

20   Ibid, p. 595.

21   Ibid, p. 595.

22   Dan O'Connell, 'Religious Education and the Public Sphere', in *The Furrow*, Vol. 57, No. 7/8, July/August 2006, pp. 391–402.

23   Oliver Brennan, 'The Cultural Context for Religious Education Today', in *Critical Issues in Religious Education*, Dublin: Veritas, 2005.

24   Anne Holton, 'Teaching Religion in the Examination System', in *The Furrow*, Vol. 53, No. 9, September 2002, pp. 469–478.

25   Thomas Groome 'Shared Praxis – a way towards educating for spiritual wisdom', in *Religious Education Leaving Certificate, Guidelines for Teachers,* Dublin: The Stationery Office, no date, pp. 110–112.

26   The Irish Catholic Bishops' Conference, *Guidelines for the Faith Formation and Development of Catholic Students*, 1999.

27   See Robert Dunne's Chairperson's Address to the A.G.M. of the Religion Teachers' Association as reported in their subsequent newsletter, p. 1.

28   Deenihan's reply to Micheál de Barra in 'Religious Education and Catechesis – the view from the middle ground', in *The Furrow*, p. 299.

29   Junior Certificate Syllabus Rationale, p. 3.

SECTION 3

CATHOLIC EDUCATION AS INCLUSIVE
EDUCATION AT THE HEART OF EUROPE

CHAPTER 9

RELIGIOUS EDUCATION FROM
A EUROPEAN PERSPECTIVE

Peter Schreiner

How can one profile the situation of Religious Education in Europe? In order to attempt to answer this question it is important to uncover the main concepts and current developments that underlie and shape Religious Education in contemporary Europe. This is the major and challenging task with which I am involved, as a professional educational researcher, at the Comenius-Institut in Münster, Germany.[1] My research has shown that greater understanding of, and dialogue about, the concepts underpinning Religious Education and the objectives of Religious Education in Europe, is necessary. Furthermore my work argues that it is vital to promote children's right to religion and Religious Education in Europe and to encourage knowledge and understanding of their own and other religious traditions. Current European collaborative approaches to Religious Education, tend to link students' personal concerns to broader social and political issues at local, national and global level.

Introduction and Overview
SIX KEY CHARACTERISTICS OF RELIGIOUS EDUCATION IN EUROPE

1.   Religious Education as a complex, varied European phenomenon manifests different concepts of, traditions about, and approaches to, Religious Education, in nearly all of the states of Europe.

In many schools in Europe, Religious Education is a contested issue. It is helpful to frame current debates on Religious Education in Europe in terms of two overarching perspectives. According to the first perspective, Religious Education is seen as a relic of former times and proponents of this view argue that in a neutral and impartial state it should no longer have any place in public or state schools. A second perspective sees Religious Education as making a vital contribution to *identity formation, orientation and dialogue* in Europe. It argues that this is especially relevant at a time where there is an increasing plurality of worldviews in Europe. From this perspective Religious Education is an indispensable part of a general education. In both perspectives the quality of existing approaches to Religious Education is a central theme. In general, when surveying the European situation, one can say that the necessity of Religious Education in schools is not contested in the majority of European countries, yet the nature of Religious Education and the appropriateness of different approaches to it gives rise to serious debate.

It is helpful to begin with a general overview of Religious Education in Europe.[2] One discovers a range of approaches to Religious Education that are linked to one of three main basic models of organisation:

a. Teaching organised by religious communities that have exclusive responsibility for Religious Education (confessional/catechetical)
b. Teaching organised in collaboration between state and religious communities (confessional/non-confessional; voluntary and/or obligatory subject)
c. Teaching organised exclusively by state authorities (non-confessional, religious studies).

One can further refine one's classification of Religious Education in Europe by exploring the different emphases in the three terms: 'learning religion', 'learning *about* religion' and 'learning *from* religion'. The first term 'learning religion', refers to a confessional approach to religion or an introduction to a specific faith tradition. The second term 'learning *about* religion' encompasses religious studies, in other words, knowledge about religion and its meaning for its adherents. The final term 'learning *from* religion' explores religious experience and religious life as well as the meaning of religion for identity formation, orientation and dialogue. However it must be noted that some religious educators view the separation of these three terms as somewhat artificial when it comes to classroom practice where aspects of all three overlap.

2. Existing approaches to Religious Education in Europe are shaped by national and regional contexts.

When we survey Religious Education in Europe by moving from specific local situations to the general regional, national or European context, it becomes evident that these specific contexts are highly influential in shaping particular approaches taken at local level. This may, at first, appear to be an obvious insight yet its significance means that each approach to Religious Education is contextual and is shaped by a specific history, a 'biography' or life-story created by the interplay of multiple factors. Furthermore there is a distinct rationale underpinning the existing diversity of Religious Education in Europe. Therefore it is necessary to outline some key pointers that facilitate an understanding of

Religious Education in European countries. In general one can state that:

a. There are differences in the religious landscape of the countriesof Europe. The south tends to be dominated by Catholicism (Austria, Italy, Spain, Portugal and to some extent France, as well as Poland, Ireland and Lithuania) whereas the north is more Lutheran-Protestant (Scandinavia). Central European countries tend to have mixed religious landscapes (Germany, Hungary, the Netherlands, etc.) while Orthodoxy dominates most countries in Eastern Europe, including Greece. Finally Islam is the major religion in countries like Turkey, Albania and Bosnia-Herzegovina.

b. There are differences in the *relationship between the state and religion* in European countries, ranging from a more hostile encounter (France) to a relationship of sympathy (Poland, Ireland). Furthermore different countries present different understandings of the nature of religion in society as well as having different educational systems e.g. in the number of private or state public schools in a country. For instance in countries where there is a majority religion as is the case in Italy, Ireland, Norway, Poland or Austria, the issue of the relationship between the majority religion and the religion of the minorities is discussed differently than in mixed confessional countries with a more equal distribution of religious affiliation. There is an observable contrast between a country where a state-church system exists or has been in existence for a long time, and the situation of a country with a strict separation between state and religion or where (fractional) collaboration exist.[3] Where religion and state are strictly separated one finds that religion has no place in public schools. While one might be inclined to suggest that France illustrates this situation, the issue is complex and in France there is a current debate about a so-called intelligent *'laicité'* and an initiative focusing on implementing more religious knowledge in the existing curriculum and subjects has commenced.[4] France also has a high proportion of Catholic schools, attended by about 20 per cent of all pupils. Where state and religion are closely related, as in Poland, the teaching of Religious Education in schools is not very different to parish-based catechesis. In countries that have been under a socialist regime up until 1989, new or renewed approaches to Religious Education have been developed and implemented in schools. It is interesting to note that many of these approaches have faced difficulties and experienced tensions.[5]

c. Existing approaches to Religious Education in Europe one can also observe that existing approaches depend on the *structure of the school system* within a country. For example, in the Netherlands two-thirds of schools are religiously affiliated while one third is religiously 'neutral'. History has an important part to play in interpreting this data. The emphasis on the parent's right to select appropriate education for the child led to a debate about the place of Religious Education in schools at the beginning of the nineteenth century. The result has been what is termed the 'pillarisation' of schools along denominational lines. Pillarisation refers to the denominational segregation of society into small vertical pillars where all the main social institutions (newspapers, schools, hospitals, banks, universities etc.) are organised according to people's religious convictions. Thus 'pillarisation' still shapes the contemporary Dutch school system where almost thirty Islamic schools exist.

3. It is helpful to use a comparative perspective to take account of differences and commonalities in Europe and to provide ground for dialogue on further perspectives.

Every comparison of different approaches to Religious Education should be highly sensitive to the complexity of existing approaches, as well as national and regional contextual issues. Dialogue and assessment should take careful cognisance of the strengths and weaknesses of each existing approach. At an international level exchange and dialogue in Religious Education is developing in existing networks, conferences and projects. While exchange about methods and experiences in the classroom can encourage teachers to look beyond their own territory, researchers perceive an increasing need to engage in comparative research into international Religious Education. International studies like the OECD International PISA survey, which investigated learning 'outcomes' in the form of the skills and knowledge of fifteen-year-olds in fifty-seven countries, highlighted issues around the 'success' of Religious Education. Whereas obstacles like the problem of language or how theory and practice fit together should not be underestimated, the value of a comparative perspective has to be promoted to take account of the increasing Europeanisation and internationalisation of the field of education. The Open Society Institute in Ljubljana/Slovenia has engaged with south eastern European countries in a comparative project on experiences and developments in Religious Education throughout Europe. The project aims to explore the possible role of Religious Education in state-based community schools as well as the role of Religious Education in promoting an open, democratic society. This institute has produced a significant publication titled *Religion and Schooling in an Open Society*.[6] This publication is particularly intended for policymakers who have little prior experience or comparative information on religion and schooling. Among its findings it presents the right to establish private sponsored schools and a preference for the model of 'teaching about religions'. The publication also underlines the need for more comparative research on the social impact of various approaches and methodologies to teaching about religions. However comparative research does not have the goal of a future-oriented perspective aimed at creating one model of Religious Education for the whole of Europe. Such a model would ignore the range of diverse conditions for Religious Education in different countries, each with their own unique historical context.

4. Labels like a confessional, a non-confessional or a religious studies approach to Religious Education fail to distinguish adequately between different approaches.

Simple binary distinctions between confessional/non-confessional Religious Education only represent one dimension of Religious Education. What is perceived as confessional in one country can differ significantly from the mainstream understanding of the same term in another country. For example in England the term confessional is often seen as involving indoctrination.[7] This in itself highlights the need to develop a more subtle and differentiated view about the involvement and participation of religious communities in the education system in a country. Also in some contexts religious studies has a negative image, whereas knowledge about religious issues and religious traditions is of high importance for every approach to Religious Education. More significantly, labels do not necessarily indicate underlying hermeneutical approaches that show how students are made aware of their own religious tradition as well as the manner in which they are given knowledge and understanding of traditions other than their own.

5. There are convergent tendencies in Religious Education in Europe.

A survey of different objectives and goals for Religious Education in different European countries reveals that they share much in common and so one can speak of a tendency towards coming together or convergence. The general rationale for Religious Education in most countries is based on strong educational principles and Religious Education is no longer viewed as having exclusively theological roots. This means that religion is seen as a significant part of education in general and faith has a subordinated value in this respect. However the pupil's perspective on religion and belief is highly significant in the teaching of Religious Education. The following objectives can be found in most syllabi governing the teaching of Religious Education in Europe:

- To encourage pupils to be sensitive to religion and the religious dimension of life
- To provide orientation on the variety of existing religious opportunities (including ethically-oriented guidelines for life that are based on religious convictions)
- To provide knowledge and understanding of religious beliefs and experiences.

All approaches are challenged by the need for concepts that can respond to and accommodate an increasingly plural European society. All existing models must address how they can facilitate and respond to existing diversity while enabling deeper understanding to occur. In many cases the situation of plurality gives impetus to the further development of existing approaches.

The following issues are central to such discussion:

- Developing an openness toward other religions and inter-religious learning
- Presenting a dynamic understanding of religion and culture (taking into consideration the intra-plural situation of religious communities)
- Raising the question of how to integrate students' experiences and attitudes.

6.   A Europe-wide debate about standards in Religious Education?

If we are serious about working towards high quality Religious Education as well as the convergence of objectives for Religious Education in Europe we must raise the question of whether it is appropriate and desirable to speak of establishing common standards for Religious Education that extend beyond national boundaries. These common standards could clarify what Religious Education professionals might expect children and young people to achieve in the area of Religious Education in different European contexts. Friedrich Schweitzer, a German scholar involved in international comparative research, has suggested five examples of such professional criteria:[8]

a.   Religion must and can be taught in line with the criteria of general education (educational quality)
b.   Religious Education is of relevance to the public and must be taught accordingly (contribution to general education)
c.   Religious Education must include some type of interdenominational and inter-religious learning which are in line with the increasingly

pluralist situation of many countries (dialogical quality, contribution to peace and tolerance)

d. Religious Education must be based on the children's right to religion and Religious Education (child-centred approach based on children's rights)

e. Religious Education teachers must be professionals in the sense that they have reached a level of self-reflexivity based on academic work which allows for a critical appropriation of their religious backgrounds and biographies (professional teaching).[9]

Schweitzer's five important criteria focus on the educational quality of Religious Education, its contribution to general education, its dialogue-oriented, child-centred nature and its delivery by professional teachers. Effectively these criteria form a preliminary type of *benchmarking* for Religious Education in Europe that can help to provide guidance and orientation on issues that have already proved to be significant in different approaches. This approach, which outlines common standards in Religious Education, has much to offer the European context and merits serious discussion.

A Profile of the situation of Religious Education in three selected European countries (England, Norway, Switzerland)

ENGLAND

In Britain, Religious Education is part of the curriculum in all Local Authority Schools (LEA) and while it has equivalent status to foundation and core subjects in the National Curriculum, it remains outside the national curriculum. Parents have the right to withdraw children from Religious Education and teachers have the right not to teach Religious Education. The content of Religious Education in Local Authority schools focuses on Christianity and the other main religions in the United Kingdom. These religions include Islam, Hinduism, Sikhism, Buddhism and Judaism. Standing Advisory Councils on Religious Education (SACRE) operate at a local level and determine the content of Religious Education in LEA schools.

In recent years there has been widespread discussion of models of Religious Education in England and Wales where there is a rich diversity of approaches and debates.[10] As an illustration of this diversity, Michael Grimmitt has presented eight main approaches to Religious Education.[11] While no single approach is evident, in all places one can say that the dominant approach to Religious Education is phenomenological (non-dogmatic and non-denominational) and it has been further developed towards a more systematic and theme oriented-approach. Religions are no longer seen as fixed entities but their variety and dynamic nature is now more in focus.[12] Authentic material from ethnographic studies about the religious life of children and young people is used to generate school books.

Development in Religious Education in England and Wales, as in other parts of Great Britain, is widely presented and debated at European and international conferences. In conformity to other countries, two attainment targets comprising 'learning *about* religion' and 'learning from religion' are viewed as being equally significant when it comes to developing a curriculum for Religious Education in England and Wales. The *non-statutory national framework* (published in 2004) puts Religious Education in the wider frame of the school curriculum and introduces its contribution to learning across the curriculum. In October 2004, the public presentation of the framework emphasised the central role of Religious Education 'in providing pupils' with a range of experiences that enable them to develop a realistic and positive sense of their own beliefs and ideas.[13] The Qualifications and Curriculum Authority (QCA) document firmly outlines the nature and function of Religious Education in England and Wales:

> Religious education provokes challenging questions about the ultimate meaning and purpose of life, beliefs about God, the self and the nature of reality, issues of right and wrong and what it means to be human. It develops pupils' knowledge and understanding of Christianity, other principal religions, other religious traditions and other world views that offer answers to questions such as these. It offers opportunities for personal reflection and spiritual development. It enhances pupils' awareness and understanding of religions and beliefs, teachings, practices and forms of expression, as well as of the influence of religion on individuals, families, communities and cultures. Religious education encourages pupils to learn from different religions, beliefs, values and traditions while exploring their own beliefs and questions of meaning. (…) Religious education encourages pupils to develop their sense of identity and belonging.[14]

In the debate about the non-statutory national framework it has been proposed to merge learning 'about' and learning 'from' to 'learning *through* religions and world views', to emphasise that the teaching of Religious Education contains more than themes and issues, but takes in the questions and interests of the pupils and from these creates links to the content of the religious traditions.[15]

Even critical voices see many positive trends emerging from developments in England. However, the level of appreciation for the English model differs. Some see the religious studies model as too distanced from the individual experiences of the pupils and students while others see the involvement of religious communities in the Standing Advisory Councils on Religious Education (SACRE) and their responsibility for the local agreed syllabus as an important element of collaboration between state and civil society.

NORWAY

Norway is a country with 4.5 million inhabitants, 86 per cent of whom are members of the State Lutheran Church. There are sizeable groups of members of other world faiths and other Christian churches including sixty-two thousand Muslims, forty-three thousand Pentecostals and forty-two thousand Catholics. Norway has an established and important tradition of ensuring human rights at a domestic and at an international level (Nobel Prize). It specifically focuses on generating a national climate where minority and majority groups can live together constructively. 'Education for all' is the motto of its educational system where each child begins school at six and is guaranteed a minimum of thirteen years education. Emphasis is placed on the inclusion of all children regardless of social and cultural background or level of ability.

In 1997, the confessional approach to Religious Education in Norway was displaced by a new, non-confessional approach called 'Christianity, other religions and moral education'.[16] This new approach emerged as a consequence of an intense and protracted public debate about religious and cultural plurality in Norway's relatively homogeneous culture. As Norwegian society became more intercultural and inter-religious so too did its student population and its schools. There are good reasons behind the reform of Religious Education.[17] An increasing number of students had previously opted out of Religious Education and some suggested that the content of Religious Education and 'Ethics', an alternative subject, was almost identical. Since its introduction, the new syllabus has focused on enlarging the range of issues while providing an introduction to Christianity, other religions and world views 'according to their own specific character.'[18] The syllabus has a two-fold aim of enabling students to deal with the existing plurality of Norwegian society while simultaneously recognising Norwegian 'cultural heritage'. In terms of content and methodology, it was hoped that knowledge about other religions and world-views would be enlarged while teaching methods would take greater account of the narrative and aesthetic dimension of religion. This syllabus allows a partial opting out when 'faith issues' are part of the teaching. This right to opt out is a controversial rule, as it is the perspective of the parents that determines whether a song, a prayer, or a visit to a church is a 'faith issue'. Questions arise as to the practicality and feasibility of this opt-out clause. Religious minorities demand the right to opt-out completely because they see that in comparison to the former subject area, the new syllabus does not offer a radically new approach. To date court decisions have not supported their opinion.

At the end of 2005, a new reform of the general curriculum took place in Norway with more emphasis being placed on 'knowledge promotion' combined with a change of perspective which moved from content and teaching methods towards teaching and learning *outcomes* as well as competences and standards. The syllabus for Religious Education has been quick to respond to these new emphases and there is genuine desire, among those involved in Religious Education in Norway, to find a solution to the 'problem' of the partial opting-out system.

New subject in the canton of Zurich: Religion and Culture
In Switzerland the responsibility for education lies with the government of the twenty-six cantons. On the basis of different Church traditions, and the religious landscapes within those cantons, the following approaches governing Religious Education can be found:

- Denominational Religious Education provided by religious communities
- Teaching organised in collaboration with state (canton) and religious communities
- Teaching organised exclusively by the canton.[19]

The profile of the subject
In August 2004, the Education Council of the canton of Zurich decided that the existing confessional-cooperative Religious Education approach at secondary level should be replaced by a new subject entitled 'Religion and Culture'. Since 2007 the obligatory subject of 'Religion and Culture' has dealt with the content, forms, ceremonies and festivals of different religions in an impartial perspective. Teaching *in* religion is excluded from state-maintained schools where the main religious traditions are presented from the Religious Studies perspective (non-confessional) while simultaneously being related to the lived experiences of the students. The syllabus contains three perspectives:

- The historical-descriptive perspective: Religions and their main characters
- The societal-political perspective: Religion and the community
- The life-world oriented perspective: Religion and the individual.

The subject 'Religion and Culture' is designed in such a manner that students 'who come from different cultural, religious and ideological backgrounds will be able to participate.'[20] It combines two didactical concepts:

a. 'Religion and Culture' is based on the concept of religious studies, in which young people can learn about the origin of the religions, their main elements, their impact on culture (literature, music, architecture, aesthetics) and their relevance for society today ('teaching about religion').

b. The starting point of the subject 'Religion and Culture' can also be young people's life questions. They should learn about their life-world and the values that shape life-world issues as well as understand ways of living differently to their own. They should deal with questions that are important to their own experiences of life and also at the same time with religious traditions. The subject addresses topics of values in society that are also important for people who do not belong to a religion. The students should learn a critical and a respectful attitude towards different religions ('learning from religion').[21]

Religious experiences and the students' personal perspectives are also intended to play a role in teaching and learning and this poses the question as to whether a 'neutral' and objective view – not to mention learning about religion – is possible at all.

Didactical conception of Planning and instruction – exploration courses
In Switzerland, the syllabus for Religious Education favours an exploratory method. According to this rationale, students learn by exploring phenomena or connections about cultures and religions in a holistic sense.[22] This method promotes exploring and learning about religious traditions in order to gain a better understanding of one's own world-view. This can be done by:

- Dealing with a specific religious tradition (e.g. Judaism)
- Comparing a common issue in different religions
- Theme oriented exploration e.g. war and peace
- Life history oriented exploration
- Religious life in a specific context.

EUROPEAN DEVELOPMENTS AND PERSPECTIVES
In summary, one can state that there is a recent recognition of religion as a significant cultural fact and a major public issue in Europe. Moreover there are many recent signs that suggest that at a legislative, political and research level Religious Education is being appreciated as a positive force within Europe. For example one can say that the Council of Europe, the oldest political institution in Europe (founded in 1949) and a watchdog concerning democracy, human

rights and the right of law, is now more open to the phenomenon of religion than it has ever previously been. It is widely recognised that the tragic events of 9/11 in New York and Washington along with other subsequent brutal attacks in Madrid and London, have placed religion at the centre of the European stage in an unprecedented manner. In recent years there has been a general interest in religion in the discipline of education. In 2007, the Council of Europe gave prominence to religion by publishing a reference book for schools on Religious diversity and intercultural education.[23] Earlier in 2005 the Parliamentary Assembly of the Council of Europe adopted a recommendation entitled *Education and Religion*, which supported the religious studies approach to Religious Education and recognised the involvement of religious communities in the teaching of religion. A positive relationship between religion and democracy underlay its recommendation, which emphasised the common roots and sources of the world religions.[24]

> The Assembly observes moreover that the three monotheistic religions of the Book have common origins (Abraham) and share many values with other religions and that the values upheld by the Council of Europe stem from these values.[25]

These examples document a remarkable enhancement of the Council's policy that had previously tended to deal with religion mainly as a problem or a source of conflict. However, other initiatives served to further reinforce the position of Religious Education at a European level. At a conference of the Coordinating Group for Religion in Education in Europe (CoGREE) in November 2005, Jan Figel', EU-Commissioner for Education, Culture and Multilingualism, expressed the 'close relationship between education and religious and moral values' as decisive for the future of Europe. He further stated:

> Above all, our Union must live up to its aspiration to be a community of values: peace, solidarity, democracy, respect for human rights, including religious rights. And all these values are centred on the human being ... The shared values of different religious traditions can provide a collective sense of good conduct in private and public life. Getting to know about each other's beliefs and values can also raise our mutual respect for the principles of cultural and spiritual diversity.

The fact that a high-ranking European politician can present a convincing argument for Religious Education at European level indicates how religion has become central to public debate in recent years. Moreover, in a historic move the European Commission has supported a research project about religion in education.[26] The project which organises research on religion in education and Religious Education from universities in Estonia, Russia, Norway, France, the Netherlands, Spain and Germany, is entitled *REDCo – Religion in Education: A contribution to Dialogue or a factor of Conflict in transforming societies of European countries.* This European funding marks an important development and witness to the fact that the role of religion in education is seen as highly relevant in Europe. Furthermore it recognises that it is vital to research the contribution that Religious Education can make to peaceful social co-existence in an intercultural and inter-religious Europe. Finally in 2005 a thematic trans-national cooperation project was established under the heading of *Teaching Religion in a European multicultural society* (TRES). This network consists of over fifty partner institutions spread across almost every European country. The general purpose of this network is to strengthen the professional profile among scholars in the field of Theology and Religious Studies and to develop a common strategy as well as common educational standards on how to teach religion in a multicultural European society.

These developments signal that religion and Religious Education are not marginal to educational, social and legislative endeavours at a European level. The increased research activity, the renewed emphasis on Religious Education as a force for social harmony and for developing respect and tolerance in society are welcome departures. It remains for religious educators in local, regional and national contexts to respond positively to the challenges posed by an intercultural and inter-religious European society by working imaginatively and collaboratively for a better future.

Notes

1   I am also involved in existing religious and educational European networks and organisations as well as in intercultural and inter-religious learning and alternative approaches to education which integrate a spiritual and/or religious dimension.

2   Peter Schreiner, 'Entwicklungen im RU in Europa [Developments in Religious Education in Europe]', in *Entwurf*, No. 1, 2000, pp. 7–14. Peter Schreiner, *Religious Education in Europe: A collection of basic information about Religious Education in European countries*, Münster, 2000. Peter Schreiner, 'Religionsunterricht in Europe: Wie bleibt er zukunftsfähig?' [Religious Education in Europe. How to be sustainable?], in *Ru intern, Informationen für evangelische Religionslehrerinnen und – lehrer in Westfalen und Lippe*, 33. Jg. 2/2004, pp. 2–4.

3   Gerhard Robbers, *Staat und Kirche in der Europäischen Union* [State and church in the European Union], Baden Baden, 1995.

4   Régis Debray, *L'Enseignement du fait religieux dans l'école laïque*, Paris: edition Odile Jacob, 2002.

5   Pille Valk & Olga Schihalejev, 'Using Narratives in Primary Religious Education in Estonia', in P. Schreiner, F. Kraft, A. Wright (eds), *Good Practice in Religious Education in Europe. Examples and Perspectives of Primary Schools*, Münster: Lit, 2007, pp. 59–75.

6   Kodelja, Zdenko & Bassler, Terrice, *Religion and Schooling in Open Society. A Framework for Infomed Dialogue*, Ljubljana, 2004; available as download through: http://www.espblackboard.org/webapps/login/ (accessed 10.08.08).

7   Terence Copley, *Teaching Religion: Fifty years of Religious Education in England and Wales*, Exeter: University of Exeter Press, 1997, p. 101.

8   Friedrich Schweitzer, International Standards for Religious Education, in: *PANORAMA. International Journal of Comparative Religious Education and Values*, Vol. 14, No. 1, Summer 2002, pp. 49–56. See also Friedrich Schweitzer, 'Comparative Research in Religious Education: International-Interdenominational-Inter-religious' in R. Larsson/C Gustavsson, *Towards a European Perspective on Religious Education*, Skellefteå: Författarna, 2004, pp. 191–200.

9   F. Schweitzer, *Comparative Research in Religious Education*, p. 196.

10   Werner Haußmann, *Dialog mit pädagogischen Konsequenzen* [Dialogue with pedagogical perspectives], Hamburg: ebv, 1996; Karlo Meyer, *Zeugnisse fremder Kulturen im Unterricht*, [Testimonials of strange cultures in the Classroom]: Neukirchen-Vlyun: Neukirchener, 1999; Karl Ernst Nipkow, *Bildung in einer pluralen Welt*, Bd. 2, *Religionspädagogik im Pluralismus*, [Education in a plural world, Vol. 2, Religious Education in Pluralism] Gütersloh: Gütersloher Verlagshaus, 1998, pp. 448–486.

11   Michael Grimmitt (ed.), *Pedagogies of Religious Education*, Great Wakering: McCrimmon Publishing, 2000.

12   Robert Jackson, *Religious Education: An interpretive approach*, London: Hodder and Stoughton, 1997.

13   Ken Boston, *Religious Education: The non-statutory national framework*, London: QCA, 2004. See www.qca.org.uk (accessed 10.08.08).

14   *Religious Education: The non-statutory national framework*, London: QCA, 2004, p. 7.

15   Joyce Miller, 'Editorial' in *Resource*, 27:2, Spring 2005, pp. 3–4.

16   Sissel Østberg, 'Religious Education in a Multicultural Society: The Quest for Identity and Dialogue' in T. Andree, C. Bakker, P. Schreiner (eds), *Crossing Boundaries: Contributions to Inter-religious and Intercultural Education*, Münster: 1997, pp. 147-153; Heid Leganger-Krogstad, 'Religious Education in the Norwegian School System' in Religious Education Kristiansen, N.M. Terebikhin (eds), *Religion, Church and Education in the Barents Region*, Arkhangelsk: 1997, pp. 171–183; Geir Skeie, 'Some Aspects of Religious Education in Scandinavia and Norway' in T. Andree, C. Bakker, P. Schreiner (eds), *Crossing Boundaries: Contributions to Inter-religious and Intercultural Education*, Münster: Comenius, 1997, pp. 155–160.

17   Østberg, *Religious Education in a Multicultural Society*, p. 149.

18   Ibid., p. 150.

19   Hans Eggenberger, 'Switzerland' in P. Schreiner, *Religious Education in Europe. A collection of basic information about Religious Education in European countries*, Münster: 2000, pp. 165–170.

20   Bildungsdirektion, Zürich, 2006, p. 3.

21   Bildungsrat, 2006, p. 4.

22   *Pestalozzi*: learning by head, heart and hand.

23   John Keast (ed.), *Religious diversity and intercultural education: a reference book for schools*, Strasbourg: Council of Europe, 2007.

24   Recommendation 1720/2005, available through http://assembly.coe.int/Documents/AdoptedText/TA05/EREC1720.htm

25   Recommendation 1720/2005, point 12.

26   EU's Sixth Framework Programme for Research and Technological Development, Priority 7: Citizens and governance in a knowledge-based society.

CHAPTER 10

LEARNING IN DIFFERENCE: INTER-RELIGIOUS LEARNING IN THE SECONDARY SCHOOL

Bert Roebben

Introduction

Cultural and religious diversity shape our living and learning environments. In recent years they have become the subject of considerable debate. Indeed, in many parts of Europe the explosive ingredients of multicultural conflicts and multi-religious tensions have been given significant media coverage. Nonetheless it is interesting to note that in schools and other places of social empowerment, the steady work of mutual exchange and enrichment between culturally and religiously diverse groups seems to enjoy far less media attention. Since 9/11, societies are acutely sensitive to the destructive power of religious fanaticism and inevitably this sensitivity has permeated European classrooms. Indeed some scholars claim that Religious Education can no longer be omitted from the curriculum of modern state schools and should be provided as an examination subject for *all* students.[1] This chapter concurs with this argument and adopts a pragmatic approach to Religious Education. It argues that since religion is a worldwide phenomenon, young people in school are entitled to be educated in the dynamics of religion. They must also be educated about how to handle the possible 'dynamite' that might ignite when people play dangerously with 'religious fire'. Information and interpretation are key words in this regard. It is vital that young people are given information and interpretative skills to enable them to learn how to recognise, understand and respect their own and other people's religious backgrounds. In such an environment successful education contributes to mutual understanding in the midst of differences.

Learning about religious difference is a multi-layered task. Those who engage in the encounter with the other will not only be confronted with diversity and with the other's 'difference' (*la différence*), but also with the other's radical strangeness or otherness (*l'altérité*). In class, students meet each other in a direct way, as a classmate, as a person and as a human being with their own origin and future. The students are not first and foremost representatives of ideological and religious groups. They are human beings, blossoming in pursuit of happiness, starting to develop as moral people. I am convinced that young people not only learn to recognise and respect the *origins* of the other, they also learn how to become open to the inalienable authenticity and life project or *future* of the other. This future will resound most strongly in the other's (non-)religious convictions. In these convictions, a glimpse of the mystery of the other will be revealed. When this glimpse occurs in class it often occurs as an invisible and unintentional pedagogical outcome. It happens when a student in the encounter with the other, begins to address the fundamental question 'Who do I want to become as a human being, and what is *my* future?' In the wake of 9/11, the authoritative Dutch rabbi, Raphael Evers, phrased it as follows:

> We have here a culture in which we think highly of tolerance. (…) And that is what you should teach young people. To learn in school (how) to live together with one another is of even greater importance than to learn how to read and write, or to know where Paris lies. We all make a huge mistake if we look at each other and think: there sits a Muslim. And: there sits a Jew. We forget that the other is a human being in the first place, who happens to be raised in a Muslim or Jewish culture. In our religious zeal we often forget the human being.[2]

This deep layer of inter-religious learning involves learning to recognise, know and appreciate differences. It implies an encounter, at a profound level, with the otherness of the other. Mary C. Boys refers to this as *learning in the presence of the other*. This encounter usually happens after preliminary acquaintances have taken place, and after one has done one's best to acquire information about the other and to talk with the other about differences and similarities. Those who then dig deeper come across differences in interpretation that require clarification. Through this encounter students not only learn to perceive these differences and to communicate with others so that they can have a better understanding of their positions, they are also invited to open up their own religious experience to one another. The encounter involves posing the question 'Who are you, I want to become captivated by you?' and the response 'Come and see, let yourself be captivated!' The encounter presupposes difference and enables the perception, communication and holding of different positions represented by fellow human beings. In this regard inter-religious learning is, without doubt, a stimulating invitation to learn how to articulate and take responsibility for one's own (non-) religious point of view.

A Contemporary Profile of Religious Education as a School Subject
In a plural society, Religious Education can no longer be considered exclusively from a catechetical orientation. After all, explicit initiation into one (for instance Catholic) religion requires a community of believers, yet many modern state

schools are not composed of a community of faith. A model of pure application or adaptation to the secularised culture also falls short. As a subject Religious Education is not identical to social or moral education and it necessitates that religion, as a complex reality, should be studied from a critical perspective. Religious Education helps young people to listen more carefully to 'slowly fermenting questions' within their own multifaceted lives. In a classroom context it enables them to vocalise their own questions in a reasonable manner. In a plural and often religiously indifferent culture, young people are not only entitled to receive solid information and guidance concerning life-questions, but also to learn to ask their own critical religious questions. In 'children's theology' [the German *Kindertheologie*], a recent development of 'children's spirituality', the skill of asking critical questions is deliberately stimulated in early childhood.[3]

Generating religious questions embraces two competences focusing on: (i) a hermeneutical nature which concentrates on identity clarification and (ii) a communicative nature which looks at the communication of worldviews.[4] It is important to spend some time exploring these two areas.

(i)   Contemporary young people grow up in a European society where many intersecting and competing ideas exist. The co-existence of multiple ideas does not only occur within groups of youngsters, but also within the lives of individuals themselves. Today, identity is formed in radical plurality. The master narratives that once imparted meaning are no longer plausible and people are now entrusted to one another and to their own inner compass in order to obtain clarity in their quest for meaning.[5] As a school subject Religious Education offers students advice relating to their own lives, along with a safe place where they can learn to deal with confusing and compelling experiences and questions.[6] After all, the environment in which they grow up is often threatening, confusing and overwhelming.[7]

(ii) Young people must also learn to express and account for themselves in their relationships to others. They must be challenged to examine critically the world of hazy opinions and to position themselves within a solidly grounded and well-documented vision of their interaction with others. The class group plays an important role in the process of religious communication, as it is the locus for a learning process where opinions are clarified, explained and substantiated. Class group interaction provides insights into pivotal questions such as: 'What are religious people really talking about? What motivates believers into seeing their lives from a perspective of radical commitment? How do I formulate the questions of life which concern *me* unconditionally?' In this sense the dialogue never takes place exclusively in the class group, but ties in with the ongoing dialogue of humankind which poses the great life-questions as well as the answers that religions and secular world-views offer.

Religious Education Embedded in the Educational Dynamics of the Modern School

Religious Education is part of the intercultural dynamics of the contemporary school, which in turn responds to great social and cultural questions. Just as schools never stand alone neither do school subjects. Since 9/11 religion cannot be considered a private issue, but is placed at the core of education, and must be considered as a part of intercultural dialogue. In Europe, Religious Education has become a matter of public awareness, and this extends to the mind of politicians and legislative bodies.[8] It should offer students the opportunity to identify, describe and clarify concerns about their living environment while operating as a valuable building block for a new world. It invites students to transform the chaotic field of talked-about opinions and threatening information, into a powerful living environment of insights and skills, which have both a liberating and invigorating effect, and which make a positive future possible. In order to understand Religious Education's role in the public space of the school, the traditional paradigm of handing over (religious) information and life patterns to the next generation should be radically transformed into a paradigm of (religious) awareness of the social context of this and other (more secular) forms of 'handing over'. Traditionally Religious Education was about initiation into one particular religious tradition. Today, Religious Education implies: a recognition of the unique resilience of education in society; an awareness of the attractive and frightening presence of religion in society; and the unavoidable need for religious communication in society, at the heart of modernity.

Learning to deal constructively with differences is a primary objective of the present-day school, all the more because dialogue with other beliefs takes place, not only in the depth of time (intergenerational), but also in the breath of space (intercultural) and in the perspective of hope for the world (global). The factual presence of people from other cultures (via migration and asylum), the large mobility of people and services, the supply of the media (TV, film and internet etc.), ensure that our living environment remains in an ongoing atmosphere of cross-fertilisation. This process shapes our outlook and way of life, and creates both challenges and tensions. Values Education, Education for Citizenship, Personal, Social, Moral and Spiritual education are partial answers to this intercultural and plural situation. In schools, one strives to create a safe space to address this situation so that differences are not evaded but examined in their directness and power while being tested for their ability to promote humanity. This means that threatening and closed concepts of the 'good life' can also be critiqued and freed from fanatical and fundamentalist biases. Religion is not immune from the process of interpellation (the process whereby human subjects are constituted by pre-given structures).[9] As the whole social and cultural horizon of meanings shifts, religion also changes. Nevertheless, this process of awakening runs its course slowly and laboriously, and religions tend rather to neglect the existing state of affairs and mask the contingency of existence.[10]

Christianity faces the historical challenge of confronting this situation directly. The temptation to escape into religious or ecclesial 'platonism' (i.e.'this situation does not affect us so just carry on as if nothing ever happened') is great.[11] After all, for centuries Christianity has determined the agenda of Europe's social and cultural systems, and as a consequence it now finds it difficult to disentangle its internal truth-claims from their institutional interpretations. The role of women in the Church and society is one example of this. Despite forceful statements from the Church about emancipation and equal rights for all human beings in society, women do not enjoy equality of opportunity when it comes to ordination to the priesthood in the Catholic tradition. The great challenge for the Christian tradition is to re-contextualise itself in an environment of moral and existential plurality and indifference. This view of tradition as a 're-sourcing process' implies that Christians are prepared to review and re-experience the internal reflective, affective and dynamic strength of their tradition against the background of social and cultural developments. They will fulfil this task especially with a strategy of encounter that goes further than doomed self-preservation on the one hand, and half-hearted adaptive behaviour on the other.[12] Therefore the primary task of the contemporary Christian school is to put its learning resources at the service of its students' quest for meaning.[13]

The Post-Modern Multi-Vocal Identity of Young People
Contemporary children grow up in a world of difference. As a result, their personal identity frequently comes under pressure. They must perform the vulnerable developmental task of self-clarification in the context of a society and a culture that is unclear about its own perspectives on development. We may question if this situation is qualitatively different from situations in previous times. In response we can say 'perhaps not'. In previous times children's identity conformed to the self-image that they received from others ('generalised other'). Contemporary children also draw the other-pole into the self-pole: they weave the stories told and attributed to them by others, into a web of intertextuality. When someone asks young people what they are like, they turn the text material of significant others in their environment into a personal texture and conclude: 'This is just the way I am'.

However, a plurally structured environment is more confusing to grow up in than a background that is neatly and clearly singular. Some children lose themselves in fragmentation (the other-pole outstrips them), others cling obstinately to one perspective (the self-pole takes in all the differences). For a contemporary, well-considered outlook on education and the life cycle, one therefore speaks of a 'balanced identity' or 'multi-vocal identity'.[14] One can describe it as follows: I try to keep myself in sight by acquiring insight into the attitude and background of the many significant others who shape my self. I try to be aware of where I come from and what my life story is thus far (*diachronic* multi-vocal) and I try to obtain clarity in and to live with the many and often conflicting voices that operate in me at this moment (*synchronic* multi-vocal).[15] The school's hermeneutical task in general, and the task of Religious Education in particular, is therefore accelerated and strengthened by the circumstances in which contemporary education takes place. Cultures and religions have never existed in a chemically pure condition, but today the weight of plurality breaks right through the safe initiation boundaries and impels young people and their educators into heightened reflexivity. Those who want to know where they stand must consciously go into the many voices that resound in their narrative identity.

According to this perspective, inter-religious learning is a form of intensive Religious Education. It does not replace Religious Education, but substantially deepens its dynamics of interpretation. It takes place in the first instance, not between representatives of ideological and religious groups, from a kind of outsiders' perspective but rather, in the dynamics of the worldview of the individual person. This involves intra-religious learning. Explicit religious socialisation involves setting up an interpretative search process in communication with others, where one searches in order to acquire clarity in one's diachronic and synchronic aspects of identity. Young people experience a superabundance of ideological ingredients. There is no shortage of religion and worldviews. Indeed one could posit that, if anything, there is an over-supply. Indigestion lurks round the corner unless the learning process helps young people to digest this multitude and to gradually but surely connect themselves to their own life-project, no longer in a non-committal and freely experimental manner, but intrinsically tied up with the truth-claim of that project. Pastiche, sampling and syncretism are some of the indications of the way in which youngsters try to maintain this plurality in themselves.

This search for identity in difference characterises the educational environment in which religious educators carry out their work. An often-heard lament among religious educators is that they themselves partake in this pluralism and no longer stand for uniformity in their own tradition. One cannot and should not want to resolve the crisis of tradition, the Church and of the Christian belief by assuming that the Christian heritage is one and undivided and can therefore be passed unproblematically onto young seekers. Discourse about whether children first of all need their own religious feeding ground before they can deal with inter-religious dialogue and learning, is often ideologically tinted.[16] One must ask 'What is the underlying idea of religious responsibility and commitment to tradition?' 'Is it true that children must first "know" everything about their own tradition before they can be truly responsive to others?' 'Does the crisis of Christian belief instead not render us sensitive to the fact that trouble-free initiation zones no longer exist and that even the most closed religious congregation is intruded upon by the "world" of religious pluralism and secular worldviews?'

Three Learning Models Dealing with Religious Diversity in School
Religious Education should contribute to an understanding and appreciation of religious differences between people. Two key objectives in Religious Education involve learning about all that religion implies and learning how religion influences the lives of people. In this way Religious Education can deal with ignorance and indifference, two negative developments that hamper the peaceful coexistence of people. In the broad sense of the word inter-religious learning refers to the religious insights that youngsters gain when encountering others. In a narrow sense it refers to the element 'interpretation through communication' (*learning from religion*), that follows the element 'information through documentation' (*learning about religion*). Inter-religious learning attempts to make the student sensitive to the unique nature of a religious position and, in (dis-)agreement with others, invites them to situate themselves within this field.

In general there are three models which outline the learning tension between particularity and plurality in Religious Education. These are 1) the mono-, 2) the multi- and 3) the inter-religious models.[17] In addition three key questions help to critically assess these models. These are: 'In which way do they do justice to the particularity of one's own tradition?' 'How do they deal with the phenomenon of religious plurality?' Finally, 'How do they situate themselves in the tension between these two?'[18]

1. The mono-religious model ('learning in religion') consciously aims to immerse young people in the dynamics of a particular tradition and render them full-fledged participants of that tradition. A possible exclusive variant of this model radically ignores other life views, while an inclusive variant is salvifically optimistic and claims that salvation – perhaps in fragments, never in *extenso* – is to be found also in other traditions. In evaluating the mono-religious model critics argue that its underlying concept of tradition is extremely static. For even in the most

closed community, crises occur in the manner in which people understand themselves. Further in this model the uniqueness of others is not recognised, and there is a strong correlation of this attitude with forms of ethnocentrism. Moreover, people are blind to the possible tension between what is familiar and what is strange.

2. The second significant model is termed the multi-religious model ('learning about religion'). Here one assumes that young people can be introduced simultaneously or successively to various religious traditions and world views, since they have no specific affinity with one or other tradition and can thus decide for themselves purely on the basis of information given. A variety of approaches have developed from this model in the last decades including 'Religionskunde' in Germany, 'multi-faith education' in England and 'geestelijke stromingen' in primary education in the Netherlands. Critics of this model suggest that it leads to indifference. Further no conscientious commitment is stimulated between the child and the tradition. If all viewpoints are the same, if nothing makes any difference, then there is absolutely no reason to consciously engage with and interest oneself in any one particular perspective. Finally, this model does not take seriously the pluriformity of religious experiences. Students adopt, as it were, a religiously clinical attitude and study the religious phenomenon from a spectator's perspective. It is akin to learning about the digestive system by devouring information, without ever being tempted at any single moment in the process to really taste and savour the flavour of food, let alone to alleviate hunger.[19] An emergency exit is substituted for a search for truth. This model runs the risk of being ideologically misused. In a non-committed presentation of various religions and views of life, the idea that it does not matter whether one is engaged or not threatens to resonate throughout. This kind of education is counter-productive as it does not inform, but deforms. It renders young people into a species of religious tourists who put themselves through the anecdotic, exotic, adventurous and 'kick-generating' facades of religions. Differences between traditions become levelled and depoliticised, and their potential as moments of learning on the road to a more conscious humanity, is lost.[20]

3. The inter-religious model ('learning from religion') thematically explores the deep questions of life, to which religious traditions and worldviews answer in parallel and/or differently. The outlook of a religion or worldview can be analysed and communicated in four forms through a) story, b) community, c) moral outlook and d) ritual. At these four levels, the internal-argumentative strength of interpellation of religions and

world views can be investigated and tested in one's own life and brought before conversation partners for investigation and testing in an ongoing dynamic of perspective exchange. Real pluralism assumes a multitude of beliefs that are deeply significant to real people. These beliefs cannot be swept into one pile and labelled as being 'all the same', but must be acknowledged as being able to deepen and broaden the vision of various conversation partners in conflict and convergence. Critics of the inter-religious model state that an intrinsic commitment to one's own tradition, however minimal, is expected from the students, so that people are prepared to study and present this to the group for perspective exchange. There is much openness to other beliefs, but the question remains whether a real rapprochement in the religious realm is possible, and if the post-modern multi-vocal self is capable of withstanding this diversity. Will the multi-vocal self be sufficiently socially agile to resist collapse into indifference or fundamentalism? In evaluating this model it is important to keep in mind what could be termed the 'shady' side of inter-religious learning based on a realistic view of pluriformity, which analyses the negative aspects of inter-religious contact such as non communication and oppression.[21] While these negative aspects exist it is important to recognise the positive developments evident in the spontaneous multicultural sensitivity of young people who express themselves in world music festivals, international exchanges, root- and folk-music and folk-culture etc. Furthermore many young people seem to recognise polyphony in their own life, and integrate and celebrate it as spontaneous energy.

From Multi-Religious Learning to Inter-Religious Learning

Since Religious Education no longer takes place in a trouble-free zone and interactions with the outside world criss-cross the life patterns of young adults, in my opinion, the inter-religious model has the best chance of success. This model supposes a thorough knowledge of the religious backgrounds of fellow-classmates and when this happens prejudice is inhibited and respect for the opinions of others flourishes. This inter-religious model does not exclude but rather includes the multi-religious model. Observing religion as a societal phenomenon ('What does religion do to people and what do people do with religion?') (*learning about religion*) offers students the opportunity to gauge the life questions to which religious people, over the course of time and in the depth of society, have given answers (*learning from religion*). This contributes to a better understanding of one's own worldview and can help to clarify one's multi-layered identity. Therefore one can say that multi-religious learning and inter-religious learning presuppose and complement each other.

In this dialectic, two forms of inter-religious learning regularly occur in the classroom. Some students are strongly convinced that their religious beliefs and behaviour emphasises the necessity of providing others with information. Other students are more timid and insecure when it concerns their own religious position and they require more help with the interpretative aspect of the learning process. Both of these forms of inter-religious learning occur in the classroom and pulsate the teaching and learning environment. The German Religious Educationalist, Karl-Ernst Nipkow, called these forms respectively the (a) hard and (b) soft form of learning in plurality.

(a)   The hard form of learning in plurality invites young adults, through conversation, to rename, document, and clarify their religious origin in conversation. For instance they are asked to think about the implications of their baptism for themselves by consulting their parents and/or grandparents. The presupposition is that those who have a traceable religious history and origin must also be able to relate to it, and respond to questions such as: 'Does this mean something to you or does it leave you indifferent? Do you know what you are talking about when you say that you are non-religious, when in fact you have been baptised?' In this process of documentation young adults bring their religious backgrounds into focus. Through the search for similarities and differences they learn to understand and express the richness of their religious backgrounds to each other. While for many their religious origin may not be relevant to their own life-quest, neither can it be denied. For those who are religiously convinced, it is often a closed chapter. It is up to them to open the book again and learn to communicate its story.

(b)   The soft form of inter-religious learning connects more with the polyphonic identity of young adults. After all, a lot of young people know so little about their own religious background that they may not know which religious 'nest' they may have been hatched from. Therefore it is pointless to enter into conversations about (supposed) elements of explicit religious initiation. This form opts for a broad perspective on worldviews, and from there it searches for connections and invites young adults to identify where they fit into these worldviews. It presupposes that religious ties, which are often not expressed in words and images, interconnect people. This form of clarification is essentially a communicative issue. It is about teaching young adults to ask pertinent questions about their own existence and to put their own perspective between parentheses and through conversation with others to learn to accept its relative status.[22] According to the British Religious Educationalist Robert Jackson, this leads to the *edification* of the person:

Through the challenge of 'unpacking' another worldview one can, in a sense, become a new person.[23]

Barriers to Inter-Religious Learning

Three issues exemplify that inter-religious learning in any given circumstance may be difficult and that it is not automatic. One difficulty relates to classrooms that students perceive to be unsafe for the disclosure and discussion of diversity. In such instances students might feel themselves and their religious position threatened, disrespected, and even ignored in the classroom. If trust is absent, especially when it comes to the vulnerable domain of exchanging experiences and ideas in religion, then inter-religious learning will not occur. On a more profound level it is important to ask how students and teachers cope with competing truth claims in the classroom. In the name of tolerance and for the sake of continuing a respectful conversation, one must ask how far a teacher or student should go before criticising and challenging an intolerant position.

A second problem which may arise in inter-religious learning relates to the individual development of the student. In some sense inter-religious communication in class supposes an advanced degree of personal development. Only those who are able and willing to represent their own position can fully participate in the dialogue. This does not imply that all students need to be pocket-theologians. Moreover it does not mean that they should be able to present a neat and fully worked out map of their lives. However, it does imply that students should be willing to reflect on their worldview and their own religious story, both in a synchronic and diachronic perspective. Or to put it in Kohlbergian terms, they should be able and willing to grow from a conventional viewpoint – through clarification – to a post-conventional viewpoint. From sixteen years onwards this approach has significant advantages. That is not to say that children and pre-adolescents cannot be sensitised to the plurality that surrounds them. In inter-religious learning to date, a crucial question that has not been satisfactorily addressed is the question of whether there is a definite moment in the person's transition from monophony to polyphony. In other words, how many different voices can a child withstand before it hears a deafening cacophony?

Finally young adults may feel insecure and 'socially disabled' from engaging in inter-religious conversation with others. Hans-Günter Heimbrock asks 'How far can one walk in the shoes of the other?'[24] Certain aspects of the conversation might remain inaccessible and radically different because they stem from completely different religious traditions or because they cannot be expressed. Moreover when one listens to other religious stories one can become confronted with the internal fallibility of one's own religious conviction. Certain elements of one's own conviction might in principle be incompatible with those from other traditions (for example resurrection versus reincarnation). One could also fall into the hands of *holy envy*, a sort of religious jealousy, 'experiencing something so profound one wishes that his or her own faith community also had or practiced it'.[25] In summary one can become quite entangled, not only within the conversation, but also within oneself.

Learning in Difference and Inter-Spiritual Dialogue

'What can I learn from you if we cannot be different from each other? Why would I learn at all when it does not make a difference where you come from, who you are, and what you stand for?' Educational meeting places originate where differences in interpretation occur. 'You are different from me, your way of acting is strange to me, but I want to know you, you intrigue me. This is where I stand, where do you stand?' These questions can open up the learning process of religious 'diversity' in class (this involves multi-religious and inter-religious learning) and form it into 'learning in difference'. Here the sole objective is not a transfer of information that enables interpretation to occur through communication. One also has to challenge the authenticity of the human being and enliven the soul. When this happens people are ushered into the unfathomable mystery of the uniqueness, immanence and transcendence of the human being as a member of humankind. In this exchange of dialogue each person is initiated into religious experiences and the mystery these experiences relate to. It is obvious that this 'learning in difference' is diametrically opposed to 'learning in indifference'. Learning in indifference does not only happen when differences do not stand a chance, it also happens when diversity is wiped away. Students will then drop out of the process because there is nothing for them to learn. They are not stimulated through a diversity of perspectives and neither are their soul's energised by the radical 'otherness' of the other.

This new type of learning can be called 'learning through encounter' or as the American practical theologian Mary C. Boys terms it 'learning in the presence of the other'.[26] Such 'inter-spiritual' – dialogue is not about having the last word on doctrinal or disciplinary matters, on the contrary it involves a sharing of spiritual experiences that lie beneath the different positions. I am convinced that, considering the eagerness, ease, and interactivity of the spiritual search of contemporary young adults, this inter-spiritual model can be easily implemented and practiced in classrooms. The Indian theologian, Raimon Pannikar, suggests: 'It is about having an inner religious conversation with myself, an encounter in the depth of my own religiosity after I have met another person on the same intimate level'.[27] One might wonder if 'inter-spiritual' dialogue is an unachievable aim in class. Perhaps it is a challenging and worthwhile aim for the future. For if one ushers young adults into the realm of the soul, the demands of class instruction are high, the desire for information great, and the longing for communication with peers limitless. Perhaps the most noticeable aspect of the process will be young adults' underlying questions of hope and the future: 'Is there a perspective possible that connects and unites people globally, that transcends humankind, and that at the same time helps human beings to respect and cultivate both their individuality and their difference from others?'

Such critical encounter with the other encourages me to look more thoroughly at myself. Inter-religious learning is not a youthful version of a 'mature' inter-religious dialogue, but a religious learning process in which religious plurality (in class groups, but also in the individual person) is taken seriously. This critical encounter reinforces the ability to look deeper into one's own meaning-giving system and to explore further the existential resilience it offers. Through the intercultural and inter-religious encounter, I am challenged to re-define myself, to know myself better, and respect myself more, as a human person with dignity, who makes a difference through encounter with others. Another person's view on a given (religious) question can only inspire me when I myself am committed to that question and begin to answer it. That is a point of departure. One has to start somewhere. Nobody can see and honour all perspectives at the same time. Without one's own spiritual view, it is even impossible for one to converse with another. It would not be worth the effort for nothing (new) would come out of it. So, in this approach the multi- and inter-dimensions are interrelated to the intra-dimension of religion. Encounter implies difference. Without difference there can be no encounter. So one could argue that the intra-religious dimension is re-incorporated in this approach to inter-religious learning.[28]

Inter-spiritual dialogue teaches people modesty and fortitude where the other is radically different and they can learn from them. For a truthful presence in this learning process, I need to be secure and honourable in encountering the other, in the hope and trust that the other will be secure as well. Learning through encounter is not easy. It requires time and energy to learn, recognise and respect other's views while not losing oneself in the euphoria of universal brotherhood ('alle Menschen werden Brüder'). On the other hand it implies a fundamental willingness to let the other be a unique and authentic self, and to respect their point of view, trusting that the other will be willing to express their own opinions. It requires a leap into the unknown, a hope for a willingness of communication with the other; a hope that can only be verified through an actual involvement in conversation. In this conversation one does not wait for the other but has the courage to start it oneself. It is this mutual vulnerability that has urged Mary C. Boys to speak of a *hermeneutic of affections*, a willingness to lend one's ear, not so much to the opinions of the other, but to the inspiration (the 'spirit') that the other demonstrates by talking about their point of view.[29] It generates space for mutual acknowledgment, for admiration and respect for the unique way in which fellow human beings, each in their own manner, hear, experience, and fulfill the religious call without feeling obliged to take on or annul the authenticity of the other.

By way of summary we can say that this 'new' approach to the 'old' inter-religious learning can be schematised as follows. Inter-religious in the 'old' sense of the word relates to the middle column. Inter-religious learning in the broad 'new' sense of the word expands over the three columns.

Learning about religion	Learning from religion	Learning in religion
Multi-religious learning	Inter-religious learning	Intra-religious learning
Knowing the other	Respecting the other	Knowing/respecting myself
Information through documentation	Interpretation through communication	Encounter through confrontation
Heuristic competence	Social competence	Existential competence

Conclusion

Will education succeed in overstepping the contemporary accent on one's own ego? Will the other truly come into my life and touch it, no longer in function of my own ego and formation of my own narrative identity, but in the figure of the radical other, who gives me food for thought, who leads me away from old certainties and foreknowledge, and who refreshes me with new, 'bestowed' identity? In this chapter I have pleaded for an inter-spiritual learning process through 'learning by encounter' or 'learning in difference'. In this learning process there is room for impeding elements (conflict, disharmony, holy envy) as well as elements that are beyond didactical command. Is this learning of the 'practices of dispossession', this 'learning in dedication', possible and doable?[30] Is there mental space for it in our high-tech educational systems? Is there enough creativity to implement a teaching of learning in difference? These are some key questions that Religious Education must address.

Notes

1   S. Miedema, 'Levensbeschouwelijke vorming voor alle leerlingen op alle scholen', in H. Alma e.a.,
        Zin op school. Zingeving in het voortgezet onderwijs, Nijmegen: 2000, pp. 72–87. S. Miedema,
        'Contexts, debates and perspectives of religion in education in Europe. A comparative analysis',
        in R. Jackson, S. Miedema, W. Weisse, J.P. Williaime (eds), *Religion and Education in Europe*,
        Münster: Waxman, 2007, pp. 267–283.

2   J.M. Sjah, 'Axis mundi', in *Narthex. Tijdschrift voor levensbeschouwing en educati*, 2 (1), 2002, p. 29
        (present author's translation).

3   G. Büttner, 'Kinder-Theologie', in *Evangelische Theologie*, 67, 2007, pp. 216–229. A. Dillen,
        'Religious participation of children as active subjects: toward a hermeneutical-communicative
        model of religious education in families with young children', in *International Journal of Children's
        Spirituality*, 12 (1), 2007, pp. 37–49 ; F. Schweitzer, *Das Recht des Kindes auf Religion. Ermutigungen
        für Eltern und Erzieher*, Gütersloh: Kaiser/Gütersloher Verlagshaus, 2000; F. Schweitzer, 'Children
        as Theologians. God-Talk with Children, Developmental Psychology, and Inter-religious
        Education', in D. Bates, G. Durka & F. Schweitzer (eds), *Education, Religion and Society. Essays in
        Honour of John M. Hull*, London, New York: Routledge, 2006, pp. 179–190.

4   B. Roebben, 'Religious education through times of crisis. Reflections on the future of a
        vulnerable school subject', in B. Roebben & M. Warren (eds), *Religious Education as Practical
        Theology. Essays in Honour of Professor Herman Lombaerts*, Leuven, Paris, Sterling (VA): Peeters,
        2001, pp. 245–272; H. Lombaerts, D. Pollefeyt (eds), *Hermeneutics and Religious Education*, Leuven:
        Peeters, 2004.

5   M. Crawford, & G. Rossiter, *Reasons for Living: Education and young people's search for meaning,
        identity and spirituality. A handbook*, Camberwell: ACER, 2006.

6   N. Mette, 'Religionsunterricht am Ort der Schule – Möglichkeiten, Grenzen, Ambivalenzen,' in
        Religionspädagogische Beiträge, No. 58, 2007, pp. 5–26 [Religious education at school: possibilities,
        boundaries, ambiguities]; F. Schweitzer, *Die Suche nach eigenem Glauben. Einführung in die
        Religionspädagogik des Jugendalters*, Gütersloh: Gütersloher Verlagshaus, 1996, pp. 164–178; F.
        Schweitzer, Religionspadagogik Lehrbuch Praktische Theologie 1, Gütersloh: Gütersloher
        Verlagshaus, 2007, pp. 81–96.

7   One only has to think of the impact of the media on youth culture cf. B. Roebben, 'Spiritual and
        Moral Education in/and Cyberspace: Preliminary Reflections', in *Journal of Education and Christian
        Belief*, Vol. 3, No. 2, 1999, pp. 85–95; M. Crawford & G. Rossiter, Reasons for Living, 2006, pp.
        322–367.

8   R. Jackson, S. Miedema, W. Weisse & J. P. Williaime (eds), *Religion and Education in Europe.
        Developments, Contexts and Debates (Religious Diversity and Education 3)*, Münster, New York,
        München, Berlin: Waxmann, 2007.

9   H. Lombaerts, 'Religion, Society, and the Teaching of Religion in Schools', in M. Warren (ed.),
        Sourcebook for Modern Catechetics, Vol. 2, Winona: Saint Mary's Press, 1997, pp. 306–329.

10   J.A. Van der Ven, & H.-G. Ziebertz (eds), *Religiöser Pluralismus und interreligiöses Lernen*,
        Weinheim/Kampen: DSV/Kok, 1994.

11   P. Valadier, 'Identité chretienne et morale', in J. Doré (ed.), *Sur l'identité chrétienne*, Paris: Desclée,
        1990, p. 97.

12   B. Roebben, 'Shaping a Playground for Transcendence. Postmodern Youth Ministry as a Radical Challenge', in *Religious Education*, Vol. 92, 1997, pp. 340–346.

13   B. Roebben, *Bewogenheid in beweging. Een visie op de spiritualiteit van een christelijke school.* Brussels: Licap, 2003.

14   W.A. J. Meijer, 'The Plural Self. A Hermeneutical View on Identity and Plurality', in *British Journal of Religious Education*, 17, 1995, pp. 92–99; H. Streib, 'Erzählte Zeit als Ermöglichung von Identität und seine Implikationen für die religionspädagogische Rede von Identität und Bildung', in D. Georgi, H.-G. Heimbrock & M. Moxter (hrsg.), *Religion und die Gestaltung der Zeit*, Kampen: 1994, pp. 181–198.

15   Diachronic and Synchronic are terms that refer to two logics or ways of ordering things. Diachronic involves looking at sequences, origins, history and change, whereas Synchronic refers to connections and patterns at a particular moment.

16   R. Mokrosch, Brauchen Kinder und Jugendliche einen konfessionell geöffneten Religionsunterricht oder werden sie damit überfordert?', in R. Frieling & C. Th. Scheilke (hrsg.), *Religionsunterricht und Konfessionen (Bensheimer Hefte 88)*, Göttingen, 1999, pp. 24–28.

17   M. Grimmitt, *Religious Education and Human Development*, Great Wakering: McCrimmon, 1987; J. A. Van der Ven & H.-G. Ziebertz (eds), Religiöser Pluralismus und interreligiöses Lernen, Weinheim/Kampen: DSV/Kok, 1994.

18   C. Sterkens, C.A.M. Hermans & J. A. Van der Ven (eds), 'Formation of the Religious Polyphonic Self: Inter-religious Learning in Religiously Affiliated Schools', in P. Ploeger & C. Sterkens (eds.), *Search for Meaning: Education into Realms of Meaning in a Plural Society*, Kampen: Kok, 1999, pp. 163–165.

19   Streitgespräch zwischen Albert Biesinger und Jürgen Lott, *Den Religiösen Hunger Stillen – in der Schule?* in *Publik Forum*, 10 April, 1998.

20   H.A. Giroux, *Living Dangerously. Multiculturalism and the Politics of Difference*, New York et. al.: Peter Lang, 1996.

21   J.A. Van der Ven, *Formation of the Moral Self*, Grand Rapids/Cambridge: Eerdmans, 1998, p. 273.

22   F. Rickers, 'Interreligiöses Lernen. Die religionspädagogische Herausforderung unserer Zeit,' in F. Rickers & E. Gottwald (hrsg.), *Von religiösen zum interreligiösen Lernen: wie Angehörige verschiedener Religionen und Konfessionen lernen*, Neukirchen-Vluyn, 1998, pp. 135–137; Van der Ven, Formation, 1998, pp. 266–282.

23   R. Jackson, *Religious Education: An Interpretive Approach*, London: Hodder and Stoughton, 1997, pp. 130–131.

24   H. Streib, 'Inter-Religious Negotiations: Case Studies on Students' Perception of and Dealing with Religious Diversity', in H.-G. Heimbrock, C. Th. Scheilke & P. Schreiner (eds), *Towards Religious Competence. Diversity as a Challenge for Education in Europe*, Münster: Lit, 2001, p. 140.

25   M. Boys, *Has God Only One Blessing? Judaism as a Source of Christian Self-Understanding*, New York/Mahwah NJ: Paulist Press, 2000, p. 276; S. Lubarsky, 'Identity: confronting truth and ambiguity dialogue – "Holy insecurity"', in *Religious Education*, 91, (4), 1996, pp. 539–546.

26   M. Boys, *Jewish-Christian Dialogue. One Woman's Experience*, New York: Paulist Press, 1997, pp. 6–60.

27   R. Pannikar, *The Intra-Religious Dialogue*, New York: Paulist Press, 1978, p. 40.

28   A. Halsall & B. Roebben, 'Intercultural and Interfaith Dialogue Through Education', in *Religious*

Education, 101, 2006, pp. 443–452; B. Roebben, *Living Together in a Post-Secular Europe [Proceedings of the CoGREE Meeting in Berlin (5–6 October 2005)]*, Münster: Comenius-Institute [cd-rom], 2006; B. Roebben, *Godsdienstpedagogiek van de hoop. Grondlijnen voor religieuze vorming* [Religious Pedagogics of Hope. Foundations of Religious Education], Leuven: Acco., 2007, pp. 156–160.

29   M. Boys, 'Authenticity, not Demonization: An Education for Paradox', in *Journal of Ecumenical Studies*, 34, 1997, p. 353.

30   I. Geerinck, 'God Embarrassed by the Pastor? A Search for New Practices in Religious Education', in D. Nauer, R. Nauta, & H. Witte (eds), *Religious Leadership and Christian Identity*, Münster: Lit Verlag, 2004, pp. 143–153.

CHAPTER 11

HOW WORLD RELIGIONS TEACH RELIGION

Joseph McCann

Catholic teachers can sometimes lose the sense of what is distinctive about Christianity. Christian education has a unique view of God, the universe, human beings and the world of knowledge. This unique view is not just reflected in the religion class, it is reflected in the classroom and in the school. It can only be appreciated when it is seen in comparison to Religious Education in other world religions. This chapter places Christian Religious Education in the context of Other World Religions (OWR).

Religion is a complex human activity, involving distinctive activities, beliefs and rituals. Scholars have listed principal religious activities as follows: What people believe; How people worship; How people live; How people associate with each other; How people experience life and How people express their identity. As a short-hand these are summed up in six 'C' words for religion: Creed; Cult; Code; Community; Consciousness and Culture. In this chapter I suggest that each major world religion stresses a different activity, and so, these six approaches can help us appreciate each religion's distinctive approach to Religious Education. It would be an interesting 'thought experiment' for you, the reader, to choose now, which of these six activities is closest to the characteristic approach of Christian or Catholic Religious Education.

Hinduism
Hinduism is the religion of India but it shares its world-view widely throughout Asia and beyond. Hindu sages combined many different religious beliefs and practices in a peaceful and sensible way. Two common insights helped them to do this. They believed that everything has divinity within it, and that everyone suffers from delusion. This makes Hinduism a tolerant religion. Hindus believe that each person has some of the truth, but no one has it all.

HINDU WORLD-VIEW
Hindus are devoted to many divinities, because they see the divine everywhere.

People labor under the illusion that things are all different and very real. On the contrary, deep down every single thing, is really *Brahman*, the Supreme Being. Individuals are bubbles on the stream of life, destined to merge into the great ocean of *Brahman*. When talking about Hinduism perhaps we should not say 'God', because that would suggest the Christian or Jewish or Muslim God who is a Creator God. A Creator God is 'other than' the created universe, but *Brahman* is the reality at the core of everything and everyone.

Humans are the victims of illusion (*Maya*) because they cannot see *Brahman*. They are trapped in a world of shadows. Death is no release because another life quickly follows, another bubble forms as each bubble bursts. Hindus believe in 're-incarnation' or being reborn. Fate means that our bad actions bring us back to life as a lower being in a reincarnated life. Good actions, of course, mean that we can climb higher on the ladder of being for our next life. This fate is called *Karma*. Escape from the cycle or wheel of life and death (*Samsara*) happens when we see that *Brahman* is within us and that all life is divine. That insight brings happiness because individuality (our bubble) is bypassed. Then we are truly free and really happy. We flow freely like water to the sea.

In Hindu society, everyone's status has been earned in a previous existence. The caste system is a social hierarchy of priests, rulers, merchants, labourers and outcast menials. Liberation comes through the discipline (*Yoga*) of good thought, devotion and action. Each caste requires different duties from its members. The Hindu scriptures say that it is better to do the duty of one's own caste badly than the duty of another caste well.

HINDU RELIGIOUS EDUCATION

The goal of all Hindu education is religious. The Hindu teacher traditionally began with the study of the sacred books – the *Vedas* – to alert the student to the hidden realm of the spirit and the proper ceremonies to recognise it. Students lived with their teacher (*guru*) to be trained in simple living and their ceremonial obligations. The *guru* used oral methods to teach the books, instructing students in pronunciation, memorisation, grammar and the practice of meditation. The stages of learning involved: first, listening to the teacher, then questioning and reflection, and finally, rational thought and meditation.

Secular learning was necessary to earn one's living, but it was specific to one's caste. Hindu educators concentrated on personality development rather than academic learning. Ancient and modern Hindu schools include training in (1) silence and meditation, (2) exposure to nature and contemplation of the world, (3) simple chores, tasks and crafts, (4) self-discipline and a respectful obedience to the teacher.

Hinduism values personal rituals, family devotions, and community ceremonials as a window into reality. Rite and ceremony reveals the divinity in every person, place and moment. Hence, the role of *Cult* (or worship) is especially significant in Hindu Religious Education.

Buddhism

Buddhism originated with one man, Siddartha Guatama, a prince of Nepal, who lived around 500 BCE. He had sampled life's luxuries and then tried stern self-discipline, but neither brought him happiness. He concluded, after much soul searching, that sorrow can be eliminated from human life but only if the individual can recognise suffering, know its cause, and in calm determination, undertake the task of removing it. He called his prescription the 'Middle Way', because it is neither too strict nor too lax. Guatama was called the Enlightened One (*Buddha*) because he revealed the truth about life to humanity.

BUDDHIST WORLD-VIEW

Buddha's teaching is simple. However the experience that lies behind his teaching is difficult to achieve. The Buddha preached the Four Noble Truths:

1. To live is to suffer.
2. Suffering is caused by desire.
3. We can eliminate the cause of suffering.
4. The Eightfold Path is the solution to suffering.

Buddhism advises a training regime that takes you to the roots of your person. It comprises wisdom, morality and contemplation. The Eightfold Path is directed towards individual consciousness.

Selfish attachment is the only cause for sorrow. Our internal clinging to things gives us pain. This is true both of the obvious sorrows of living, such as failure, loss, illness, pain and death, and also to the less obvious sorrow of our short and fleeting existence. Each of us is a collection of random elements that will soon dissolve. Once I thoroughly realise this truth, I can quench completely my longing for pleasure and power and permanence. Then I will not care what happens. I will be completely detached.

BUDDHIST RELIGIOUS EDUCATION

Buddhist Religious Education is based on the practice of the Buddha himself. He spent his life teaching and he employed very modern pedagogical methods. He was very aware, for instance, of the individual differences in his students. On one occasion, he explained how a question was to be answered depending on the previous state of mind of the questioner.

The challenge for Buddhist education is the achievement with a group of something that can be accomplished only by the individual. Oral instruction holds pride of place along with memorisation, questioning and analysis. Since debating skills were so important for missionaries, argument came to play an important role. To this day training in debating has continued in parts of the Buddhist educational world.

An element of Buddhist education often involves withdrawal from ordinary life to a monastery, if only for a short period. The common life of a monastery provides support for soul and spirit. This helps one to give full commitment to meditation with the hope of achieving enlightenment. To be a Buddhist, though, each person must stand on their own feet, depending on no one else, not even a god. Enlightenment is possible for all but an individual must achieve it for oneself. The Buddhist teacher is concerned with consciousness. Nothing else matters. All information and any opinion that is not contained in the Four Noble Truths, is unnecessary.

The gods play no part in classical Buddhism. Nevertheless, the devotion to the truth and reality is religious in its motivation and commitment. Buddhist education leads to moral improvement, intellectual independence and mental discipline. Completely detached, free and autonomous, the adherent can face fleeting existence with equanimity in full mindfulness. Buddhist Religious Education is about *Consciousness.*

Confucian Religion
The Chinese sage Kung Fu Tzu or Confucius also lived in the fifth century BCE. He was a philosopher and administrator. He tried to get the divided small kingdoms of ancient China to accept his ideas for peace but none agreed with him. Confucius then turned to teaching, committed his ideas to writing, and founded the school of thought that bears his name. Confucianism has lasted for over two thousand years, and it became the official philosophy of China. Even today, after sixty years of Communism, Confucian ideas deeply influence Chinese culture.

CONFUCIAN WORLD-VIEW
Confucius did not claim to be inspired with a divine revelation. He said only that he had reclaimed the ancient wisdom. He taught that people's yearning for eternal life and personal comfort could be achieved on earth rather than in heaven. Immortality is available in two ways: survival of the family line and the memory of posterity. These values are at the heart of history, close to the needs of people and relevant to the tasks of government.

The core of Confucian thought is 'humane virtue' (*Jen*) which is a respect for human dignity. This is achieved by 'an adherence to moral rule and ritual obligation' (*Li*). Chun Tzu 'the ideal man or superior person' is the product of Confucian formation. The authorities do not rule by force but by the power of moral example (*Te*) expressed in the 'arts of peace' (*Wen*).

Confucianism does not believe in supernatural beings. Yet it too is religious and its teaching relies on religious beliefs: ancestor worship and the will of Heaven. A strong bond between generations leads to a peaceful social order. We do things in honour of our forebears and for the good of our children. When this happens, people have physical security and spiritual confidence. Respect for ancestors is the glue that holds person, family, state and universe together.

Confucian Religious Education

For two thousand years Confucianism framed Chinese education and schooling. Confucian teaching is hopeful about society. People are fundamentally good but can be corrupted by bad example, weak teaching and external temptation. The aim of Confucian education is to form citizens of the nation, servants of the state, heirs to the family, balanced individuals, superior people who act at all times with honesty and a deep sense of humanity.

Traditional Confucian education was straightforward. It was not utopian or revolutionary. It emphasised precise training rather than original thought. Its focus was moral strength. Confucius claims that a stable nation depends on good families, comprised of virtuous people, with pure motives, sincere thoughts and wide knowledge. Confucian education works to make this happen. Personal destiny and social progress are both advanced by determined study and sustained discipline.

Confucian education inculcates a high esteem for teachers and a deep regard for learning. This respect survives among many contemporary Asian students. Chinese education is directed to the written rather than the spoken word and Chinese script bears no relationship to the language as spoken. There is much emphasis on memorisation and less on discussion. The commitment to attain a high standard of literacy produces erudite scholars. It also produces a stable civilisation. We may contrast Chinese with Western education on this point.

In Confucian education, ceremonies play an important part but their purpose is social rather than personal. They serve the collective good rather than individual devotion. Confucian Religious Education is concerned to support the pillars of public culture and civilisation. Thus Confucian Religious Education is concerned with *Culture*.

Judaism

The Bible tells us that God Himself chose the Hebrews as his own people, rescued them from slavery, formed them into a nation called Israel, taught them the law and a way to live, and promised them a land and posterity. However the Jewish people enjoyed peaceful possession of their Promised Land for less than one hundred years during the kingships of David and Solomon. Ever since, they suffered internal division or external invasion. Despite those setbacks, the Jewish people (*Qahal*) is entrusted with a special relationship with God.

JEWISH WORLD-VIEW

The memory of Abraham, Moses, David and the prophets shapes the Jewish world-view. Abraham recognises the Creative Presence in the Universe as a caring God and Father. Moses experiences that God acts in history and seeks friendship with humanity. The reigns of David and Solomon afford a glimpse of what God wants for Israel. Finally the prophets teach that God is concerned with justice and peace.

Justice is at the root of creation. God shall, in God's own time, inaugurate a permanent era of justice and peace. Yet Jewish religion is practical. It provides a law, intended to remind people of the power of God, the demands on human beings and the values at the heart of creation. The destruction of the Second Temple in 70 CE caused a crisis and many Jews were scattered to other countries (*Diaspora*). The Rabbis thereafter taught that faithfulness to the law and the preservation of Jewish tradition is a substitute for the Promised Land and Temple. Jews living outside Palestine could continue to be God's chosen people if they stayed holy and separate, retained their tradition and kept their Law.

JEWISH RELIGIOUS EDUCATION

Traditional Jewish primary schools were called *Hadarim* and secondary schools *Yeshivot*. Jewish education is religious in purpose and content. Some Jewish schools around the world began including secular subjects in their curriculum, trying to balance Jewish identity with the needs of immigrants in their new lands. Stricter religious schools refused to compromise. After the foundation of Israel in 1948, similar anxieties about religious and secular aspirations for the new nation resulted in the emergence of different types of schools: traditional religious schools; Jewish schools that teach religion and general subjects; and schools that teach Jewish material to serve a nationalist ethos.

In the *Diaspora* many Jewish children attend regular secular schools. Jewish Religious Education is then taught part-time in schools. Such schools stress Jewish identity, Jewish culture, religious holidays and synagogue prayers. At ages eleven to thirteen, supplemental schooling includes preparation for the *bar mitzvah* or *bat mitzvah* (the ceremony of entry into adulthood). Out-of-school activities such as summer camps, preschools, tours to Israel and youth groups, allow children to develop a commitment to Jewish culture and values.

Teaching is a central value in Jewish culture. Jewish education is concentrated on the sacred texts of the Bible. Education of children is training in prayer and observance. Induction into adult life, with the obligation of the commandments, is a crucial part of Religious Education. Discussion and debate, explanation and application are all part of the process.

Jewish Religious Education, then, involves immersion in Jewish experiences, recall of Jewish memories, awareness of Jewish identity, and participation in Jewish traditions; in short, becoming a member of the Jewish *Community*.

Islam
Islam means 'obedience' or 'submission'. 'Obey God' was the message brought by Muhammed from Mount Hira near Mecca in Arabia in 610 CE. The theme was simple, the preaching was powerful, the effects stunning. Arabia was converted within a century. Islam spread to neighbouring regions with extraordinary rapidity and an impressive Muslim civilisation was established. Much of the origins of modern science and mathematics and the intellectual stimulus for the European Renaissance are credited to Islamic scholarship.

MUSLIM WORLD-VIEW
Muslims believe that there is an infinite gap between the divine and the human. *God (Allah) only communicates with humanity to give us His commands.* Even then, God employs an angel as a go-between. Muhammed, a caravan driver in Mecca, received the revelation from God through the Angel Gabriel. God had already warned humanity through previous messengers – including the Jewish prophets and Jesus. Muhammed is the last messenger and greatest prophet, the bearer of the final warning to obey God's law.

A Muslim obeys God and acknowledges Muhammed as God's final prophet. Human beings need no help from God to do this, other than to heed God's word. Though merciful and compassionate, God is also just and fair. Human beings will receive the reward for their actions, good or bad. Humans know what God wants by using their intellects, or by visions but the best way is through the revelation revealed to Muhammed and written in the *Qur'an*. The *Qur'an* records God's word and is sacred beyond every worldly reality.

Obeying God is the sign of the true Muslim. The Five Pillars express the duties of the Muslim. These Five Pillars consist of:

- the Creed or *Shahadah* ('There is no God but God, and Muhammed is His Prophet.)
- Prayer five times a day (*Salat*)
- the annual 2.5% Levy for the poor (*Zakat*)
- the Fast at the month of Ramadan (*Sawm*) and
- the once-in-a-lifetime Pilgrimage to Mecca (*Hajj*).

Obeying Muslim law or *Sharia* is the sign of a Muslim society. Men and women should live like brothers and sisters as they form part of the universal community of Muslims (*Umma*). Muslims want Islam to be supported by public order as well as practised in private life yet Islam adopts different political stances in different countries. There is diversity in the Islamic world. There are fully secular states such as Turkey, officially Islamic states such as Saudi Arabia and Pakistan, and states with a Muslim majority such as Indonesia, Nigeria and Syria. These differences have implications for Muslim Religious Education.

Muslim Religious Education

The institutions of Muslim Religious Education are the *kuttab* (elementary school) and the *madrasah* (secondary school and higher education). Originally the core of the curriculum was the *Qur'an* but the elements of reading, writing and counting were added. The *kuttab* made a major contribution to literacy. The *madrasah* came later with a broader curriculum, which included astronomy, medicine and the sciences.

The *Qur'an* is written in Arabic. Accordingly, Muslims of many nations learned Arabic in order to be able to read the word of *Allah*. Recitation of the *Qur'an* was the typical pedagogical method employed in Muslim Religious Education. Muslim Religious Education is concerned with the formation of the person. Both the discipline of obedience and the drilling of common recitation play a major part in that effort. The incantation of the syllables, understood or not understood, brings mind, body, spirit and heart close to the divine. The Muslim educator looks for practical compliance to God's command first, in the confidence that understanding and knowledge will follow.

The introduction of Western schooling in some Muslim countries and recent Muslim emigration to the West, has challenged Islamic educational practice. Islam has more energetically confronted secularism than other world religions, but some commentators suggest that the concentration of Muslim Religious Education on deed, rather than idea, has left Islam somewhat unready to meet the modern world. There is therefore much discussion about the place of science and secular subjects in modern Islamic education.

Generally speaking, for Muslims secular learning is subordinate to religious knowledge. The primary obligation of the human being is to obey, to carry out the commands of God in everyday life. Muslim Religious Education emphasises the *Code* aspect of religion, or how people live.

Christianity

Christians believe that God is the Creator of the universe, and so, infinitely beyond all that exists. Yet God is not separate from the universe. Christians believe that God freely created everyone and everything out of love. God then freely decided to make a personal entrance, as a Creature, into the world He had made. This is an incredible belief. The author becomes a character in the story. In stating that Jesus is the Son of God, Christians are asserting that the Creator became a Creature. There is more. God is present, everywhere and always, in creation through the Holy Spirit. While God is beyond us (Father and Creator), God is also among us (Son and Human Being), and within us (Holy Spirit). The Trinity – three persons in one divine nature – is the essential Christian teaching.

CHRISTIAN WORLD-VIEW

From this revelation springs the Christian world-view. The Christian perspective has shaped European civilisation, framed the philosophical and social horizons of Western thinkers, and laid the foundations for the world's contemporary scientific and political landscape. The de-divinisation of the universe (recognising that the world is not divine) has endowed creatures with autonomy so that things can exist as authentically themselves. That released science from the darkness of magic. On the other hand the Fathers of the Church noted that the Incarnation (the life of Jesus, true God and true man) divinised humanity so that every human being is irreducibly sacred. That instilled a high respect for the individual person. The Spirit, deeply involved in human history, alerted humanity that universal justice and peace is possible.

CHRISTIAN RELIGIOUS EDUCATION

These insights inform Christian and Catholic Religious Education so that *Creed* (what people believe) is the focus for Christian education. Indeed the cognitive dimension – Religious Knowledge – typifies Christian teaching. Catholic teachers, for instance, have traditionally organised their curriculum around the Ten Commandments, the Seven Sacraments and the Twelve Articles of the Creed. These cover three of the religious dimensions (Code, Cult, and Creed), but the Creed is generally given most attention. The educational emphasis on the Creed is, of course, true of other Christian Churches, and not just the Catholic Church. Yet it should be noted that the educational commitment is not to mere cognition or knowing but to personal conversion.

This follows from the life of Jesus Christ. Jesus proceeded by persuasion. He began with the Twelve, and ended with eleven (not very courageous) champions for the Kingdom. Christians learned that the Kingdom is built, person-by-person. There is no short-cut. Each one has a chance to make up his or her mind. Each one must, in freedom, respond to the call for conversion. Each must hear the Word and receive the Spirit. Christian Religious Education is founded on personal conviction, is patient with gradualism, but convinced of the possibility of radical change at the end of the day. For the word 'Creed' (*cor dare* in Latin) means not 'What one believes' but 'What one gives one's heart to'.

Another feature of Christian and Catholic education has been the weight given to the secular subjects. Since the world is the work of God's hands and is also independent of God, humanity can learn about God, the universe and human life by the study of creation. Hence, the secular subjects, alongside Religious Education, are another way to the truth. They are not just useful for earning a living, or necessary for assimilation with other citizens. By knowing things about the world and its workings, students can discover God, because the Spirit is there too. The wise men followed the star, and arrived at the stable just the same.

Lastly, Christian and Catholic education is poised in the 'time between'. The Kingdom has already come, but is, also, not yet come. Our hearts cling to the loving purpose of God for justice and peace. That leads to hope here and now. Life is not suffering, but neither can suffering be ignored nor eliminated. Suffering is the birth-pang of the New Creation.

Further Reading

Burke, P., *The Major Religions: an Introduction with Texts*, Oxford: Blackwell, 1996.

Cole, W.O. (ed.), *World Faiths in Education*, Guildford: Allen and Unwin, 1978.

Dorr, D., *Divine Energy: God Beyond Us, Among Us, Within Us*, Dublin: Gill and Macmillan, 1996.

McCann, J., 'Religious Perspectives: An Analysis of the Perspectives of World Religions' in de Souza, M., Durka, G., Engebretson, K., Jackson, R. and McGrady, A. (eds), *International Handbook of the Religious, Moral and Spiritual Dimensions in Education, Part Two*, Dordrecht: Springer, 1996, pp. 917–935.

Smith, H., *The World's Religions*, San Francisco: Harper, 1991.

Tulasiewicz, W. & To, C.Y. (eds), *World Religions and Educational Practice*, London: Cassell, 1993.

CHAPTER 12

INVISIBILITY AND INCLUSIVITY:
APPROACHES TO RELIGIOUS DIFFERENCE IN SCHOOLS

Patricia Kieran

> The Religious Education of the future generations is of crucial importance. It is important to teach them respect for the religious other, so that they learn to tolerate, but that is not enough. Whenever possible, we need to teach them also about the truth, the good and the holy as reflected in other religions, so that they will learn to appreciate them.
>
> Peter Schmidt-Leukel

This chapter provides an overview of alternative approaches to religious difference or to what Schmidt-Leukel terms 'the religious other' in schools. The debate focuses on two key themes as they are embodied in the legislation and educational systems of selected countries. The first theme concerns legislation prohibiting or excluding public displays of religious symbols, of religious otherness, in state schools in a number of European countries. Religious symbols and clothing are a visible and public manifestation of religious difference. In many instances the impact of the legislation is to eliminate signs of religious difference and to render it invisible in the public school context.[1] This European legislation forms a general contextual backdrop for the second theme that explores approaches to religious difference in Catholic primary schools. Here the Church's teaching on Catholic schools as centres of inclusivity provides a framework for understanding religious otherness.[2]

Faith and Symbols of Faith in European Schools
In recent years a renewed emphasis on the importance of religion in contemporary Europe has resulted in many positive developments. In 2002, the Council of Europe focused on the religious dimension of Intercultural Education (ICE) and posited that inter-Religious Education might help to contribute a solution to intercultural problems. In 2003, European Education Ministers made ICE, including its religious dimension, a priority for further work. In 2007, the Council of Europe published a reference book for teachers on religious diversity in Europe.[3] Significant networks such as Teaching Religion in a Multicultural

European Society (TRES), the European Community Framework Six project on Religious Education, Dialogue and Conflict and The European Network for Religious Education through Contextual Approaches, have initiated large scale research into documenting and improving the teaching of religion in Europe.[4]

Many European countries have hosted recent debates on the role of religion as well as religious symbols and clothing in their societies and in their educational systems.[5] The association of religion with acts of terrorism such as 9/11, the Madrid (2004) and London bombings (2005) has also had negative consequences. It goes without saying that many dispute the legitimacy of the link between religion and violence. At the 2004 Parliament of World Religions 'the use of violence, especially when it is given a religious justification, was ritually denounced by almost every speaker'.[6] However other commentators conclude that religion contributes to social conflict and potentially inhibits adherents from integrating into society.[7] Indeed it is estimated that religion was 'a contributory cause in more than half of the 115 armed conflicts which occurred between 1989 and 2001'.[8] Many view religious difference as a potential cause of social, cultural and political conflict. John Bowker argues that without religion:

> it is impossible to understand the nature of so many bitter conflicts in the world today. For years I have been pointing out that religions are likely to destroy human life as we know it now on this planet ... [9]

Bowker states that one can predict future conflicts of a serious kind by taking a map of the world and drawing the boundaries where religions or sub-systems of religions meet. Wherever these points of religious difference converge, fault lines emerge indicating possible future sources of conflict. While Bowker is not advocating the elimination of religious difference in the hope of avoiding conflict, he stresses that Religious Education is crucial in facilitating a deep understanding of religious difference with the consequence of avoiding future conflict.

Within many European societies proponents have argued that religion, and in some cases explicit symbolic indicators of religious faith (wearing headscarfs, crucifixes, turbans etc.), should play no role in the formal public or state school system.[10] In effect there is nothing new in these lines of argumentation.[11] For instance the French Republic is based on the principle of *Laicité* or non-confessionalism and while the Alsace and Moselle regions have state-funded optional confessional Religious Education in their schools, they represent the exception rather than the rule.[12] In France, the public or government operated school is a religiously neutral space. A law that came into effect on September 2, 2004, banned the wearing of conspicuous religious symbols in French public, primary and post-primary schools.[13] The legislation was intended to accord equality of opportunity and treatment to all students and teachers regardless of religious affiliation. This meant that the wearing of large Christian crosses, Sikh turbans, Jewish yarmulkes, Muslim headscarfs (*hijab, khimar* or *burqa*) as well as any other ostentatious or noticeable religious symbol was prohibited. This controversial law was resisted and amid protests and public debate in August, 2004, Iraqi Islamic militants kidnapped two French journalists, Georges Malbrunot and Christian Chesnot. The militants demanded that the French government revoke the ban on religious symbols and clothing. France upheld its ban and in December 2004, both hostages were released. However the debate over the right to a religiously neutral learning environment depleted of religious clothing and symbolism continues in France. In a controversial letter to teachers and parents in 2007, a letter which threw secularists into disarray, President Nicholas Sarkozy spoke of a radical reform of the French school system so that the teaching of religion would not be excluded from school.

> The birth of the great religions and their visions of humanity and the world must be studied, not of course to proselytise in any way, or as part of any theological approach, but in the context of a sociological, cultural and historical analysis which can give pupils a better understanding of the concept of religious faith. Spirituality and a sense of the sacred have accompanied the human adventure since the dawn of time. They are at the wellsprings of every civilisation. It is easier for us to open up to others, to talk to them when we understand them.[14]

The German state school has also become the locus for a conflict between secular ideology and religious commitment as expressed through the wearing of religious clothing and symbols. In 2003, Germany's constitutional court ruled that individual states in Germany could pass independent legislation to ban teachers wearing religious apparel in schools which might unduly influence children. While there is no uniformity in the German legistlation, some states provide teachers with a limited right to wear Christian symbols (e.g. Hessen) while others ban religious symbols which are not harmonious with Christian values (e.g. Bavaria). In Germany, the legislation has had greatest impact on female Muslim teachers who wear the headscarf. It is worth noting that while Germany is home to the largest ex-patriot Turkish community in the world, as a secular state Turkey prohibits the wearing of male and female religious headcover in its schools and government buildings.[15] By 2006, Muslim teachers in half of all German States were forbidden to wear headscarves. An exception was made for Religious Education class where the wearing of the hijab was permitted. Furthermore, a distinction can be seen between states in the former east Germany who seem disinterested in banning the veil and those in the west of Germany where the veil is mainly banned. Critics argue that what really lies beneath the law banning the headscarf or veil is an unsubtle conflation of ideas about terrorism, extremism, political fundamentalism and Islam. Wearing the veil appears to symbolise political activism and fundamentalist Islam. Also in Germany there appears to be a greater level of tolerance towards symbiology associated with Christianity.

In the Netherlands, the Christian Democratic Appeal (CDA) party's pledge to ban the full-length veil or *burqa* became a major issue during the 2006 elections. Since then the Dutch government pledged to introduce legislation to enforce the ban. The ban concerns all forms of coverings of the full face including motorcycle helmets with visor down, ski masks and *burqas* when they are worn in public places including schools. Islam is the religion of six per cent of the Netherland's population and only a tiny minority (some estimates suggest as few as thirty people) of these wear the *burqa* or full Islamic head-to-toe dress. After the murder of the Dutch filmmaker Theo Van Gogh, an outspoken critic of Islam, the banning of the burqa became a major political issue. The Netherland's immigration minister Rita Verdonk, stated that it was not desirable 'that face-covering clothing – including the *burqa* – is worn in public places for reasons of public order, security and protection of citizens ... From a security standpoint, people should always be recognisable and from the standpoint of integration, we think people should be able to communicate with one another'.[16] The banning of face-covering clothing, including the *burqa*, in public places, including schools, was interpreted by some as a vital reassertion of the principles of a secular Dutch society as well as a protection of the equal status of females.

In 2007, the Italian Government issued guidelines for immigrants which, although not legally binding, nonetheless outlined what it viewed as undesirable religious clothing.

> Types of clothing that cover the face are not acceptable because they prevent the identification of the person and are an obstacle to the interaction with others.[17]

While Italy has stopped short of a ban on the *hijab* or other conspicuous religious emblems in school, its concern that the *hijab* might pose a risk to national security as well as the lack of assimilation of the religious other is consistent with many European countries. In Belgium, in the city of Antwerp, municipal staff working as counter clerks were banned from wearing visible religious symbols, including Christian crosses and Muslim headscarves. Meanwhile, in the United Kingdom the Government, in the interests of effective learning, security and safety, has given school principals the right to prohibit Muslim girls from wearing a full covering of the face (*niqab*). In a high profile case in 2006, a Muslim bilingual support worker, Aishah Azmi, lost the case of religious discrimination that she took against a school which asked her to remove the full-veil in the classroom while working with children. Supporters of the ban emphasise that there are circumstances where it is inappropriate for a teacher or student to have their whole face covered, for instance where it impedes the teaching and learning of hearing impaired children, English as an Additional Language children, visual learners or where it might pose a health and safety risk in laboratory work. In Ireland, there have been successive calls for the Minister of Education to issue guidance on the wearing of the *hijab* in schools and in August 2008 the DES announced that it would not be issuing guidelines on this matter. Each school will decide its own policy.[18]

Any analysis of these debates in European countries must be sensitive to the specificity and complexity of each context. Legislation is not uniform and even within individual countries interpretation and implementation of it varies. In French state schools wearing the symbol of a religious community is interpreted as resistance to social integration, dilution of the secular principles of the state's educational system and a cause of potential offence to other faith and secular groups. In Holland and the UK, the rationale behind the ban tends to focus on security, health and safety as well as issues of integration. In France the ban focuses on teachers and children while in Germany it focuses on teachers. While Italy presents guidelines, Germany provides legislation that is variously interpreted and implemented in different states. In the UK the school principal uses discretion to enforce the ban whereas in France, in state schools the ban is blanket. In all countries the ban impacts on Muslim women more than any other group. This has led some to allege that what is operative here is a form of post-9/11 Islamaphobia[19] inspired by the association of Islam with political fundamentalism and terrorist attacks. Governmental attention has linked religious symbols to political activism with a clear focus on Islam.[20]

In all countries where religious symbols and clothing are banned, a major issue that arises is the status and role of religion within society and within the public school system. This prohibition of religious symbolism raises the question of the treatment of religious and cultural difference. Many view the elimination of all visible religious symbols and therefore evidence of religious difference as an important prerequisite for equality of opportunity in secular state schools. It is ironic that legislation designed to foster tolerance and equality has resulted in what many perceive as the discrimination, marginalisation and suppression of religious believers. For the religious believer, the wearing of a religious symbol is a natural, private and public expression of religious faith and belief. Article 30 of the United Nations Convention on the Rights of the Child reads:

In those States in which ethnic, religious or linguistic minorities or persons of indigenous origin exist, a child belonging to such a minority or who is indigenous shall not be denied the right, in community with other members of his or her group, to enjoy his or her own culture, to profess and practice his or her own religion, or to use his or her own language.[21]

Forbidding the expression of religious identity that is interconnected with cultural and personal identity has serious implications, not just for one religious community but for all religious communities and indeed for the whole of society. Furthermore the assumption that the wearing of religious symbols is offensive to or invasive of others needs to be challenged. Mona Sahlin, Swedish minister for democracy and integration issues emphasises that:

By stressing the factors that separate people rather than those in common, ethnic conflicts can be stirred up. Better instead that respect for difference apply not only to groups but to individuals, and that integration policies therefore be based on the rights of individuals. In short, respect for human rights should be equal, regardless of ethnic or cultural group or religion.[22]

One could argue that legislation directed at the elimination of religious symbols associated with the 'religious other' in schools fractures the relationship between home and school and signals a lack of equality for religious believers who become marginal and invisible in status.

Catholic Schools as Centres of Inclusivity
The word catholic originates from the Greek *kath'holou* which means 'according to the whole' or 'universal'. To be Catholic is to be called to live a life focused on inclusivity. It recognises the unity and dignity of all human life since 'humankind form but one community and all stem from one stock which God created'.[23] Chapter seven has outlined successive recent Church documents which testify to the fact that inter-religious dialogue is not an option but a crucial imperative for Catholics.[24] Addressing the Foundation for Inter-religious and Intercultural Research and Dialogue in 2007, Pope Benedict XVI insisted 'research and inter-religious and intercultural dialogue are not an option but a vital necessity for our time.'[25] In a sense, the controversy surrounding his Regensburg address in September 2006 has served to augment and reinforce the Pontiff's emphasis on the need for inter-religious dialogue.[26]

When it comes to schooling the Church sees that there is no such thing as a value or a religiously neutral school since 'To claim neutrality for schools signifies in practice, more times than not, banning all reference to religion from the cultural and educational field ... '[27] The goal of Catholic education 'focuses on the human person in his or her integral, transcendent, historical identity'.[28] This involves the promotion of the physical, moral, intellectual, emotional, spiritual and religious welfare of the human person. An individual or group's religious identity, as expressed through the wearing of religious symbols and clothing, is respected by the Church. However the Church acknowledges that in a Catholic school not all members of the school community are Catholic and it offers general principles on how Catholic schools might include and celebrate the religious other while being true to its own mission and teaching.[29] The Vatican II Declaration on Christian Education, *Gravissimum Educationis* (GE), makes it clear that 'the Church considers very dear to her heart those Catholic schools, found especially in the areas of the new churches, which are attended also by students who are not Catholics.'[30] The Church affirms that the Catholic school is not restricted exclusively to Catholics and is open to all those who appreciate and share its qualified educational project.[31]

Catholic teaching on religious freedom is consistent with other foundational texts on religious freedom including Article Two of the Declaration of Human Rights (1948) and Principle One of the Declaration of the Rights of the Child (1959).[32] The Church is at pains to stress that catechesis or leading people to maturity of faith is incompatible with coercion and the Church teaches respect for the religious freedom of all. This includes non-Catholics in a Catholic school environment. Neither does the Catholic Church wish to render invisible the 'religious other' in the Catholic school or to coerce the religious or non-religious other into conformism to Catholic belief and practice. It teaches that the:

> Catholic school offers itself to all, non-Christians included, with all its distinctive aims and means, acknowledging, preserving and promoting the spiritual and moral qualities, the social and cultural values, which characterise different civilisations.[33]

This does not mean that the Catholic school relinquishes its mission for evangelisation or proclamation of the gospel of Jesus Christ in deference to the students of other world faiths that it serves. *Redemptoris Missio* (1990) asserts that while elements of truth can be found in world religions, this does not cancel the call to faith and baptism in the Catholic Church.

> (...) a Catholic school cannot relinquish its own freedom to proclaim the Gospel and to offer a formation based on the values to be found in a Christian education; this is its right and its duty. To proclaim or to offer is not to impose, however; the latter suggests a moral violence that is strictly forbidden, both by the Gospel and by Church law.[34]

So the manner in which a Catholic school includes and educates members of different faiths is crucial and it prohibits coercion. The Church places emphasis on the Catholic school as a lively centre of proclamation, apprenticeship and dialogue between people of different social and religious backgrounds.[35] The Catholic school has a variety of approaches and methodologies to enable it to welcome and educate the 'religious other' in its schools. A respect for the religious other should permeate the entire curriculum of a Catholic school and includes ICE as well as recognition of the inter-cultural diversity of Catholicism and Christianity. This involves a respect for the religious symbolism and clothing of other religious traditions. It also includes the teaching of Other World Religions (OWR).

Religious Education in a Catholic school involves providing children with accurate knowledge and respectful understanding of the beliefs and practices primarily of the Catholic faith but also, and inevitably to a lesser extent, of a variety of world faiths. This is an important part of the Religious Education of Catholic children as well as children of other faiths. In Scotland, the guidelines for Catholic Schools focus on the three areas of:

- Christianity
- OWR
- Personal Search

While the main focus in the Scottish Catholic school system is on the Catholic faith, time 'should also be found within the programme to lead pupils to an understanding of and respect for the beliefs and traditions of other Christian traditions and other major religions.'[36] For Catholic primary Schools in England and Wales using the 'Here I am' scheme of work, this translates generally into five per cent of the total time allocated for Religious Education.'[37]

> The study of Other World Religions, where appropriate, can help pupils to appreciate that religious questions are universal, addressed not only by Catholics and other Christians, but also by people of all faiths. Catholic Religious Education, which aims to communicate the fullness of the revelation in Jesus Christ, is enriched by appreciating the search for truth, sincerely made throughout the centuries in other religions. At the same time, the study of other World Religions can help to promote attitudes of respect for others, based on knowledge of their heritage of faith and prayer.[38]

Minority Faith Children in Majority Faith Schools: The Catholic Primary School Context

While the preceding section outlined the Catholic Church's positive teaching on acknowledging and celebrating religious difference as part of inter-religious dialogue and the call to religious inclusivity, this is not matched by a large body of research on the issue of inclusion in Catholic schools. Indeed J. Kent Donleavy states that while reviewing the literature on non-Catholic students in Catholic schools:

> (…) there was a paucity of information dealing with the topic. In fact, after a search which included contacting individuals in the United Kingdom, Australia, the United States of America, and Canada, all that was revealed was a small 25-page, opinion-based pamphlet … a short comment in a recent book … a series of qualitative studies primarily from one researcher … and a tangentially relevant number of doctoral and master's degree theses … In all other respects, the academic literature was silent. Ostensibly, the topic seemed by this lack of attention to be of little significance to the Catholic community.[39]

The situation, while needing improvement, is not as drastic as Donleavy presents in his synopsis of research literature. For instance in the UK there have been a number of recent reports into teaching world faiths in Catholic schools[40] while in Ireland some small-scale research has been carried out into diversity and inclusivity in Catholic schools as well as religious minorities in majority religious schools.[41] One study argues that Ireland's denominational and confessional primary school system 'does not allow for equal recognition or respect for difference'.[42] The researcher, Anne Lodge, conducted interviews with people of minority belief including members of the Bahá'í and Buddhist communities, people of personal belief,[43] and a member of a minority Christian faith, about how they and their children experienced the denominational, largely confessional, Irish system of primary education. While Lodge's research sample was small, key issues emerging from the research were that:

- children sometimes feel alienated because of their different religious or personal beliefs
- bullying and teasing can be based on the perception of the child as religiously different and
- both participation in and withdrawal from Religious Education can be problematic.

Lodge's findings highlight the need for Catholic schools to embody Church teaching that Catholic schools should promote 'civil progress and human development without discrimination of any kind'.[44] Lodge contends that 'differences in belief are denied in the denominational primary system and those whose beliefs are different are rendered invisible and subordinate'.[45] These are serious charges and the Catholic school system must ensure that its schools do not marginalise or ignore those who are religiously different.

So how can Catholic schools act as centres for evangelisation (the call to ongoing conversion), catechesis (nurturing the faith of believers) as well as Religious Instruction (providing information about the Catholic faith and Other World Faiths)? Certain principles are important to observe:

1. It is vital that Catholic schools are securely rooted in the Catholic faith so that they are able to engage in respectful, generous and open dialogue with members of other faiths. A Catholic education is devoted to the full, complete development of the human being and has as its guide the life, death and resurrection of Jesus Christ and the teaching of the Catholic Church. The Catholic school must be anchored in its Catholic mission to care for and develop the whole human person while simultaneously proclaiming and nurturing the Christian faith.[46] Research shows that teaching children well about one religion is beneficial to other religions and children who have a personal prayer life tend to have a more positive attitude to their own religion and to the religion of others.[47] A Catholic school which is rooted in gospel values and Church teaching should be Catholic; that is inclusive, welcoming and open to others. This includes respectful dialogue with members of other religions. It is important that the Catholic school does not neglect or annul the rich spiritual and theological legacy of its own Catholic tradition. When the school community is firmly grounded in the teaching of the Catholic faith it will not marginalise or ignore people of different faith. The religious other is not invisible in a Catholic school precisely *because* it is a Catholic, inclusive school. A passive or silent tolerance of children from other faiths which never engages in consultative and supportive discussion with the child, his/her parents or guardians can not be counted as inclusive.

2. No matter how well-intentioned teachers may be and no matter how much they wish to include children of different faiths in their Religious Education class, it is vital to take the lead from the child's parents or guardians. In Ireland, the Constitution guarantees the right of any child 'not to be given inappropriate religious instruction'.[48] Since the early days

of the national school system in Ireland the right of withdrawal from Religious Education has been protected. The present Rules for National Schools state 'No pupil shall receive, or be present at, Religious Instruction of which his parents or guardian disapprove.'[49] A child's legal and constitutional right to be withdrawn from Religious Education should not simply be tolerated by a teacher who largely ignores the child for the duration of the Religious Education lesson. The child's right to withdraw should be facilitated positively in a manner that signals that this right is a legitimate important right.

3. In the same way that it is crucial for Catholic schools to acknowledge and respect other faith traditions and non-religious worldviews, it is important that everyone (staff, parents/guardians, children of Catholic, different faith or non-religious background) respect and agree to uphold the Catholic ethos of the school. Terence McLaughlin suggested that a Catholic school has a distinctive institutional framework (statements of aim and mission, recruitment, appointment, promotion of staff, admission of students, marketing of the school, prioritisation of resources), a distinctive ethos and life (culture of the school, liturgy and worship) as well as a distinctive curriculum (in areas such as catechesis and Religious Education, sex education). All members of the school community have a role in upholding the school's distinctive Catholic ethos.[50]

4. The Catholic classroom should be one where everyone is respected, valued and cherished. Part of the education of children in a Catholic school involves learning about faith, principally the Catholic faith, but also, albeit to a lesser degree, the faith of other believers. This can be done in a variety of ways including Religious Education. 'It should be remembered that to introduce children to religion via Christian faith is not to demean or deny the insights of other faiths. Indeed such a way of teaching will affirm and celebrate such insights, although this is not the same as affirming everything that another faith holds dear.'[51] Learning about diverse faiths in a classroom context is a complex activity. Often, when it comes to different faiths, the experience and knowledge of the children exceeds that of the teacher. Furthermore the teacher may have a symbolic or theoretical understanding of a world faith tradition whereas children practicing that faith will have a more intimate, nuanced and practical knowledge of it. It is possible, in such circumstances, for children to feel alienated even when the focus of the lesson is on their faith. Julia Ipgrave's research suggests that teachers must enable children to learn from each other and to 'make room for the pupils' own experiences and perspectives on those traditions, even when they

challenge the teacher's own'.[52] Ipgrave suggests establishing rules of engagement for discussing religious topics in an inclusive manner. She provides an example of the rules that emerged from discussion with a Year Five primary class.

- Respect each other's religion.
- Talk and think seriously about differences.
- Listen to what other people say.
- Be ready to learn new things even about your own religion.[53]

5. It is important to acknowledge that Religious Education is just one manifestation of the ethos and mission of a Catholic school. Rather than administering a once-off injection on inter-Religious Education during Religious Education class, it is more effective and important to teach all topics in a manner that celebrates and respects diversity. A once-off lesson on Islam or Hinduism can confuse children unless it is integrated with the whole ethos of the classroom and the Catholic school which openly, positively and explicitly addresses issues of religious, ethnic and cultural diversity.[54]

Conclusion

While recent debates and legislation in some European countries has resulted in a prohibition of religious clothes and symbols in selected schools, thus rendering invisible the religious other, other state schools provide effective ICE and inter-Religious Education which values the religious dimension of life. The debate on the prohibition of religious symbiology and the treatment of the religious other in European state school systems is of significance to all those involved in Religious Education. There is an intimate inter-dependence between different religious traditions so that when 'one religion is diminished all religions are diminished.'[55] Catholic educators should not be indifferent to the prohibition, invisibility or marginalisation of religious clothes and symbols in any school sector. The European debate on the role of religion in society and in state schools provides a broad contextual backdrop to current thinking on the status of the religious other in Catholic schools. When it comes to Catholic schools, the Catholic Church has a body of positive teaching on inclusivity which provides guidelines for Catholic schools to value, respect and acknowledge the religious other. Unfortunately research into the treatment of members of other faiths in Catholic schools is in its infancy and some of the existing research suggests that religious minorities can be marginalised in Catholic schools that are not as inclusive as they should be. With this in mind Catholic schools need to revisit seminal Church teaching on respecting the religious other, and to translate this body of teaching into praxis, so that they can become genuinely Catholic.

Notes

1   Here I use the term 'religious other' to refer to anyone explicitly professing religious belief or wearing religious clothing and symbols in a state or public school context which is founded on secular or non-confessional principles.

2   In the Catholic school context any member of a non-Catholic tradition or faith represents the 'religious other'. This includes other Christian denominations as well as members of other world faiths.

3   John Keast (ed.), *Religious Diversity and Intercultural Education: A Reference Book for Schools*, Strasbourg: Council of Europe, 2007.

4   TRES is a trans-national cooperation project in the form of a thematic network funded by the Socrates Programme commenced in 2005 and held a launching conference in Uppsala, Sweden, in 2006. Further examples of research groups and networks include: Oslo Coalition's project on education for freedom of religion or belief; the European Community Framework 6 project on Religious Education, Dialogue and Conflict; The European Network for Religious Education through Contextual Approaches and the International Seminar on Religious Education and Values (ISREV).

5   For a synopsis of the debate on faith based schools in England and Wales see Robert Jackson 'Should the State Fund Faith Based Schools: A Review of the Arguments' in British Journal of Religious Education (henceforth BJRE), Vol. 25, No.2, Spring 2003, pp. 89–102.

6   Cf. Marcus Braybrooke, 'The Interfaith Alternative to Terror and the war Against Terror' in *Inter-religious Insight A Journal of dialogue and engagement*, Vol. 5, No. 2, April 2007, p. 41.

7   A study of discrimination and racism post–9/11 concluded that 'religion may sometimes be a stronger motivator for discriminatory sentiment and behavior than race or ethnicity' see L. Sheridan, 'Discrimination and Racism, Post-September 11', University of Leicester, 2002, http://www.le.ac.uk/ua/pr/press/discriminationandracism.html (accessed 23.08.08).

8   Oliver Mc Tiernan, *Violence in God's Name*, New York: Orbis, 2003, p. xiii.

9   John Bowker, 'Introduction' in Brian Gates, (ed.), *Freedom and Authority in Religions & Religious Education*, London: Cassell, 1996, p. 3–4.

10   Terry Sanderson, president of the National Secular Society in Ireland has lamented that 'it still seems beyond the imagination of most educators in Ireland – even the ones who recognise there are problems with religious influence – that a secular system that requires pupils to leave their religion (if they have one) at home would be the answer' see Newsline, National Secular Society Newsletter, http://www.secularism.org.uk/irishpollshowsparentsnolongerwan.html (accessed 16.08.08).

11   Europe has been ravaged by conflicts in which religion has played a significant role – from the Balkan crisis that acted as an ignition point for World War One, to the holocaust of World War Two, to the re-eruption of the Balkan states into war in the 1990s. On a global scale recent atrocities such as the wars in Rwanda, Iraq and Darfur, reinforce the link between tribal group, religious faith and conflict.

12   Kevin Williams, 'Religious Worldviews and the Common School: The French Dilemma' in *Journal of Philosophy of Education*, Vol. 41, No. 4, 2007, p. 676. While up to one third of the schools in France are Catholic and are subsidised by the state (on condition that they do not impose

religion on students or discriminate on religious grounds) the majority of French schools are public or state schools.

13   *Loi n° 2004-228 du 15 mars 2004 encadrant, en application du principe de laïcité, le port de signes ou de tenues manifestant une appartenance religieuse dans les écoles, collèges et lycées publics.*

14   A Letter to Educators, President Sarkozy, 4 September 2007.

15   In November 2005 the European Court of Human Rights upheld Turkey's legislation as legitimate in the case of Leyla Sahin v. Turkey.

16   http://timesofindia.indiatimes.com/World/Rest_of_World/Holland_bans_burqa_Muslims_enraged_/articleshow/468955.cms (accessed 10.06.08).

17   Scientific Council, Ministry of the Interior, Charter of Values, Citizenship and Immigration, Italy: 2007.

18   *The Irish Times*, 19 May 2008; *The Irish Times*, 9 June 2008.

19   'In 1997, The Runnymede Trust (the UK-based independent think-tank on ethnicity and cultural diversity) coined the term 'Islamophobia'. Islamophobia constitutes a two-stranded form of racism - rooted in both the 'different' physical appearance of Muslims and also in an intolerance of their religious and cultural beliefs.' See L. Sheridan, *Discrimination and Racism*.

20   Recent research reveals a correspondence between anti-Islamic feeling and consent to banning the veil. In the Pew report (2005) people who held a negative view of Islam were more likely to favour the banning of the scarf than those who held more positive views. See Pew Global Attitudes Project, *'Islamic Extremism: Common Concerns for Muslim and Western Publics'*, 14 July 2005.

21   Article 30, United Nations Convention on the Rights of the Child, adopted and ratified by General Assembly resolution 44/25 of 20 November 1989. For a child-friendly illustrated and simplified version of this text with a foreword by Archbishop Desmond Tutu, see Caroline Castle, *For Every Child*, New York: Phylllis Fogelman Books, 2000.

22   Richard Barltrop, *Muslims in Europe, Post 9/11 Understanding and Responding to the Islamic World*, St Anthony's College: Oxonian Rewley Press, 2003, p. 6.

23   *Nostra Aetate Declaration on the Relation of the Church to Non-Christian Religions*, Vatican II, 1965, par. 1 (henceforth NA). Many other faith traditions also emphasise the unity of humanity. This is evident in the following Bahá'í prayer which comes from 'Abdu'l-Bahá, 'O Thou kind Lord! Thou hast created all humanity from the same stock. Thou hast decreed that all shall belong to the same household … O Thou kind Lord! Unite all. Let the religions agree and make the nations one, so that they may see each other as one family and the whole earth as one home. May they all live together in perfect harmony. ' Abdu'l-Bahá, *Compilations, Bahá'í Prayers*, Wilmette: BPT, 1991, p. 102.

24   NA; Dialogue and Mission, 1984 (henceforth DM).

25   Zenith, *The World Seen from Rome* (Vatican News Agency), 1 February 2007.

26   Cardinal Tauran, newly appointed President of the Pontifical Council for Inter-religious Dialogue told Vatican Radio: '"I think it [the Regensburg address in September 2006] had a decisive influence, because thanks to the reactions, the Pope was able to clarify his words," the cardinal said. "By reading the Pope's speeches to the ambassadors of Arab countries, and also to those who have come from Asia to present their credentials, you can see a common thread in the thought of the Pope, who thinks that inter-religious dialogue is important for peace, and that religions are at the service of peace."' *Zenith*, 27 June 2007.

27   *Catholic School on the Threshold of the Third Millennium*, Congregation for Catholic Education, 1997, par. 10 (henceforth CSTTM).

28   Ibid.

29   *Lay Catholics in Schools: Witnesses to Faith*, 1982, par. 3 (henceforth LCS); *The Religious Dimension of Education in a Catholic School*, 1988, par. 6 (henceforth RDECS), CSTTM, par. 16.

30   *Gaudium et spes*, The Pastoral Constitution on the Church in the Modern World, Vatican II, 1965, par. 9 (henceforth GS).

31   CSTTM par. 6.

32   Article 2 states, 'Everyone is entitled to all the rights and freedoms set forth in this Declaration, without distinction of any kind, such as race, colour, sex, language, religion, political or other opinion, national or social origin, property, birth or other status'. Principle one states, 'The child shall enjoy all the rights set forth in this declaration. Every child, without any exception whatsoever, shall be entitled to these rights, without distinction or discrimination on account of race, colour, sex, language, religious, political or other opinion, national or social origin, property, birth or other status, whether of himself or of his family'.

33   This mirrors NA Par 2 which states 'Sons and daughters to enter with prudence and charity into discussion and collaboration with members of other religions. Let Christians, while witnessing to their own faith and way of life, acknowledge, preserve and encourage the spiritual and moral truths found among non-Christians, also their social life and culture.'

34   RDECS, par. 6.

35   John Paul II, *Ecclesia in Africa*, 1995, no. 2; cf. CSTTM, par. 11.

36   *Religious Education* 5–14: Roman Catholic Schools, Hamilton: Scottish Office Education Department, Scottish Catholic Education Commission, 1994.

37   'As to the teaching of world religions in the primary school within the "Here I am" scheme of work other faiths are taught in two weeks of the year – Judaism is taught for a week in the autumn term, and Sikhism or Islam for a week in the summer term; the religions are approached in a systematic rather than thematic way. This works out at approximately 5% of a year's RE time is devoted to other faiths.' Anne Cassons, *The Teaching of Other Faiths in Catholic Schools in the North East*, Farmington: Farmington Fellowship, 2003; Catharine Speroni Teaching Other Faiths in the Catholic Primary School, Farmington: Farmington Fellowship, 2005.

38   Anne Cassons, *The Teaching of Other Faiths*.

39   J. Kent Donleavy, 'Ten Dimensions of Inclusion: Non-Catholic Students in Catholic Schools', in *Catholic Education*, Vol. 10, No. 3, March 2007, pp. 293–4.

40   Anne Cassons, *The Teaching of Other Faiths*; Catharine Speroni, *Teaching Other Faiths in the Catholic Primary School*. Also J. Astley , L.J. Francis, C. Wilcox , & L. Burton 'How different is Religious Education in Catholic schools?', in *International Journal of Education and Religion*, Vol. 1, No. 2, 2000. Deirdre Mc Govern, *Hospitality to the Other in Faith-based schools*, Ph.D. research, St. Andrew's College, University of Glasgow.

41   Micheál Kilcrann, 'Welcoming the "New Irish"', in Raymond Topley & Gareth Byrne (eds), *Nurturing Children's Religious Imaginations: The Challenge of Primary Religious Education Today*, Dublin: Veritas, 2004, p. 86ff; P. Kieran, & A. Hession, *Children, Catholicism and Religious Education*, Dublin: Veritas, 2005; Patricia Kieran, 'Promoting Truth? Inter-faith education in Irish Catholic

Primary Schools', in *Teaching Religion in the Primary School: Issues and Challenges*, Dublin: INTO, 2003, pp. 119–130. Masters Theses at St. Patrick's College, Drumcondra: Micheál Kilcrann, 'The Challenge to Primary Religious Education' posed by a Multicultural Society (2003), Helen Bhreathnach, 'Living with Difference & Discovering a Common Heritage: Bringing *Nostra Aetate* into the Primary School Religious Education Programme in the light of the Writings of James Dunn' (2004).

42   Jim Deegan, Dympna Devine & Anne Lodge (eds), *Primary Voices: Equality, Diveristy and Childhood in Irish Primary Schools*, Dublin: Institute of Public Administration, 2005, p. 32. Michael Cooke, 'Interfaith Perspectives: More questions than answers' in M. Hayes (ed.), *Contemporary Catholic Education*, Leominster: Gracewing, 2002; J. Egan, *Opting Out: Catholic Schools Today*, Leominster: Gracewing, 1998.

43   Anne Lodge in Jim Deegan, *Primary Voices*, p. 22, fn. 8.

44   See Chapter 6 on 'Religious Belief' especially section 6.4 on 'Harassment' in A. Lodge, & K. Lynch, *Diversity at School*, Dublin: Institute of Public Administration, 2004.

45   Anne Lodge in Jim Deegan, *Primary Voices*, p. 32.

46   GS par. 35–6.

47   Kay W.K.D. Linnet Smith, 'Classroom factors and attitudes to six world religions', in *British Journal of Education*, Vol. 24, 2, 2002, p. 121. See also Kay W. K. D. Linnet Smith, 'Religious terms and attitudes in the Classroom', in BJRE, Vol. 22, 3, 2000, pp. 181–191.

48   Lynch & Lodge, *Diversity at School*, p. 50.

49   Rules for National School, No. 69 (2) (a).

50   Terence McLaughlin, 'Distinctiveness and the Catholic School: Balanced Judgement and the Temptations of Commonality' in James C. Conroy (ed.), *Catholic Education inside out outside in*, Dublin: Veritas, 1999, p. 71f.

51   Penny Thompson, 'Whose confession? Which tradition?', in BJRE, Vol. 26, No. 1, 2004, pp. 61–72.

52   Julia Ipgrave, 'Religious Plurality Including pupils' faith background in primary Religious Education', in *Support for Learning: British Journal of Learning Support*, Vol. 19, No. 3, August 2004, p. 116.

53   Ibid. p. 117.

54   Kay Linnet Smith's research has shown that the more religions children studied, especially if this involved four or more, the less positive their attitude to the religions and the greater their sense of confusion. See also Kay Linnet Smith, 'Religious terms and attitudes in the Classroom', in BJRE, Vol. 22, 3, 2000, pp. 181–191.

55   Dermot Lane, *The Irish Times*, 22 January 2002.

CHAPTER 13

CATHOLIC RELIGIOUS EDUCATION IN IRELAND

Patrick M. Devitt

The Historical Background and the Legal Basis

During the nineteenth century, Ireland was under British rule. Shortly after Catholic Emancipation in 1829, a system of interdenominational 'National schools' was introduced, to provide primary education for all Irish pupils. This system proved unsatisfactory to most religious bodies; so, by the end of the nineteenth century, the 'National schools' had become denominational schools, and, in respect of the Catholic community, parish priests were responsible for their staffing and upkeep. 'Religious Instruction' was always an integral part of the curriculum in these schools. Nothing in this regard changed radically after Irish Independence and the establishment of an Irish Department of Education in the nineteen-twenties. As late as 1956, one reads that:

> ... of all the parts of a school curriculum religious instruction is by far the most important ... As, however, the prescribing of the subject matter of Religious Instruction, the examination of it, and the supervision of the teaching are outside the competence of the Department of Education, no syllabuses of it are here set forth.[1]

The Catholic Bishops of Ireland, as the recognised experts, regularly published local catechisms outlining what was to be learnt; and appointed Diocesan Examiners to inspect the quality of teaching being done, during the obligatory thirty-minutes a day class period.

Second-level schools in Ireland today reflect this long evolution, and now consist of four major types:

- *Catholic Voluntary* (sponsored by various Religious Orders, or individual Dioceses and usually offering Religious Education as part of the normal curriculum)

- *Voluntary* (sponsored by other faith communities and often accepting Catholic pupils)
- *Community/Comprehensive* (often amalgamated from existing smaller schools; governed by a Board of Management and obliged by ministerial order to appoint qualified Religion teachers)
- *Vocational Schools/Community Colleges* (under the control of the local Vocational Educational Committee and also obliged by ministerial order to engage qualified Religion teachers).

When this structure of second-level schooling was recently given a firm legal basis through the *Education Act* (1998), the importance of religion in the overall school ethos was clearly recognised: all schools should 'promote the moral, spiritual, social and personal development of students ... in consultation with their parents, having regard for the characteristic spirit of the school'.[2] From the perspective of Religious Education, the major effect of this Act was the abolition of the ban on state examinations in religion, dating from the *Intermediate Education (Ireland)* Act of 1878. Accordingly, Religious Education can now be taken as a State Examination subject in both Junior and Leaving Certificate cycles.

Influences from Abroad
The Catholic Church in Ireland is part of the Universal Church, and therefore, bound by its laws and values. The most significant recent event in the long life of this Church was the *Second Vatican* Council (1962–65). A large gathering of bishops from all over the world took place in Rome under the inspiring leadership of Pope John XXIII. Its purpose was to renew the Church and enable her to be more articulate in the world of today.

Inspired by this vision of renewal, Pope Paul VI issued a *General Catechetical Directory* in 1971. Its purpose was to lay down the principles of faith formation that should underpin every attempt at teaching and handing on the faith throughout the world. Each country was expected to apply these general guidelines to its own particular situation.

The Irish response has been, *firstly*, to establish a Commission of Bishops to overview the work of catechesis and Religious Education. *Secondly*, Veritas was established as publishing house for the Irish Church: its major purpose is to develop catechetical programmes, syllabuses, and textbooks for schools (both primary and second-level). *Thirdly*, Diocesan Advisors for Primary Schools, as well as Diocesan Advisors for Second-Level Schools, have been appointed in each diocese. The task of these advisors is to support the teachers, and foster links between school, parish and home. *Fourthly*, the bishops appointed a Director of the Catechetics Office, Columba Centre, Maynooth, Co Kildare.[3] This Office promotes the use of the web for e-learning, and publishes relevant documentation online. A fifth major development has been the appointment of Dr Gareth Byrne to draft the first Irish *National Directory for Catechesis*.

The Primary School Sector (ages 4–13)

The teaching of religion has been described in many ways: the official legal term (both in Ireland and in the Vatican) was 'religious instruction', but most Catholics talked about 'religious knowledge' or 'Christian Doctrine'. More recently, the terms 'catechesis' and 'Religious Education' have gained in popularity. Catechesis is handing on or sharing Christian faith, which usually includes clarifying its meaning. Religious Education (RE) is largely clarifying the meaning of religion, and may or may not involve handing on a faith tradition.

A typical pupil in Ireland spends eight years in Primary School (ages 5–13). Each year has one dedicated teacher, whose teaching remit includes the daily thirty-minute religion lesson. In Catholic schools the basic resource for all this teaching of religion is the *Alive-O* programme,[4] published by Veritas on behalf of the Irish Bishops. *Alive-O* is based on sound educational, theological and catechetical principles, and is highly regarded internationally. It is rooted in what is often called 'the double fidelity': fidelity to God, and fidelity to humanity. Though a vast array of creative pedagogical approaches, it brings the Word of God to the mind, heart and imagination of young children, so that they can taste it, digest it, and assimilate it in ways that foster their humanity and the divine life of grace throbbing within them. Faithful to the vision of the *General Directory for Catechesis* (no. 85), it promotes among pupils a deep knowledge of the Catholic faith, provides liturgical and moral formation, teaches pupils how to pray, educates them for community living and inspires their missionary spirit. In the spirit of ongoing renewal, so typical of *Alive-O*, a new syllabus is now being written for Catholic Primary Religious Education.

The Catholic ethos of a primary school extends far beyond the daily religion class. Pupils' faith is also nourished through regular prayer services and school liturgies. Furthermore, because of the nature of the 'integrated curriculum', religious themes can surface during the teaching of any subject. However, perhaps the most significant fostering of pupils' religious sensitivity takes place during sacramental preparation, which, ideally, is a joint effort by parents, teachers and priests. Parents send their children to Catholic schools because they want them to be prepared by the teachers in school, and by the local priest in the parish, for First Penance, First Eucharist and Confirmation. In a changing Ireland, with numbers of active Catholics declining, this long-standing arrangement may begin to change.

The Second-Level Sector (ages 13–18)

Before Vatican II, most Catholic second-level schools in Ireland were sponsored by a religious order, or by a Bishop. Consequently, Religious Education was usually taught by members of that order or by diocesan priests. Most of them had no specific preparation for Religious Education: they relied entirely on their years of spiritual formation. The religion classes they taught followed no state syllabus (there was none), and led to no state certification. However, a Religious Knowledge examination did take place each year, which was devised by the Bishop and corrected by his seminarians.

A major change occurred in the late sixties with the development of the Mater Dei Institute of Education. Its purpose was to offer potential religion teachers the best of modern theology, the best of educational theory and practice, and a thorough grounding in one Arts subject (each student must choose either English, History or Music). After a four-year concurrent professional course, the graduates of the Bachelor of Religious Education degree are fully qualified for the teaching of Religious Education and one other subject. In contemporary Ireland, students can also be prepared for a career in teaching Religious Education at University College Dublin; All Hallows; NUI Maynooth; Saint Angela's; Saint Patrick's College, Drumcondra; University College Cork; Mary Immaculate College, etc.

Before Religious Education became a subject for State examination, the Bishops had already published their own *Syllabus for the Religious Education of Catholic pupils in Post-Primary Schools* (1982). This, however, gave little practical assistance to teachers, who struggled to build up their own resources for a subject taught to all but valued by few. Teachers now have the support of two excellent new state syllabuses,[5] which were developed by the National Council for Curriculum and Assessment (NCCA) for assessment in Junior and Leaving Certificate examinations. All the major religious traditions in Ireland were consulted in the construction of these syllabuses, so that every religious community would support their introduction into Irish schools. All the great world religions can be studied, including one's own. The non-religious life-stance is also studied. Here is the shape of the Leaving Certificate Religious Education syllabus:

Section A (obligatory) is called *The search for meaning and values.*
Pupils choose one of the following:

- Christianity: origins and contemporary expressions
- World religions
- Moral decision-making.

Pupils also select one of the following:

- Religion and gender
- Issues of Justice and peace
- Worship, prayer and ritual
- The Bible: literature and sacred text
- Religion: the Irish experience
- Religion and science.

As well as answering examination questions on the above, pupils also submit one piece of personal coursework, for which twenty per cent of the total mark is awarded.

Most Irish second-level schools now prepare pupils for the Junior Certificate examinations in Religious Education, but, so far, only very few schools have attempted Religious Education at Leaving Certificate level. There is a wide range of excellent textbooks for pupils at both levels, as well as a series of teacher commentaries on each of the ten sections of the Leaving Certificate course.[6] Some schools prefer not to prepare pupils for state examinations in Religious Education, concentrating instead on other (formational) aspects of Religious Education. They are assisted here by the NCCA's new non-examination Religious Education Curriculum Framework for Senior Cycle.

Adult Faith Development
For a century and a half, the Catholic Church in Ireland has made generous investment of money and personnel into general education, and, in particular, the teaching of religion in school. However, very little support has been available for adults to continue their Religious Education after school. The Irish Bishops commissioned Ann Hanley to research the state of Adult Religious Education (ARE), and this led to an unpublished report, called *Faith for Life: Adult Religious Education in Ireland*.[7] Hanley describes what she found as follows:

> If we were to put together a composite picture of a typically successful adult Religious Education programme in Ireland today, it would look something like this: it would be a course dealing with spirituality, and it would meet the needs of those taking it by developing their sense of participation in a community of faith. It would last for a relatively short period of time (i.e. less than three months), producing a deepened experience of faith on completion. It would almost certainly use group discussion in some form as a teaching technique and would be well supported by clergy at both a parish and a diocesan level.[8]

In their general reflections on this report, the Bishops stated the following:

- The survey thus confirmed what everybody knows, that adult catechesis is available to very few Irish adults
- The survey also shows that there is a great lack of appropriate processesand methods specific to adult modes of learning
- There is a great lack of appropriately qualified religious educators for adults
- There have been many reports strongly recommending that greater attention be given to ARE, in accordance with the official teaching of the Church, but these still await implementation.

Everyone now agrees that fostering ARE is one of the greatest challenges facing the Irish Catholic Church. A good start at national level has been made by the appointment of a resource person in the Episcopal Commission for Pastoral Renewal and Adult Faith Development.[9] Her major work at present is to coordinate and support the variety of initiatives that have already been taken.

Education of Religious Education Teachers
No renewal of Religious Education can proceed without renewed teachers. One major influence on this renewal process, during the seventies and eighties, was the *Catechetical Association of Ireland*. Meeting about four times a year, inviting expert speakers from home and abroad, it dealt with Primary, Secondary and Adult Faith Formation issues. It was well served by its journal, *The Irish Catechist* (1977–85).[10] When both Association and journal ceased to exist, the second-level teachers continued the process through their Religion Teachers Association.[11]

A major recent development in the field of Catholic Religious Education is the expansion of post-graduate courses in the fields of religion, education, culture and school chaplaincy. It is now possible for more Irish teachers to do masters and doctoral work in these disciplines in Ireland.

Looking Ahead in Hope
The title of the Irish *National Directory for Catechesis* is 'Be Good News'. It captures the excitement of the good news as proclaimed by Jesus, and as now lived by his followers. Its purpose is to speak about the changing Irish culture of today, and to help people understand their Catholic faith as a treasure to be shared in freedom and love. Two major cultural changes in Ireland are already influencing both religion as lived and the teaching of religion: firstly, the spectacular economic growth associated with the 'Celtic Tiger'; and, secondly, the large numbers of immigrants who bring new cultures and new religions to Ireland. While wealth is welcome, it brings with it the temptation to forget God and

create false idols. While newcomers bring many blessings, they can sometimes be resented too. In a post-Celtic Tiger era it remains to be seen how cultural shifts will interact with the phenomenon of religion.

Everybody engaged in Religious Education in Ireland today must respond to this rapidly changing context. Catholic Religious Education also faces one other major challenge: the manner in which some Bishops responded to the sexual abuse of children by some priests and religious. Hopefully, creative Religious Education will help people to see beyond such abuse and understand the common sinfulness of every human being.

The *National Directory for Catechesis* is a powerful aid to good Catechesis and Religious Education. Not only does it contextualise Christian faith, and explain the ideals behind the enterprise of faith education, but, in a very detailed final chapter it spells out some of the resource implications for implementing this ongoing catechetical journey. Supported by a wide variety of practical faith development initiatives (at home, in school and in the parish community) all Irish Catholics will be helped to advance on their faith journey.

Notes

1   Ireland, Department of Education, *Programme of Primary Instruction,* Dublin: Stationery Office, 1956, p. 2.

2   Ireland, *Education Act 1998,* Dublin: The Stationery Office, 1998, 9(d).

3   See www.catechetics.ie (accessed 10.08.08).

4   *Alive-O* is the direct descendant of an earlier programme entitled *Children of God* (1973). This was re-presented in 1983, and again, as Alive-O, during the years 1996–2004. Account was taken, not just of ongoing cultural and religious changes in Ireland, but also of two significant Roman documents: *The Catechism of the Catholic Church* (1994) and *The General Directory for Catechesis* (1997).

5   See the NCCA website, www.ncca.ie/publications. An excellent resource for teachers of Religious Education is the Department of Education and Science publication, *Religious Education, Leaving Certificate Guidelines for Teachers* (2005), which has a bibliography and websites section pp. 145–48.

6   See Eoin G. Cassidy and Patrick M. Devitt, *Into the Classroom Series,* Dublin: Veritas, 2000–2005.

7   Maynooth: 1999.

8   Anne Hanley, *Faith for Life: Adult Religious Education in Ireland*, p. 18.

9   See www.renewal.ie; and also the website of the Irish Catholic Bishops Conference, www.catholiccommunications.ie (accessed 10.08.08).

10   The entire run of this journal is available in the library of The Mater Dei Institute of Education, and might be a helpful resource for any student of Religious Education in Ireland after Vatican II.

11   The Religion Teachers' Association of Ireland website is www.rtai.ie (accessed 16.08.08).

CHAPTER 14

CATHOLIC RELIGIOUS EDUCATION IN NORTHERN IRELAND

Sharon Haughey

Political progress in the North of Ireland in recent years laid the basis for The Good Friday Agreement in April 1998, The St Andrew's Agreement in October 2006 and for the establishment once again, this time on a seemingly more sure footed way, of the power-sharing Executive. Many now hope that a more harmonious society, built on reconciliation and respect for diversity will emerge. Northern Irish society is changing rapidly: in addition to the Executive there is also increased ethnic and religious diversity through the influx of people from Eastern Europe, Asia and South America and the development of a more prosperous economy. These changes need to be addressed at local level and will undoubtedly have a major bearing on education. Catholic education has a particular role to play in this new society as Archbishop Sean Brady explains;

> They [Catholic Schools] welcome people from all national backgrounds and people from various faith traditions and none. Catholic schools are not an obstacle on the road to reconciliation. They make a valuable contribution to it while maintaining the right of schools to have their own distinctive character. That right is consistent with the principle of a diverse society. In fact, it is essential to it.[1]

There is a very welcome and growing recognition of the contribution of Catholic education as a partner in the broader political and social context of Northern Irish society. The 547 Catholic schools, teaching approximately 45 per cent of all pupils, take seriously the need to promote a genuine ecumenism. Pope John Paul II on the fortieth anniversary of the 'Decree on Ecumenism' argues that this should be the concern of every Catholic, from every diocese and parish, and from every one of the Church's communities.[2] As Catholic educators we are called to a deeper Christian unity and our Catholic schools place particular emphasis on the values of justice, peace, tolerance, respect for diversity and reconciliation. These values, Archbishop Brady argues, exist at the heart of Catholic education.[3] Catholic schools share a vision where pupils and staff are valued, where young people learn to respect themselves and others and are encouraged to take their place in Northern Irish society to further reconciliation and build a brighter future for everyone.

The Education System in Northern Ireland
Historically, religious instruction was the responsibility of the different churches and was taught through local church schools. The Londonderry Education Act 1923 resulted in the different Protestant denominations relinquishing their schools. Catholics however maintained their schools; this led to the emergence of a Catholic school system for Catholic children and a separate system of state controlled schools for all predominantly Protestant children. The 1944 Education Act and the subsequent 1947 Education Act (for Northern Ireland) strengthened the position of religion in the school curriculum raising its profile as a subject and preferring to use the term Religious Education. Northern Ireland has operated an academically selective system of education since the 1947 Education Act (Northern Ireland). It differed from the selective system in Britain at that time, in that enrolment here tended to divide along religious grounds, Catholic and Protestant.

The Department of Education Northern Ireland (DENI) is responsible for the central administration of education and related services in NI, with the exception of Further and Higher education which are under Department of Employment and Learning (DEL).
The Department of Education in Northern Ireland provides an outline of the main types of school:

- Maintained (primary, special and secondary) are Catholic schools under the management of the Council for Catholic Maintained Schools (CCMS)
- Controlled (primary, special, secondary and grammar) schools are state schools and cater largely for the Protestant population. They are under the management of five Education and Library Boards
- Voluntary (grammar), Integrated (primary and secondary) and Institutions of Further and Higher Education – each school is under the management of a Board of Governors.[4]

There is also a continuing increase in demand for Irish-medium education comprising grant aided nursery, primary and post-primary Irish language schools alongside, Catholic schools teaching through the medium of Irish.

Education in Northern Ireland is divided into year groups at primary and post-primary level and also stages in learning, ranging from Foundation Stage through

Key Stages 1–4. Compulsory schooling begins when the children are four or five years old, although a high percentage of younger children receive pre-school education. Children starting primary education enter the Foundation Stage in primary one and two with a focus on interactive learning. From here they move through Key Stage one and two in the primary sector. Up until now, pupils at the end of Key Stage two transferred to post-primary school at ten or eleven through academic selection, 'the Eleven Plus'. The Transfer Test which is scheduled to be phased out by 2013, awards pupils with high grades a place in Grammar school. At the time of writing discussions are still ongoing as to what will replace this academic selection and on the role and place of Grammar schools. The Education Minister set out proposals for change to the Assembly on 4 December 2007. It is hoped that the Executive of the Northern Ireland Assembly will agree new arrangements for transfer and admission to post-primary schools. The Catholic Bishops in the North state that 'the decision to abandon academic selection will represent the most significant and far reaching change in the educational system for more than fifty years.'[5]

At post-primary level pupils continue through key stages three and four taking GCSE exams at age sixteen. For pupils remaining in education after sixteen the new Advanced General Certificate in Education (ACSE) follows a modular system wherein students complete examinations in year 13 (AS level) and year 14 (A2 level). [See Table 1, p. 178.]

A Core Syllabus for Religious Education
The 1988 Education Reform Act and the subsequent Education Reform (Northern Ireland) Order 1989 brought a new emphasis on the need to ensure that all pupils receive a broad and balanced curriculum. As a direct result the Core Syllabus in Religious Education in Northern Ireland was first implemented in 1993 and reviewed in 2007. The drafting group composed of primary, post primary teachers, lecturers from St Mary's and Stranmillis University Colleges, Diocesan Advisors, members from the four main Christian denominations in Ireland (Catholic, Methodist, Presbyterian and Church of Ireland) and identified personnel from the Education and Library Boards met to draw up a core syllabus for religion in all schools. Their aim was to establish a common entitlement for pupils and to compile a comprehensive Religious Education programme to be used by all schools. For most of the Catholic schools the current Veritas programmes, *Alive-O* in primary and *Fully Alive* – a programme especially devised for the North – in years eight to ten in post-primary, incorporate the aims and content of the Core Syllabus for Religious Education in Northern Ireland and are widely used by them. Many primary schools in the controlled and integrated sector also use *Alive-O* as a basis for their Religious Education, though they usually omit lessons specifically related to Catholic belief and sacraments.

Table 1 Current Education Provision in Northern Ireland

School	Age	Key Stage/Year	Curriculum areas for learning
Pre school	3–4	Nursery schools/ classes and/or reception classes for children under four	
Primary Compulsory school age 4–5	4–6 6–8 8–11	Foundation Stage – Primary 1 and 2 Key Stage One – Primary 3 and 4 Key Stage Two – Primary 5–7	– Religious Education – Language and literacy – Maths and Numeracy – The Arts – The World Around Us – Personal Development and Mutual Understanding – Physical Education
Post-Primary	11–14	Key Stage Three – Years 8–10	Religious Education Language and Literacy Maths and Numeracy Modern Languages The Arts Environment and Society Science and Technology Learning for Life and Work Physical Education
	14–16	Key Stage Four – Years 11 and 12	GCSE syllabus for pupils at the end of compulsory schooling
	16–18	AS and A2 level syllabus – Years 13 and 14	

Religious Education is part of the statutory curriculum in Northern Ireland and should be taught in all schools. The new curriculum for primary and post-primary education introduced in 2007 includes a range of areas for learning as noted in Table 1. The compulsory common syllabus for Religious Education (which was phased in from September 2007) for children in Foundation Stage through to Key Stage four outlines the study of Christianity under three sections: The Revelation of God, The Christian Church and Morality with an additional section on World Religions at Key Stage 3. Key Stage four covers the GCSE (General Certificate Secondary Education) examinations for sixteen year olds. The syllabus from the NI Examining Board adheres to the broad and balanced range of subject areas outlined in the Core Syllabus for Religious Education. In the Maintained sector Religious Education comes under the remit of the Catholic Church, and Diocesan Advisors (DAs) are appointed to provide support and advice in Catholic schools at primary and post-primary levels. All schools should have Religious Education co-ordinators to manage each school's Religious Education resources, organize in-service training, and provide information on current thinking and developments. Developments in the area of catechesis have meant that the religious programmes available in schools are continually restructured to meet the changing demands of education.

Teaching in Catholic Schools
Northern Irish society, in common with similar developments in the South, has undergone many changes in the last ten to twenty years not least with the influx of people from different countries, cultures and faith backgrounds. We now live and work in an inter-cultural society in which engagement with a variety of cultures is a vital part of our daily experiences. In Catholic schools it is important to not only educate young people about other cultures but to positively welcome them and offer opportunities to Catholic pupils to engage with people of different faiths and cultures in a positive and meaningful way. While some may be tempted to label Catholic schools as being isolationist and sectarian, it has to be insisted that they contribute richly to the common good by placing strong emphasis on building a community of tolerance and respect where all are valued.

> Indeed, the presence of children from other denominations is seen as an enrichment of the education experience offered by the [Catholic] school and as a practical expression to the commitment to inclusivity.[6]

Catholic schools are open to and embrace all denominations developing strong links with parents as partners in education; engaging in active learning; demonstrating a commitment to pastoral care and positive discipline policies; encouraging and facilitating links with other schools. Catholic schools have been active in promoting cross community initiatives on local and international levels as part of the statutory curriculum at primary and post-primary level. As Archbishop Brady stated:

> No one approach to education has a monopoly on forming children in the virtues of tolerance, understanding and reconciliation. All sectors have their part to play. As the Catholic sector we are fully committed to playing our part with others in healing the divisions of our society.[7]

Primary and Post-Primary Level

Religious Education at primary and post-primary level embraces knowledge of Catholic faith alongside active personal faith development. Christopher O'Donnell, writing for *Le Chéile A Catholic Ethos Journal*, argues that religion 'both offers and calls for a profound, true and existential knowledge that will transform us'[8] and in response to this Catholic schools need to offer a Religious Education that hopefully empowers and enables young people to both live out and learn about their faith. Since 2003 work has begun on a new programme which aims to follow on from the work of the *Alive-O* series in primary school and to develop a rich source of materials to complement teaching and learning at Key Stage three level in post-primary. The *Fully Alive* Programme has been introduced in years eight to ten. Having completed the GCSE course – roughly equivalent to the South's Junior Certificate – students who remain in education after sixteen may follow the A level syllabus. Religious Education for A level is strongly academic in content and many students will select this to support their university courses. How religion is taught in schools is important as there should be a balance between both academic content and personal faith formation. Students who do not choose Religious Education at AS or A2 level are often offered a non-exam programme designed to support their faith development. This is a topic based approach which promotes discussion and interaction at a more personal level and may involve specific voluntary work in the local community.

Third Level Education

St Mary's University College, Belfast is the only third-level Catholic institution in Northern Ireland and while its primary function is educating teachers for Catholic schools it also offers a BA degree in Liberal Arts. All teachers teaching Religious Education in Catholic primary schools are required to have a Catholic Certificate in Religious Education as part of their qualifications. St Mary's University College offers a three year Certificate course for teachers preparing to teach Religious Education in Catholic schools. It also offers a Post-Graduate Certificate in Education for students who hope to teach in Irish Medium schools, and for teachers from the Republic who support the Irish language at primary and second level. The Religious Education Certificate course at St Mary's is a three-year programme that may be taken in addition to the BEd course and a one year programme which runs concurrently with the PGCE course.

Alongside students taking the Religious Education Certificate there are those who dedicate themselves to the teaching of Religious Education following a four year Religious Studies degree at primary or post-primary level. Religious specialists are vitally important at all levels but particularly at post-primary level: Catholic schools need qualified and experienced teachers to interact with students to encourage and help them to take more ownership of their faith.

Conclusion

It is no cliché to say that young people are the future of the Church and their personal faith development is of critical importance to the ongoing life of the Church. The Catholic Church has a complex infrastructure in place which hopes to meet this need. The partnership between the three key players in Catholic education, namely, parents, school and parish is often a challenging one. However when we witness the strength of these partners working together in support of each child we see a growth of personal and community faith. It is of course unclear as to whether these structures are adequate to the task of handing on the faith in our increasingly secular society. The challenge now for those engaged in Religious Education is to be more understanding of the needs of young people and proactive in exploring new approaches to Religious Education and faith development. Teaching Religious Education and promoting the faith development of young people can be a challenge for teachers. Teachers lead by example: 'as a witness of faith in Christ, the teacher walks with each person sharing his or her questions and fears as well as celebrating joys and achievements.'[9] They need to remain strong in their faith in order to sustain and enrich the faith of their pupils. Teachers too need support to reflect on and consider their own Christian calling to be educators in faith. As Christopher O'Donnell points out 'there is still a lot of faith, but it needs nurturing and challenge.'[10] Catholic education must rise to meet this challenge.

Notes

1   Address by Archbishop Seán Brady at the Launch of the website for the Consultative Group on Catholic Education, 21 September 2007. www.catholiceducation-ni.com (accessed September 2007).

2   John Paul II, *Ecumenism as a Pastoral Priority of this Pontificate*, 2004, www.strssa,cua.edu (accessed September 2007).

3   Address by Archbishop Seán Brady, September 2007.

4   www.deni.gov.uk, accessed March 2006.

5   The Catholic Bishops of Northern Ireland, *A Response from the Catholic Bishops of NI to The Post-Primary Review 'Education for the 21st Century'*, June 2002, p. 4.

6   The Catholic Bishops of Northern Ireland, *Building Peace Shaping the Future* Armagh: November 2001, p. 8.

7   Address by Archbishop Seán Brady, September 2007.

8   Christopher O' Donnell O.Carm, 'A Decline in Faith?' in *Le Chéile A Catholic Ethos Journal*, November 2005, pp. 6–7.

9   Council for Catholic Maintained Schools, *Life to the Full; A Vision for Catholic Education*, Hollywood: CCMS, 1991, p. 12.

10   O' Donnell, 'A Decline in Faith?', pp. 6–7.

Further Reading

Conroy, James C. (ed.), *Catholic Education Inside Out Outside In*, Dublin: Veritas, 1999.

Council for the Curriculum Examinations and Assessment (CEA), The Northern Ireland Curriculum Primary, Belfast: 2007.

Department of Education Northern Ireland, Core Syllabus for Religious Education, Bangor: DENI, 2007.

Devitt, Patrick M., *Willingly to School, Religious Education as an Examination Subject*, Dublin: Veritas, 2000.

Feheney, J. Matthew, *Beyond the Race for Points: Aspects of Pastoral Care in a Catholic School Today*, Dublin: Veritas, 1999.

Feheney, J. Matthew, *From Ideal to Action: The Inner Nature of a Catholic School Today*, Dublin: Veritas, 1998.

The Northern Ireland Commission for Catholic Education, Catholic Education: The Vision Resource Manual.

Reichert, Richard J., *Renewing Catechetical Ministry: a Future Agenda*, New York/Mahwah: Paulist Press, 2002.

Report of the Independent Strategic Review of Education, 'Schools for the Future: Funding, Strategy, Sharing', December 2006.

CHAPTER 15

CATHOLIC RELIGIOUS EDUCATION IN ENGLAND AND WALES

David Roberts

Catholic Education in England and Wales – Garden or Uphill Road?

Two years after the close of the Second Vatican Council (1962–1965), two prominent religious educators, Hubert J. Richards and Peter De Rosa, wrote the preface to an important book on Religious Education and made the following comments about the renewal of Religious Education in England and Wales:

> We have witnessed in recent years the opening of numerous catechetical centres and a full-time religious institute; summer and evening lectures are attended everywhere by serving teachers and lay catechists in their thousands; there are urgent and repeated demands for new textbooks, new visual aids, the most updated correspondence courses. On the face of it, everything in the garden is lovely.[1]

The 'on the face it' hinted, however, that there was a need for some caution. The caution came in the next paragraph. The authors noted that although they did not want to minimise the results so far achieved by teachers and catechists, 'we have travelled only a little way on a long and uphill road.'

This essay will attempt to offer some reflections on that journey so far, and outline, albeit briefly, something of the vision for Catholic Religious Education in England and Wales. It is clear that in a short chapter, we will simply be able to make a few remarks, remarks which in no way claim to give an adequate treatment of this complex subject. First, a little history will help to put our topic in context.

A Brief History

The state of Religious Education in England and Wales for a significant part of the twentieth century was very much what it was elsewhere in the Church. The printed catechism reigned supreme and the main teaching method was rote learning. Such an approach was possible when faith was defined primarily as *belief* in doctrines. It more than likely worked sufficiently well because the vast majority of children came from families with committed faith.

One of the great reformers of Religious Education was Canon Francis Harold Drinkwater. In 1922, Drinkwater was appointed Diocesan Inspector of Schools in Birmingham with the mandate from Archbishop McIntire 'to abolish that wretched parrot-system,' the memorised catechism method. It was Drinkwater and his influential journal, *The Sower*, that introduced many people in England and Wales to the catechetical reform taking place in other parts of Europe. Reflecting on the first decade of *The Sower*, he wrote: 'its aim was to spread the notion that religious instruction is not likely to have lasting effect unless it concerns itself as much with the heart as with the head.'[2]

This holistic approach to Religious Education and catechesis[3] has continued to shape the vision of Religious Education in England and Wales, although not without intense and at times heated debate.

A National Project
In their message, *The Easter People*, published after the National Pastoral Congress held in Liverpool in 1980, the bishops of England and Wales agreed to consider 'the recommendation from the Congress about the provision of a common core Religious Education curriculum for national use.' In 1980 most dioceses were using the Irish catechetical programme, the *Children of God* series published by Veritas. The programme had been well received in Catholic schools; however, many teachers and diocesan education advisors felt that it was not addressing the specific cultural context of England and Wales.

In 1982, the bishops approved a process, initiated by the National Board of Religious Inspectors and Advisors, to address the Religious Education of children up to the age of fourteen. The bishops specifically noted that the context in England and Wales required such an initiative 'in order to be in tune with the multicultural and multi-faith background of our people.' The Project was called PREP: The Primary Religious Education Programme. The aim of this programme was to provide practical help and resources for all those involved with the Religious Education of children.

In 1985, A. Patrick Purnell S.J., the National Advisor for Religious Education, published *Our Faith Story*, which offered the context and 'a kind of backcloth' to the whole project. However, those involved in the project quickly realised that the vision was too narrow and limited. There was a need to provide resources for Catholics of all ages. A consultative process was started which sought to coordinate the expertise of those working in the field of catechesis and Religious

Education. The project was renamed *Living and Sharing our Faith: A National Project of Catechesis and Religious Education*. Since 1985, there have been numerous national project publications for adults and children including Religious Education programmes for primary (*Here I Am*) and secondary (*Icons*) years.

Religious Education in Schools

In May 2000, the Catholic Bishops' Conference of England and Wales approved the statement *Religious Education in Catholic Schools*.[4] In their statement, the bishops, quoting from the *Religious Education Curriculum Directory for Catholic Schools* (1996), summarised the overall aims of classroom Religious Education. These aims included a 'comprehensive and systematic study of the mystery of God, of the life and teachings of Jesus Christ, the teachings of his Church, the central beliefs that Catholics hold, the basis for them and the relationship between faith and life.'

The bishops went on to articulate the outcome of Religious Education as a 'religiously literate young people who have the knowledge, understanding and skills – appropriate to their age and capacity – to think spiritually, ethically and theologically, and who are aware of the demands of religious commitment in everyday life.' *Religious Education in Catholic Schools* insists on the importance of the faith of the school community but is realistic that for some in the classroom, Religious Education will be received as catechesis while for others it will be evangelisation. Nevertheless, the criteria by which it is to be judged are educational. The vision is of a Religious Education that both engages the intellect and shapes the lives of children and young people.

Adult Education – The Poor Relation?

In the mid-nineteenth century, the advisor to Pope Pius IX on English affairs, Monsignor George Talbot, wrote a letter, dated April 25, 1867, to the Archbishop of Westminster. The English cleric posed an important question: 'What is the province of the laity?' His response was provocative and adamant: 'To hunt, to shoot, to entertain. These matters they understand, but to meddle in ecclesiastical matters they have no right at all.'

In 1965, the Second Vatican Council challenged the view that lay people should simply regard secular matters as their area of competence. The Council exhorted lay people 'to exercise their apostolate both in the Church and the world.' Since the Council, we have seen a great increase of lay ministries which has resulted in a need to rethink our approach to education in the Church. A Religious Education that ended with adolescents could not possibly hope to fulfil the vision of the Council. Consequently we have seen the development of numerous opportunities for adult formation within our parishes and dioceses. Less visibly, but of no less importance, a critical mass of lay people are emerging with degrees in theology.

In 1971, a Vatican document entitled the *General Catechetical Directory*, stated that 'catechesis for adults, since it deals with persons who are capable of an adherence that is fully responsible, must be considered the chief form of catechesis.' It has been noted by many, that this call for a shift in focus from children and youth to the catechesis of adults is still far removed from the present reality. A document issued by a committee of the Bishops' Conference noted that 'despite the many developments and initiatives in adult formation in recent years, the work remains under-funded, under-resourced and under-valued relative to the priority given to it in the teaching of the Church.'[5]

On the Way to Life

The final part of this essay will introduce a recent document which has helped to open up an important conversation about Catholic education and the contemporary culture of England and Wales. In an increasingly pluralistic culture and with the growing visibility of the religious dimensions to our society, such a document is timely.

For several years, the National Board of Religious Inspectors and Advisors and the Catholic Education Service, has been reflecting on the content, method and nature of Catholic education. However, more recently, there has been a strong sense of how the landscape of contemporary culture is ever-changing and the impact this has on Religious Education and catechesis. It was in response to this situation that the Department for Education and Formation of the Bishops' Conference commissioned The *Heythrop Institute for Religion, Ethics and Public Life*, to write a critical analysis of the contemporary culture of England and Wales.

In 2005, the *Institute* published their report entitled *On the Way to Life: Contemporary Culture and Theological Development as a Framework for Catholic Education, Catechesis and Formation.*[6] The document is divided into three parts. Part One is an interpretive essay which attempts to map and analyse the contemporary religious landscape of England and Wales. Secularisation – the declining influence of religion in the public sphere – is a key characteristic. However the authors also note that the culture is not without its religious dimension, although people are more inclined to speak of spirituality than religion. Religion is perceived as something narrow and institutional. Spirituality, which is approached eclectically, connotes freedom and choice. Nevertheless, the document argues that the Church has a part to play in forming this culture as well as being formed by it.

Part Two situates faith within its theological context and specifically within the vision of the Second Vatican Council. The authors suggest that the Council offers a vision and method which provides resources for engaging with the contemporary culture. The vision which is offered is a sacramental vision. The document advocates the retrieval of this Catholic vision as essential if those involved in Catholic education are going to overcome the difficulty of communicating the core symbols of Catholic faith.

The final part of the document claims that the Catholic vision of the modern age is rooted in 'the Catholic sacramental imagination.' This vision sees created reality as a 'sacrament,' that is, a revelation of the presence of God. This has profound implications for our engagement with culture. The world is never purely and simply secular; it is always oriented toward and endowed with God's presence. It is important to note that the Catholic vision is based on the language of analogy. This provides a way of speaking of God which allows for both similarity and difference between God and creation. For example, God is *not like* a father in the strict sense of the word, but God's relationship is *like* that of a parent to a child. We come to knowledge of God through our knowledge of creation. The Catholic vision goes on to stress that the objects, events and persons of our ordinary lives make God present to us and are therefore sacramental. The task of the teacher and catechist is to develop and exercise a creative *imagination*, a creative sacramental imagination, which finds infinite meaning in the great symbols, stories and images of Catholicism. It is through these symbols, stories and images that we can give adults, children and young people access to the Catholic tradition in ways which will not only engage their minds but also shape their hearts.

Conclusion

There is no question that Catholic education in England and Wales can expect further challenges in the future. This has always been the case for Catholic education. There have never been any good old days when the Church found it easy to teach. However contrary to a certain pessimism one encounters from time to time, many concur with the revised Directory for Catechesis that 'Catechetical renewal, developed in the Church over the last decades, continues to bear very welcome fruit'.[7]

Notes

1   Gabriel Moran, *God Still Speaks: The Basis of Christian Education*, London: Burns and Oates, 1967, p. 7.

2   Francis Harold Drinkwater, 'Homiletic and Pastoral Review', Vol. 34, 1933–34, p. 31.

3   For the purposes of this essay, 'Religious Education' and 'catechesis' are used interchangeably.

4   Catholic Bishops' Conference of England and Wales, *Religious Education in Catholic Schools*, St Leonards-on-Sea: Hastings Printing Company Limited, 2000, pp. 6–7.

5   Committee for Catechesis and Adult Christian Education, *The Priority of Adult Formation*, Catholic Media Trust, 2000, p. 20.

6   London: The Heythrop Institute for Religion, Ethics and Public Life, 2005.

7   Congregation for Clergy, *General Directory for Catechesis*, Catholic Truth Society, 1997, p. 26 n. 24.

Further Reading

Gallagher, Jim, *Soil For The Seed: Historical, Pastoral and Theological Reflections on Educating to and in the Faith*, Great Wakering, Essex: McCrimmons, 2001.

Kelly, Liam, *Catechesis Revisited*, Darton, Longman & Todd, 2000.

McLaughlin, Terence, O'Keefe, Joseph and O'Keeffe, Bernadette (eds), *The Contemporary Catholic School: Context, Identity and Diversity*, The Falmer Press, 1996.

Sullivan, John, *Catholic Schools in Contention: Competing Metaphors and Leadership*, Dublin: Veritas Publications, 2000.

CHAPTER 16

CATHOLIC RELIGIOUS EDUCATION IN SCOTLAND

Roisín Coll and Robert A. Davis

The arrangements for the teaching of Religious Education in Catholic schools in Scotland can be best understood against the background of the unique historical and legal settlement through which Catholic education functions in contemporary Scotland. By an Act of the United Kingdom Parliament of 1918, a network of Church-controlled Catholic primary and secondary schools was integrated into the state system in Scotland while continuing to remain under the jurisdiction of the Church in key areas of governance and curriculum. Enjoying the full benefits of state funding and support for the maintenance and expansion of its schools, the Church, under the terms of the 1918 Act, retained control over the appointment of staff and the design and delivery of the Religious Education curriculum. This accommodation of Church and State has remained in place, largely unaltered, for the best part of a century, enduring through several important and far-reaching phases of structural change in Scottish Education.[1]

Catholic schools in modern Scotland are currently overseen by the Scottish Executive Education Department (SEED), an arm of the recently devolved Scottish Parliament, and managed by the powerful Local Authorities in which the schools are located. The geographical distribution of the schools continues to reflect the demographics of the Catholic population, with concentrations in and around the big industrial towns and cities of Central Scotland, most notably Glasgow, to which generations of Irish people emigrated in the nineteenth century. The schools founded in these turbulent times were set up to meet the basic educational needs of a poor and frequently oppressed religious and ethnic minority. They were often staffed by energetic men and women of the various religious congregations charged by the Church with alleviating the formidable misfortunes of industrial society – most tellingly the problems of poverty, ignorance and deprivation. They were stamped, as a result, with the charism of those religious orders, in which the promotion of religious instruction, the nurturing of faith and the affirmation of the sacramental life of the Catholic community were central to the tasks of education.[2]

The religious orders have now almost entirely withdrawn from schooling in Scotland, passing their responsibilities to their lay successors in the teaching profession. Most Catholic primary teachers– and a large proportion of their secondary colleagues – receive their initial teacher education at the University of Glasgow, which assumed major responsibility for maintenance of the supply of appropriately qualified staff for Scotland's Catholic sector when it merged with the national Catholic teacher education institution, St Andrew's College, in 1999.[3] As a result, it is within the Faculty of Education at the University of Glasgow that most aspiring Catholic teachers today receive their own preparation in Religious Education and faith formation. The contemporary Religious Education curriculum in Scottish Catholic primary and secondary schools has been shaped by this distinguished history of mission and commitment and is heir to a rich tradition of learning and teaching from school, college and university. It is, however, neither a nostalgic nor backward-looking curriculum, but a living and evolving experience, firmly imprinted by the values and imperatives of the Second Vatican Council and proudly but distinctively positioned in the larger pattern of educational provision and policy-making in Scotland.

The most recent period of wide-ranging curricular reform in Scotland, designed and implemented in the early 1990s, saw the whole school curriculum reorganised into three broad phases, covering the age-bandings 5–14, 14–16 and post–16 (In 1998, pre–five education was subsequently added to the structure). Religious Education in both Catholic and non-denominational schools succeeded in maintaining a key place in all of these reforms, avoiding assimilation into other curricular areas and emerging with a renewed identity and vigour.[4] In the absence of the kind of legal framework provided by the National Curriculum in England and Wales, curricular reform in Scotland has always sought to work by a consensus of the main stakeholders. Not without its tensions, this approach nevertheless generally functions well in building shared values and agreed goals. In the 1990s, the decision to restructure the curriculum for the 5–14 age range (i.e. from the first year of primary school to the second year of secondary school) resulted in the consolidation of eight broad curricular areas, of which Religious and Moral Education was one. At first, it seemed as if both Catholic and non-denominational schools would share the same curricular guidelines for Religious and Moral Education, with the distinctiveness of the Catholic sector recognised and regulated in the implementation of the guidelines within the context of the Catholic school rather than in the formal design of Religious Education itself. However, this proposal proved insufficiently sensitive to the needs of Catholic schools and, in a series of complex but constructive negotiations, the Catholic Education Commission (CEC – the body which advises the Bishops' Conference of Scotland on educational matters) succeeded in creating, in cooperation with the state authorities, a separate set of guidelines for the regulation and development of Catholic Religious Education whilst adhering to the agreed national 5–14 template. *Religious Education 5–14: Roman Catholic Schools,*[5] published under the joint auspices of the Scottish Office Education Department and the Scottish Catholic Education Commission in October 1994. This was a milestone document and remains the bedrock for the teaching of Religious Education in Catholic schools for the 5–14 age range – and therefore for Catholic Religious Education as a whole.[6]

The rationale for Religious Education contained in the 5–14 Catholic Religious Education Guidelines incorporates a succinct and graceful expression of the nature and purposes of Religious Education in the modern Catholic school. Recognising that the foundation of the guidelines is the partnership of school, home and parish, the document begins with an assertion of the integrated nature of faith and learning and an affirmation of the Catholic school as a context for evangelisation, catechesis and the development of 'knowledge and understanding … related to religion and faith.' The content of the 5–14 curriculum reflects the agreed emphasis on three broad areas of enquiry and exploration, formally referred to as Outcomes: Christianity, Other World Religions and Personal Search – a pattern echoing the arrangements for Religious Education in non-denominational schools while carefully preserving the distinctive mission and accents of the Catholic school. The guidelines are laid out in accordance with the larger 5–14 framework, which disaggregates each outcome into a series of strands and, within each Strand, defines the desired Attainment Targets across a series of Levels, from A to E – with Level A corresponding to the broad ability range of the 5–6 age group and Level E to that of the 12–13 age range. A later amendment to the 5–14 curriculum introduced Level F, to address the needs of more able pupils in the upper primary and lower secondary stages.

Within the Christianity Outcome, the Strands are:
- Sacraments
- Liturgical Cycle, Celebrations, Festivals, Ceremonies and Customs
- Sacred Writings, Stories and Key Figures
- Community, Worship, Sacred Places and Symbols
- Moral Values.

Each of these is vital to the cohesion of the curriculum and, taken together, they make up the tapestry of faith and learning in Catholic Religious Education. Within the Primary School, preparation for the post-baptismal Sacraments of Reconciliation, Eucharist and Confirmation performs a vital, informing task in the work of Religious Education, bringing together school and parish, teachers and clergy and involving parents directly in the Religious Education and formation of their children. From out of the experience of sacramental preparation emerges wider participation by staff and pupils in prayer, worship and liturgy and this, in turn, shapes the approach to Scripture, to Church and to the consolidation of positive Christian relationships founded upon the Gospel values of love, justice and forgiveness. The 5–14 Religious Education Guidelines are precise and methodical and provide a solid foundation for the activities of the teacher, enabling progress and attainment to be monitored and recorded. It is important, however, that Religious Education retains an integrated understanding of faith development and offers opportunities for personal growth and commitment within the community of believers. Contemporary Catholic schools in Scotland also frequently include pupils of other faiths, or of no particular faith, whose parents have elected to have them educated in a Roman Catholic setting. 5–14 is an inclusive curriculum, which, in its emphasis on other Christian traditions, and other monotheistic world faiths, promotes tolerance and respect for others and helps combat the menace of sectarianism and racism.

Much of the learning and teaching in Religious Education in Scottish primary schools is provided through the *Alive-O* programme– the catechetical series published by Veritas – which has been adapted to the requirements of 5–14.[7] Though not without its critics, *Alive-O* has, nonetheless, been adopted enthusiastically by dioceses across Scotland. It is ably supported by the work done with student teachers in initial teacher education and also by a range of initiatives in Continuing Professional Development (CPD) coordinated by the Catholic Religious Education Advisers from the various dioceses and also by the Scottish Catholic Education Service (SCES), the agency of the CEC concerned with the operational support of Catholic education. *Alive-O* provides an effective working syllabus for the teaching of Religious Education but in no area of education does the syllabus equate to the curriculum. Successful learning and teaching in Religious Education requires, as it always has done, confident and imaginative teachers, equipped to offer a stimulating and authoritative account of Catholic beliefs and practices, who are also able to extend to pupils the invitation of faith in Jesus Christ and his Church. Reports of Her Majesty's Inspectorate into the teaching of Religious Education in Catholic schools are generally very favourable in commending the varied and versatile ways in which Catholic teachers discharge this area of their responsibility. Nevertheless, in recent years the Church in Scotland has become more conscious of the need to support teachers in their own faith witness, as the social and cultural background to Religious Education in a secular society becomes more challenging and as pupil populations in schools become more variegated in their faith backgrounds. The launch in 2003 of the Catholic CPD package, *Faith and Teaching*,[8] was a reflection of these concerns, endeavouring to renew the knowledge and understanding of school staff and further nurture an adult, professionally reflective faith among Catholic teachers.

Beyond the primary school and on into secondary education, Catholic Religious Education assumes a more plural and locally determined character. The 5–14 curriculum embraces the first two years of secondary school and there are important elements of continuity and consistency in the teaching of doctrine, Scripture and morality, including relationships and sex education. *Alive-O*, however, does not continue into secondary school and a wider variety of syllabus materials can be found across the secondary sector, including considerable diversity in the topics and themes selected for study by schools and by dioceses, albeit within nationally agreed syllabus guidelines set by the Bishops' Conference. The key to secondary school Religious Education provision generally is the team of specialist Religious Education teachers in each school, usually managed by a Principal Teacher or Coordinator of Religious Education. Though small in number, Religious Education specialists are vital to the success of Religious Education and frequently stamp their own vision and witness upon the approaches taken to materials and pedagogy. Given the larger pupil numbers in secondary schools, specialists often require to be supported by 'generalist' Religious Education teachers: staff whose teaching expertise and qualifications reside in other curricular areas but who have expressed a willingness to participate in Religious Education and have undertaken a basic course within their programmes of initial teacher education.

In a great many schools, led by head teachers for whom Religious Education is a priority, and managed by conscientious specialist Principal Teachers, these arrangements produce rewarding programmes of Religious Education for the 12–18 age range. As the pupils mature, the themes selected for study with older teenagers can become more demanding and, in consequence, more satisfying. The agreed curriculum for the last two years of secondary education is built around the themes of 'believing', 'trusting' and 'doing', a framework that can support advanced study of Christian doctrine and ethics.[9] Catholic secondary Religious Education in today's Scotland has produced accomplished and original programmes of study in issues ranging from international justice, through christology and biblical studies, to the theology of the body. These are regularly accompanied by initiatives associated with the spiritual lives of young people, offering retreats, days of recollection and deeper familiarisation with the prayer life of the Church.

Despite a record of considerable achievement in Catholic Religious Education, the need to reform and renovate the curriculum is always keenly felt. Religious Education is situated within a broader educational system that is forever subject to the pressures of the knowledge economy and the forces of global change. In almost all Catholic secondary schools in Scotland, Religious Education is a non-certificated subject, leading to no academic qualification. This is by no means inevitably a disadvantage to an area that has been modelled according to quite different priorities. It does, however, locate Religious Education at the 'value-added' end of the curriculum, where it finds increasing competition from fashionable initiatives in themes such as Citizenship Education and Philosophical Enquiry and to each of which Catholic Religious Education has responded imaginatively and constructively.[10] Some influential voices in the UK, however, have gone so far as to call for the abolition of Religious Education and its replacement with these, more 'relevant' areas of study.

In 2004, SEED announced a major review of the whole curriculum in Scotland, from 3–18, and produced an outline statement of principles and objectives entitled *A Curriculum for Excellence*.[11] Through SCES and the Faculty of Education of the University of Glasgow, Catholic educators have been able to maintain close involvement in these deliberations. In January 2006, the CEC issued an important consultation document entitled *Curriculum Guidance on Religious Education in Catholic Secondary Schools*,[12] designed to encourage debate on the modernisation of Catholic Religious Education and timed expressly to coincide with the engagement period for the *Curriculum for Excellence* proposals, with which it is intended a new Religious Education curriculum framework will eventually articulate. In May 2008, the CEC and Learning and Teaching Scotland (LTS – the Scottish Government's advisory body on the curriculum) released a set of 'draft outcomes and experiences'[13] on Religious Education spanning both primary and secondary schooling. The importance of these documents cannot be overstated. They represent the most significant revision to Catholic Religious Education in a generation and have been presented by the Church and its educational agencies as an unparalleled opportunity to reposition Catholic Religious Education, catechesis and faith formation, for Scotland, in the twenty-first century.

The rationale for the new curriculum affirms the fundamental structure and philosophy of *A Curriculum for Excellence*, underlining the convergence of Church teaching with the ambitious goals set by the Government and intended to enrich the education of the nation's children in an era of unprecedented social and economic change. The rationale recognises the distinctive purposes of Catholic education, acknowledging that, 'Religious education in Catholic schools takes place within the context of the wider Catholic faith community, in partnership with home and parish. It is an integral part of the Catholic school, which is itself a community of faith'.[14] The content of the curriculum is divided into a series of strands covering key elements of Catholic belief and practice. The methodology is modelled overtly on a Christocentric conception of learning and teaching, encouraging a process which begins in initial engagement, moves through enquiry and questioning and culminates in a personal response to the message of the Gospel. In recognition of the scale of the proposed changes, the draft outcomes and experiences are to be piloted in a number of schools in both the primary and secondary sectors in 2008/2009. This pilot programme will be accompanied by a comprehensive consultation process involving a wide range of stakeholders.

EXPLORING RELIGIOUS EDUCATION

These new proposals epitomise the issues with which this chapter has been concerned: principally the ongoing renewal of a flourishing tradition of Religious Education and faith formation, with deep roots in the proclamation of the Gospel, to meet the challenges of a new era.

Notes

1   Thomas A. Fitzpatrick, 'Catholic Education', in Heather Holmes (ed.), *Scottish Life and Society*: *Education*, East Linton, Tuckwell Press, 2000, pp. 435–456.

2   F. J. O'Hagan, *The Contribution of the Religious Orders to Education in Glasgow During the Period 1847–1918*, Lampeter: The Mellen Press, 2006.

3   J. Conroy and D. McCreath, 'The Challenge to Catholic Teacher Education in Scotland', in *Catholic Education: A Journal of Inquiry and Practice*, Vol. 2, No. 3, 1999, pp. 312–32.

4   J. Conroy, 'Religious and Moral Education' in W.M. Humes and T.G.K. Bryce (eds), *Scottish Education*, Edinburgh: Edinburgh University Press, 2nd edn., 1999, pp. 337–351.

5   Scottish Office Education Department and Scottish Catholic Education Commission, *Religious Education 5–14: Roman Catholic Schools*, 1994.

6   R. Coll, 'Examination of the Consultation and Development Process for the Scottish Catholic Religious Education Guidelines', *Catholic Education: A Journal of Inquiry and Practice*, Vol. 6, No. 2, 2002, pp. 233–250.

7   *Alive-O*, Dublin: Veritas, 1998–2004.

8   Scottish Executive Education Department and Scottish Catholic Education Commission, *Faith and Teaching*, Edinburgh, SEED, 2003.

9   Scottish Catholic Education Commission, *A Framework for S5/6 Religious Education*, Glasgow: CEC, 1998.

10   Scottish Catholic Education Commission, *Faith and Citizenship*, Glasgow: CEC, 2005.

11   http://www.scotland.gov.uk/Publications/2004/11/20178/45863 (accessed 01.04.08).

12   http://www.sces.uk.com/Download/Download.asp?file=Documents&name=ReligiousEducation_Rationale_Jan06.pdf (accessed 19.06.08).

13   http://www.ltscotland.org.uk/curriculumforexcellence/outcomes/rerc/index.asp (accessed 19.06.08).

14   http://www.ltscotland.org.uk/curriculumforexcellence/outcomes/rerc/index.asp (accessed 19.06.08).

SECTION 4

PRACTISING CATHOLIC RELIGIOUS EDUCATION

CHAPTER 17

'COME AND SEE': THE PROCESSES OF CATECHESIS

Anne Hession

What are they saying about doing catechesis today? Is there any one preferred method? What is the best approach to use in school, parish, or community group? The first thing we can say is that there is no one perfect method for catechesis: contemporary catechists employ many different approaches though all aim to foster a relationship between the participants and Jesus Christ. Furthermore, the methods used in catechesis depend largely on how teachers understand:

- the purposes of catechesis in the life of the Church;
- the nature of religious faith and of religious knowing;
- the essential facts, truths, values, skills and attitudes to be learned by disciples of Jesus.[1]

Here we consider the first and second of these issues before examining Jesus' ministerial practice as an important source of insight for catechetical method in every setting.[2] The story of Jesus and the Samaritan woman (Jn 4: 5-30) suggests that catechesis is about making people available to the working of the Holy Spirit. Catechesis is about teaching people how to *see* and *respond* to reality in a new way *because of* and *through* their relationship with God.

Purposes: Evangelisation and Discipleship

The *General Directory for Catechesis* (1997) situates catechesis within the activity of evangelisation.[3] Evangelisation is about bringing the Good News of God's Reign made evident in the risen Lord and inviting all people to conversion and discipleship with him.[4] In other words, evangelisation, as distinct from proselytising, is about encouraging people to see that the Christian narrative gives our lives meaning and that living in the 'way' of Jesus fulfils our deepest heart's desire. In this understanding, the primary goal of catechesis is to educate Church members so that they become effective disciples of Jesus for the Reign of God. Discipleship of Jesus involves encountering Jesus, understanding his 'Way', and living out one's faith as a credible witness in the world. People are catechised in order to be sent out by the Spirit to worship and serve God in their daily lives.

The catechumenate (RCIA) is the model and inspiration for all catechesis.[5] This is important for our *approach* to catechesis for a number of reasons. In the first place, the catechumenal model recognises that it is *in and through* the religious practices – ritual, aesthetic, ethical – of living, vibrant Christian communities that Christians are best formed and enabled to become disciples. Contemporary catechetical approaches assume and seek to foster the unity between doctrine and practice, between understanding and embodiment, between personal and social transformation, between worship of God and service to neighbour. This implies further that the kind of knowing which catechesis seeks to foster is primarily an affective, behavioural mode of knowing: where knowledge and action, learning and bodily practice are integrally connected. Knowing *about* the Reign of God is important, but even more crucial is the ability to decide when confronted by it. Therefore, an adequate understanding of how thought relates to action is necessary for the development of creative and effective catechetical methods.[6]

Faith

In contemporary catechesis, faith is understood to involve 'a personal encounter with Jesus Christ, making of oneself a disciple of him' (GDC 53). The focus is primarily on the relational nature of faith and secondarily on its cognitive dimension.[7] Catechesis is about inviting participants to enter a *lifelong* process of conforming their lives to the way that Christ lived and continues to live among us; a process of worship of God and of radical self-giving for the sake of others and of the world. As this kind of faith presupposes a personal encounter with Jesus it suggests that catechesis involves providing opportunities for participants to get to know Jesus better by experiencing his presence and action in their lives.[8] Furthermore, if we believe in Jesus, this should affect our way of understanding and relating to the people and situations we meet. In summary, the faith that emerges from a personal relationship with Jesus is integrally related to the ongoing personal and social transformation we call conversion.

Conversion

The core of Christianity is its fidelity to the real. For believers therefore, to be enlightened religiously is to come into a proper relationship with what is most real. This means being open to images and visions of the world that are ever more and more adequate, complex and truthful. Catholics believe that what is revealed in Scripture and in Tradition (creed, code and cult) provides adequate and truthful images of reality. Our religion offers a truthful account of human existence and proposes a way for us to relate to ourselves, other people, the world and God. Conversion could be described therefore as a transformation from self-centredness to reality-centredness by means of a new relationship with God.[9] In other words, conversion means thinking, feeling and living as Christ, adopting *Jesus'* vision of the real – the Reign of God. The implications for catechesis are clear: discipleship depends less on the moral or doctrinal propositions people hold as true, and more on the images shaping their imagination of the world.

Imagination

The image is of central importance in how we understand and interpret the world because the imaginative process provides a link between the body, the mind, and the emotions.[10] Imagination (as opposed to fantasy) does not lead us into the unreal: on the contrary, imagination is precisely that gift which allows us to truly know the real. It is the faculty of seeing reality in depth, in a new way. Ultimately, imagination is the power we have to enter into the divine dimension of reality, the fact that it is held in being by God. To see anything in its depth is to see it held in its being in love. Finally, we can say that as we attend to reality using our imagination, reality is transfigured, not altered. God has established the order of what is truly real, through the Reign of God, and we are invited to get involved in it and make its reality our own. We begin to see reality as God does and so become caught up in God's desires for the fulfilment of the world.

If conversion is about adopting a new *vision* of reality that changes how we relate to God, other persons, and the created world, what are the implications for catechetical method? The challenge of catechesis is to feed the imagination with Christian stories, images, myths and symbols through which people can see the world in depth and respond appropriately. More precisely, the heart of most contemporary approaches to catechesis will be a creative dialogue between the experience of the faith community as captured in the language, imagery and theological metaphors of Scripture and the Church's tradition *and* the language, images and metaphors of the participants' lives.[11] If catechists facilitate a creative dialogue between participants' lives and the Christian Scriptures and Tradition it will help them to see the divine dimension of reality and to become involved with God in the transformation of that reality until the fulfilment of all things in Christ.

This dialogue has an important cognitive dimension but equally important affective, creative and mystical dimensions. The perennial challenge is to effect this dialogue in a way that honours the faith tradition *and* the lived experiences of the participants. This requires a serious attempt to adapt and inculturate the Christian faith tradition in such a way that the Christian vision of the world is brought to bear in new ways through the active imaginations of contemporary individuals.[12] As we engage in this task much can be learned from how Jesus fostered a transformation of the religious imagination in his own time.

Jesus the Teacher

The Johannine story of the Samaritan Woman (Jn 4:5-30) tells how Jesus invited a woman to faith in the gift of God (the Holy Spirit), which He makes available to her. The 'living water' he offers the woman is understood by many commentators to be his Spirit in believers. The fulcrum of the story is the woman's growing relationship with Jesus, a relationship that culminates in her going forth as his disciple.

This story provides a rich source of reflection for those concerned with catechesis in any setting. It shows *how* the woman is helped by Jesus to come to faith and much can be learned from the actions and words of Jesus about what it means to come to 'know' in the Christian religion. Furthermore, the story highlights the obstacles that need to be overcome in order for faith, religious knowing and conversion to happen. Finally, the story is a reminder that at the heart of Christian faith is a relationship. Jesus makes the presence of God real and accessible, *in his manner of relating* to the Samaritan woman. The personal, relational aspect of faith is prominent; the cognitive aspect, while important, takes second place.

Overcoming Obstacles

The opening chapters of John's gospel show Jesus gathering disciples from among the Jews. In the story of the Samaritan Woman, he moves out to those who lived on the fringes of Judaism. The Samaritans were descendents of the Jewish and pagan population left in Samaria after the Assyrian conquest in 722 BCE. They revered Moses and the Torah, but did not follow the views of Judeans or centre their worship in Jerusalem. The woman to whom Jesus speaks is therefore an outcast. She is also an outsider by virtue of the fact that she is a woman in a patriarchal culture (e.g. she would have been forbidden to read Talmud). In speaking to her, Jesus crosses cultural and gender boundaries on three counts: first, by speaking to a woman; second by speaking to a Samaritan and third, by speaking to her alone.

This is a dominant feature of Jesus' ministry: he chooses to seek out the lost, the poor, the outcasts, the oppressed, and the marginalised, even in the non-Jewish world. Jesus knows both who he is and what his mission is and he does not hesitate to be counter-cultural. He breaks down the boundary between chosen people and rejected people, between male and female. He reveals his glory wherever he finds people with religious questions and yearnings, however unaware of those yearnings they may be. In this he is a model for contemporary catechists whose ministry is marked by inclusiveness, hospitality and genuine openness to all. Rooted in their own Christian faith, empowered by a strong sense of purpose, catechists immerse themselves in the lives of their students with the conviction that the gospel message will find an echo there.

Jesus' Approach

The Samaritan woman is puzzled at Jesus' request for a drink. She has been hurt by the injustice of Jewish treatment of Samaritans in general, and by the patriarchal mores that prevail in her society. How does Jesus respond? First, Jesus meets her in person, relating to her in a spirit of mutuality and love and in that engagement he makes God present. Second, he enters the woman's experience and listens to her story. He is aware of her background and of the situation of her people. He lets her know that he is aware of her personal struggles. Third, Jesus evokes in her the need to reflect upon and re-examine her experiences, convictions and values in light of his unique Wisdom-shaped vision and his own deepest truth. He invites her to learn something that will satisfy her restless spirit ('I am he' Jn 4:26). In doing so Jesus draws on imagery from his own religious tradition (Judaism) to relate to himself as the present revealer and saviour, thus according a new and deeper meaning to the images of hunger and thirst, satisfaction and refreshment used in Isaiah, Jeremiah, Amos and the Psalms.[13] Jesus discovers the Samaritan woman's desire for the gift of faith and drawing from the riches of his religious tradition, he nurtures her religious imagination.

God's Life in Us

Following Jesus here, the challenge to contemporary catechists is to find ways of awakening people to their inborn capacity and hunger for the Divine. Often, it is in the journey into self that people are made ready for the encounter with Jesus. Referring to Karl Rahner's understanding of grace, Michael P. Horan writes:

> Our human nature is the forum through which God is known; it is in ourselves, foremost, that we find the reflection of who God is – and through such reflection come to know ourselves as graced people ... For catechetical leaders, this means helping people see and name more explicitly that God's life in us is available in our human experiences of questioning, loving and hoping.[14]

Catechesis involves helping participants recover the deep questions of existence to which Christian faith responds; questions such as what is the truth? How should I live? What makes life worth living? What kind of person can I become? What can I hope for? What kind of society should I help create? And to what shall I commit myself? The surprise of knowing something of our own hungers and depths, can expand into some question about how to live our lives.

Fostering Wonder

Today, popular culture can foster an inability in people to reach those levels where they begin to experience their hunger for God. As all kinds of media vie for their attention, people need to be helped to reconnect with their depths, with those layers of listening where wisdom can be glimpsed. Karl Rahner argued that there is a preparation which a person 'must undergo to be or become a Christian, which turns out to be a receptive capacity for the poetic word,' and he saw this whole wavelength as able to 'reach the heart, the centre' where the mystery of God becomes incarnate.[15] Consequently, catechists invest much time and resources in fostering the openness, attentiveness and disposition required for a meaningful faith encounter.

The creative process (art, puppetry, movement, music, mime) is perhaps the best language we have to search out, explore and celebrate the mystery of God. The living Word is best known through what we see and feel and hear and touch. As St John points out in his first letter:

> We declare to you ... what we have heard, what we have seen with our eyes, what we have looked at and touched with our hands, concerning the word of life ... (1 Jn 1).

The creative process uses imagery and symbols which engage the whole of our being and evoke in us a sense of wonder. Wonder makes the perception of God possible because wonder helps us go always more deeply into reality. It is only through a continued and profound observation of reality that we become conscious of the depth and mystery it contains.

Sofia Cavalletti suggests that catechists who wish to foster wonder should not offer children too many stimuli. We should offer the child's wonder 'an object capable of taking the child always farther and deeper into the awareness of reality; an object whose frontiers are always expanding as the child slowly proceeds in the contemplation of it'. One such object is the parables of the Reign of God, especially parables that present the Reign of God as an extremely small reality, which almost escapes our glance but which nonetheless becomes, prodigiously, so great (the mustard seed, woman with yeast, seed of grain, farmer).[16] Another way in which we foster wonder is by making occasions for contemplation. We can arrange for times of silence in our catechetical sessions and introduce significant periods of quiet into liturgical events.

Learning to Pray
Since God's encounter with us is at the deepest level of our being (our 'heart') and since our response to that call must bring about a conversion at all levels of our being, liturgical acts and symbols which can redirect our feelings and deepest emotions, are most appropriate for such a process. Liturgical symbols (objects, gestures, utterances or complex actions) are not 'symbolic' because we use them to express our experience. The Liturgy is like a public fund of feelings and

meanings that, if we enter it as authentically as possible, makes experience possible: 'deeper gratitude, deeper awe, a greater capacity for suffering, hope and compassion'.[17] In this way liturgy helps us to refer all things to God, and to learn how to act intentionally for the Reign of God in our lives.

Engaging with Culture

A key element in helping to nurture a living relationship between learners and Jesus is a genuine engagement with the culture of the learner. Catechists read popular books, listen to popular music, and watch popular films and television programmes in order to become familiar with the culture of those they minister to and teach. They 'tune in' to the idioms of the learners' language and to what they consider meaningful and worthwhile. In short, what is required is genuine reflection on how the learners make meaning as well as a thorough knowledge of the media through which they encounter and create meaning.

Students discover and create meaning through absorbing and reshaping whatever cultural materials and expressions they are exposed to. The challenge for catechists is to invite students to draw in similar fashion from the symbolic, narrative and sacramental resources of the Catholic Christian faith community as they form and reform their identities, relationships and lifestyle commitments. Sometimes catechists will need to identify aspects of the wider culture or the culture of the student with the truth of Christ. Christ is present in every culture and responsible for the goodness therein. Alternatively, the gospel may involve a reversal of a value or custom espoused by the student or the culture. Catholics will resist anything that leads to the diminishment of people or the denial of the real.

At times, the presumptions of the wider culture will be visible within or just beneath the surface of the language and images used to announce the gospel, turning them to new uses. For example, the language of desire is one that dominates contemporary media. As a result, participants can be very open to exploring the ways in which our desire for God manifests itself today. The key is that the language and imagery we use should reach people in the depths of their experience where they encounter God.

Developing a Sacramental Imagination

When we reflect *creatively* on our experiences we acquire an ability to see that there is a divine dimension to the ordinary experiences of our lives. Such an ability to discern and believe that God is present and active in our lives and in the world is referred to as a 'sacramental imagination'. This is primarily an imaginative capacity to glimpse God's presence and providence in particular moments, places, relationships, and in the witness of other people. A sacramental imagination also enables us to experience Jesus' presence revealed to us in a special way in scripture and the sacraments. Participants in catechesis can be encouraged to develop a 'sacramental sensitivity' by *creative* exploration of their own experience in the world, through ritual, play, art, poetry, role-play, dialogue, drama, or music. The key is to find some activity that draws participants' attention to the 'more' in reality – the fact that it is held in being by God.

Critical Reflection
Teachers also need to offer participants the possibility of reflecting *critically* on their experiences. Here, the contemplative imagination is joined with the ascetic imagination and it is at this point that much can be learned through dialogue in community.[18] For example, participants may be invited to engage in a process of personal and social analysis thus becoming critically aware of the influence that their context (their culture, history, traditions, myths, etc) has on their perspectives, beliefs, opinions, identity and praxis.[19] Sometimes participants need to be offered hard facts about reality, as well as images that confront and challenge. When offered a challenging insight, image, or perspective, participants often embark on a struggle to examine whether this requires that they change their view of reality.

Creating a Community of Truth
The Samaritan woman comes to know and believe as a result of human inquiry, critical reflection and passionate conversation. Jesus does not offer his truth before she is ready for it. Instead he nurtures her desire for truth through reflection and dialogue. When the woman interprets the 'living water' metaphor literally as the natural water of the well, Jesus accepts this lack of understanding and perseveres in the discussion. He stays in tune with her and because she does not understand his symbolic language yet, he switches back to a literal level. Each time the woman speaks, Jesus uses the opportunity to clarify and elaborate what he stands for and the message he brings. She is led to a higher level of cognition through the dialogue, thus reaching the understanding, judgement and decision of faith Jesus wants to bring about.

Today, this attention to the learner will express itself in the educators' appreciation of the psychological readiness of learners. Participants are introduced to important truths of the faith when they are likely to help them encounter, understand and follow Jesus. When catechesis is understood as a lifelong endeavour, there is no need to tell children everything before they are twelve! It will also express itself in the carefully crafted questions which nourish true dialogue, such that the process of learning itself leads not only to the discovery of truth but ultimately to an experience of God.

Announcing 'Good News'

The Samaritan woman recognises a major point of contention in the history of relations between Samaritans and Judeans, namely, whether Jerusalem or Mt. Gerizim was the proper place of worship. Jesus helps her to see beyond the conflict, suggesting that geographically localised worship will eventually come to an end. Then the Samaritans will also pray to the 'father', that is, to God as revealed to them by Jesus, and then the old shrines will not matter. The woman hears the 'good news' that true worship of God is beginning now with Jesus. She can speak intimately to God as she is God's child!

Following Jesus here, catechists are responsible for ensuring that people have access to a rich presentation of the 'good news' of Christian faith. This means that the vision of the Reign of God needs to be presented with passion, a Reign that has been inaugurated by Jesus and which, though it has yet reached fulfillment, is present in our midst. As Cavalletti notes, 'The richer the kerygma, the more living its proclamation, the more [people] will welcome it with joy and wonder and the richer will their response be.'[20]

People often come in direct contact with the 'good news' through Scripture, especially when the gospels are presented in a life-giving way. The ability to appreciate and explore Scripture using appropriate exegetical skills has recently become a key catechetical competence. These skills include the ability to carry out critical analysis of the text, coming into a real encounter with Jesus (through *lectio divina* or some other meditative approach), and finally taking an active stance for the Jesus encountered. Activities which enhance participants' understanding and appreciation of Scripture include hearing a gospel text as part of a liturgy, enacting a biblical story, entering into meditative prayer, working with biblical images in an art activity, singing a hymn as part of a choir, or dancing a liturgical dance.

Fostering Religious Knowing

The discussion between Jesus and the woman progressively reveals Jesus as the Word of Life. He offers her a new religious language, centred in the powerful images of water and worship. These images are a stimulus to conversion for the woman. It is important to note that it is in the movement from a literal to a symbolic understanding of the images of water and worship in the story that the woman comes to faith in Him. The perceptive and reflective skills needed to understand Jesus' symbolic language constitute the heart of the religious knowing he evokes in her.

People think religiously by constructing or inheriting metaphors and much of the language used in the Christian religion is used metaphorically. For example, metaphor is the principal means by which Christians speak about God.[21] So too the ability to understand parables and much biblical material requires an ability to deal with metaphors. Biblical metaphors, symbols and myths evoke God's love and compassion and Jesus' vision of the Reign of God. As disciples, our attitude toward the truth of a metaphor or symbol and our ability to participate in what the metaphor or symbol points to are more important than explaining, or interpreting it. 'Knowing' God in this mediated way is not like learning to solve a problem. It is more like responding to a call. And by our response we are brought into an intimate relationship with God whose creative and life-giving Spirit continues to call us forward to fullness of life.

As this symbolic religious thinking has an inherently imaginative aspect to it, it is taught using poetical, metaphorical, ritual, and narrative strategies. These activities invite participants into the sphere of the spontaneous, the symbolic, the mysterious, the mystical, and the sacred. Participants suspend disbelief, and participate in the play of a text, symbol, image or song. The value of such activities is not always apparent as they do not easily lend themselves to evaluation and empirical measurement of outcomes. It requires an appreciation of the curriculum as *process* where activities (for example artistic play with religious imagery) are valued precisely because they enable participants to immerse themselves imaginatively *in* religious language without having to produce anything that can be seen or measured by an objective observer.[22]

Inviting a Response

At the end of our story, the Samaritan woman leaves Jesus in order to tell her kinsfolk in the city all about him. She becomes a disciple, witnessing to other people and leading them to Jesus. 'Come and See' (Jn 4:29). Her coming to 'know' is synonymous with her transformation. She allows herself, her body, mind and soul to become implicated in what it is she is coming to know. This is very different from a simple transfer of information from Jesus to the woman, where Jesus has the 'knowledge' and the woman's role is confined to receiving this deposit and repeating it back. The truth Jesus offers is not primarily a proposition but the gift of himself ('I am'). This truth affects the Samaritan woman's very being: enabling her to enter more deeply into relationship with God and with other persons. Her knowing has less to do with conceptual knowledge of religious facts, stories, beliefs, doctrine and theology (though these have a place) and more to do with being known by a loving God who transforms her perspective and way of acting in the world. Finally, this truth that she has learned, this Mystery that she has experienced, is not considered by her to be a possession: she can only be witness to it.

The implication for contemporary catechesis is that participants be given opportunities to explore the implications of the gospel for their own lives. This connection can be made either explicitly; that is through writing, movement, mime, dialogue, debate, project work, or implicitly; e.g. through symbol, movement, music, art, or in prayer. These activities enable participants to articulate the new way of seeing made possible through faith in Jesus.

For true conversion, an *explicit* discerning and naming of what that conversion entails for people's lives in the present can sometimes be necessary. This is best done in a community of dialogue with other people. Reflection on action and coming to decision about how to live out their Christian faith, in dialogue with others, helps students avoid both subjectivism and relativism in moral decision making. The key is that participants be encouraged to examine the implications in what they have learned for the way in which they live their lives.

Conclusion

Catechesis involves any activity that opens people up to the work of the Holy Spirit, who incorporates them into the very life of God, leading them to God through Christ. Understanding the goal of catechesis (discipleship), the nature of faith, and what it means to come to *know* religiously, all enable catechists to choose methods consonant with their goals. The fundamental object of Jesus' mission was the Reign of God and his disciples are those who know how to see and transform reality in the way of Jesus. Faith is an experience of *relating* to God that answers the deepest questions of our hearts, often engendering a new understanding of ourselves and of our experiences. Religious narrative, symbol, gesture and imagery offer people new frames of meaning, new images and new insights. Catechesis enables people to develop the art of using religious language as a means of seeing and responding to their reality in a new way.

Notes

1   For a comprehensive account of these see Richard Reichert, *Renewing Catechetical Ministry*, New York/Mahwah: Paulist Press, 2002, chapter 3. See also Cardinal Avery Dulles, 'The Catechetical Process in the Light of the General Directory for Catechesis' in John Redford (ed.), *Hear O Islands: Theology and Catechesis in the New Millennium*, Dublin: Veritas, 2002.

2   The GDC proposes that 'the pedagogy of God', also reflected in 'the pedagogy of Christ', should be 'the source and model of the pedagogy of faith' (cf. all of GDC, part three, chapter one, nos. 137–147).

3   GDC part 1, nos. 50, 63, 64.

4   Reichert, *Renewing*, p. 20.

5   GDC nos. 29, 59, 68, 90–91. The RCIA (Rite of Christian Initiation of Adults) was officially declared normative for all catechesis in 1972. Note that the RCIA does not recommend a particular approach to catechesis: it is literally a series of liturgical rites. See chapter three for a fuller exploration of the catechumenate as a paradigm for all catechesis.

6   See chapter twenty-one for one such holistic theory of knowing.

7   Reichert, *Renewing*, p. 8.

8   Ibid., pp. 36–39, 43.

9   David Tracy, *Plurality and Ambiguity: Hermeneutics, Religion, Hope*, San Francisco: Harper & Row, 1987, p. 89.

10   Craig R. Dykstra, *Vision and Character: A Christian Educator's Alternative to Kohlberg*, New York: Paulist Press, 1981, p. 76. Dykstra explains how we can become open to the possible transformation of our imagination through revelation. We can receive the gratuitous love of God, the gift of faith and of the Spirit, through the gift of transformative images. This transformation of our imagination is never accomplished by ourselves alone: it is an effect of grace.

11   The core process used by contemporary catechists is supported by key catechetical and Church documents since the Second Vatican Council. It is a creative process of linking peoples' life experiences with Scripture and the Church's Tradition in such a way that they may draw life-giving nourishment from the Christian 'Story' for how they must live their lives in the world. GS nos. 4, 10, 11, 44, 62. AG nos. 11 and 15. This catechetical process is described by the GDC as 'radically inspired by the pedagogy of God, as displayed in Christ … it conducts a pedagogy of signs, where words and deeds, teaching and experience are interlinked.' GDC no. 143. Cf. D2. Woven through the GDC are references to Vatican II's use of 'signs of the times' (nos. 31–32, 39, 108) and 'seeds of the Word' (nos.38, 86, 91, 95, 200) in relation to the 'light of the Gospel' or the 'Word'.

12   Inculturation describes the creative and dynamic encounter between Christian faith and culture. It is the process whereby the gospel penetrates a culture in such a way that members of the culture begin to live and express their Christian faith through the forms of their own culture. For a lengthier explanation of inculturation see A. Hession and P. Kieran, *Children, Catholicism and Religious Education,* Dublin: Veritas, 2005, pp. 245–248.

13   Images of hunger and thirst, satisfaction and refreshment are used in Is 49:10; Is 55:1-3; Is 58:11; Jer 1:25; Amos 8:11f.; Ps 107:5, 9.

14   Michael P. Horan, 'The Participants in Catechesis' in Thomas H. Groome and Michael J. Corso (eds), *Empowering Catechetical Leaders*, Washington: National Catholic Educational Association, 1999, pp. 116–7.

15   Karl Rahner, *Theological Investigations*, Vol. IV, 'Poetry and the Christian,' pp. 357–361.

16   Sofia Cavalletti, *The Religious Potential of the Child*, New York/Ramsey: Paulist Press, 1983, p. 140. For the parables referred to see Mt 13:31-33; Mk 4:26-29.

17   Don E. Saliers, *Worship as Theology*, Nashville: Abingdon Press, 1994, p. 145.

18   Maria Harris offers these terms. The contemplative imagination acts by particularising and seeing the experience or focusing theme in its radical and unrepeatable uniqueness. 'It incorporates the active intensity of the contemplative life, which calls for a totally engaged bodily presence: attending, listening, being-with, and existing fully in the presence of Being'. When we operate by way of the ascetic imagination we exercise restraint, discipline, and a certain tentativeness toward that which is before us. Maria Harris, *Teaching and Religious Imagination*, San Francisco: Harper & Row, 1987, pp. 17 and 21.

19   For an account of the place of critical reflection in catechesis see Thomas H. Groome, *Sharing Faith*, New York: HarperSan Francisco, 1991, chapter seven.

20   Sofia Cavalletti, *Religious Potential*, p. 129.

21   J. M. Soskis, *Metaphor and Religious Language*, Oxford: Claredon Press, 1987, p. 116.

22   For further explanation of the limits of scientific methods of observing, planning and assessment in Religious Education and the place of symbolic play and narrative see Anne Hession, ' Christian Religious Education: Purpose and Process' in Hession and Kieran, *Children, Catholicism and Religious Education*, pp. 171–181.

Further Reading

Berryman, Jerome W., *Godly Play*, Minneapolis: Augsburg Fortress, 1991.

Hession, Anne and Kieran, Patricia, *Children, Catholicism and Religious Education*, Dublin: Veritas, 2005, chapter four.

Pfeifer, Carl J. and Manternach, Janan, 'The Processes of Catechesis', in Thomas H. Groome and Michael J. Corso (eds), *Empowering Catechetical Leaders*, Washington: National Catholic Educational Association, 1999.

Reichert, Richard J., *Renewing Catechetical Ministry: A Future Agenda*, New York/ Mahwah: Paulist Press, 2002.

CHAPTER 18

EARLY CHILDHOOD AND CATHOLIC RELIGIOUS EDUCATION

Maurice Ryan

Catholic religious educators are paying closer attention to the ways of Religious Education with young children. This attention has been encouraged by a flourishing interest in the religious experience of young children among researchers, practitioners and education authorities. Until recent times, young children's religious and spiritual experience was not a subject of much scholarly concern. Now, a more expansive understanding of the life cycle acknowledges that Religious Education begins at least at birth and continues at least until death. This notion has encouraged the study of what happens in the early years and what religious and educational insights might be gleaned from these observations. This new attention has compelled many to see young children as profoundly religious beings. Their language and activities push at the limits of human experience and their experiences in early childhood are formative for the course of a whole life.

Early childhood is generally considered to extend from birth to eight years of age. As we will see, this time is among the richest and most educationally significant in the whole of the life span.

Official Church Policies on Religious Education in Early Childhood
An extensive consideration of catechesis – the nurturing of religious faith – in the early years is provided in the *General Directory for Catechesis*, a document published by the Vatican's Congregation for the Clergy in 1997. The document highlights the reality that catechesis of children is the work of various complementary educational agencies. The authors (GDC 178) identify the following factors that they consider to be universal for Catholic children:

- Infancy and childhood, each understood according to its own peculiarities, are a time of primary socialisation as well as of human and Christian education in the family, the school and the Church. These must then be understood as decisive moments for subsequent stages of faith.

- In accordance with accepted tradition, this is normally the time in which Christian initiation, inaugurated with Baptism, is completed. With the reception of the sacraments, the first organic formation of the child in the faith and his or her introduction into the life of the Church is possible.
- The catechetical process in infancy is eminently educational. It seeks to develop those human resources which provide an anthropological basis for the life of faith: a sense of trust, of freedom, of self-giving, of invocation and of joyful participation. Central aspects of the formation of children are training in prayer and introduction to Sacred Scripture.
- Finally, attention must be devoted to the importance of two vital educational loci: the family and the school. In a certain sense nothing replaces family catechesis, especially for its positive and receptive environment, for the example of adults, and for its first explicit experience and practice of the faith.

This extract identifies a number of significant issues for early childhood religious educators. First is the fundamental importance of early childhood to the person's subsequent human and faith development. Large quantities of time, money and energy will be expended on later educational endeavours that will be largely wasted if the young child has been neglected or mistreated. The document outlines how early childhood is a time of primary socialisation: the care and concern of parents and other carers is formative for later development. All the feeding, clothing, talking, caressing and disciplining are educational. Also formative for their later religious development are the prayers and religious rituals that the child learns in the family circle. Of course, to the extent that this form of Religious Education is neglected, subsequent catechetical formation can be impeded.

The document's authors emphasise an understanding that is fundamental for all official Catholic teaching on education: parents and family are the first and foremost educators of children. The *Catechism of the Catholic Church*, published in 1992, indicates that 'family catechesis precedes, accompanies and enriches other forms of instruction in the faith' (par. 226). The family educates in the multiplicity of life experiences – verbal and non-verbal – that a child experiences. The role of the Catholic school is complementary to and supportive of the family's educational role. The teacher has a distinctive role in the whole education of the child. For young children, the lines between the family and the Catholic school will often be blurred. There is more continuity between the education in the home and that of the school than at any other stage of life. The teacher shares many of the same responsibilities for the young child as parents and families. However there is a pressing need to define clearly the boundaries of those responsibilities. In effect, the teacher's responsibilities should decline, as the child grows older.

One aspect of the education and care of young children that can be noted here is the significance of the relationship between grandparent and grandchild. We should not underestimate the power of a young child sitting quietly with a grandparent or other elder, talking about their lives. This relationship brings together people at either end of the life spectrum. Both have a unique relationship to the young child's parents. Both have much to teach the other about life and its meaning.

Influential Theories and Theorists
Catholic early childhood religious educators draw their ideas and approaches from a range of influential thinkers and practitioners. The work of some of these influential thinkers is described in this section.

Maria Montessori (1870–1952) was a trained physician who worked in the fields of psychiatry, education and anthropology. She believed that each child is born with a unique potential to be revealed and not as a 'blank slate' waiting to be written upon. She believed that the environment exerts a profound influence on the growing child and that it could be continually adapted in order for children to fulfil their greatest potential physically, mentally, emotionally and spiritually. Her convictions led her to argue that a child's imagination is developed through the senses and this base could lead to a creative and life-giving intelligence. In order to encourage and stimulate the child's intelligence, she created materials that children could use to learn by trial and error. Instead of passing on information to the child, a Montessori teacher endeavours to put children in touch with their environment, helps them to make intelligent choices and encourages them to conduct research in a prepared environment.

Sofia Cavalletti was a student of Maria Montessori. She adopted Montessori's use of the symbol of Jesus as the Good Shepherd in her own theory and practice of Religious Education with young children. From the mid-1950s in Rome, Cavalletti began to develop Montessori's ideas into an approach to catechesis for young children that became known as *The Catechesis of the Good Shepherd*. Cavalletti believes that the child possesses a natural spiritual capacity that precedes any religious instruction. She recounts examples of children as young as three, from backgrounds with no perceptible religious influence, who exhibit a 'metaphysical intuition' about God. This experience is embedded in Cavalletti's approach. *The Catechesis of the Good Shepherd* is directed to the needs of the three- to six-year-old child for love, protection, care and the presence of God. Cavalletti emphasises scripture in her approach, especially the gospel parables. A parable is presented without embellishment or additions. Then, the meaning of the parable is explored along with the richness the text contains. Children are then given concrete materials with which to play to help them make meaning. Those materials could be small wooden figures that represent the elements of the text. As the story is re-read, the child moves the figures, telling the parable as they do so. This inner dialogue personalises what has been presented and applies it to the child's own life.

Another theorist in the Montessori tradition is Jerome Berryman, an Anglican priest from Houston, Texas whose best known work is contained in a book entitled, *Godly Play*. Since the early 1970s, Berryman has developed his ideas, resources and strategies in the light of the work of Montessori and Cavalletti. He describes 'Godly Play' as a method of Christian education and spiritual direction primarily for children aged 2–12. The goal is to teach the art of using religious language, parable, sacred story, silence and liturgical action so that children might become more aware of God's presence around them and in their lives. Berryman thinks that if adults can communicate to young children a belief in a benevolent, loving God, the children can develop the ability to face the existential issues they will confront in their lives, such as death, freedom, aloneness and meaninglessness.

A further influential source of research support has come from the Religious Experience Research Unit in Britain who began researching children's spirituality in the 1960s. Their interest in the religious experience of young children began when researchers noted adults' responses to their surveys, such as: 'The most profound experience of my life came to me when I was very young, between four and five years old'; and: 'I just know that the whole of my life has been built on the great truth that was revealed to me then' (at the age of six). Principal researcher Edward Robinson explored these reports further by means of questionnaires and interviews to determine the influence of childhood experiences. In 1977 he published a book titled, *The Original Vision: A Study of the Religious Experience of Childhood*. The title points to the belief that each child has a picture of human existence that is particular to themselves. While they may not remember it after they have lost it, it still provides an image of a world in which all things are in harmony – an original vision.

Instead of seeing religious experience as the preserve of intellectual giants or the especially holy, Robinson reported the ordinary experiences of people that they unquestionably described as religious. In one account, a woman in her fifties remembered an experience that occurred when she was aged five. She sensed in the mist on the moors that everything was tied together and that she was somehow part of the whole. Some people reported childhood experiences that related to church buildings and ceremonies, though no one place or set of experiences or any particular set of words was identified as specific or consistent. Robinson thought that being religious is a condition known to children inclusively, regardless of religion, culture or social background. According to Robinson, adults need not be concerned with instructing children in the beliefs, narratives and practices of a particular tradition. In early childhood, the child's education and Religious Education are not distinguishable. Whatever education is for the young child it is also Religious Education. Later, in more appropriate settings, children's Religious Education needs to afford them an understanding and appreciation of the beliefs, narratives and practices of a particular tradition.

The tradition established by Edward Robinson and his team has been continued and amplified in the work of two British researchers, David Hay and Rebecca Nye, who established the Children's Spirituality Project at the University of Nottingham. They published the results of their extensive research into children's spiritual dispositions in a book titled, *The Spirit of the Child*. Nye and Hay claim that, in spite of a decline of formal religion in the United Kingdom, spiritual experience is widespread among a large proportion of the population. Their work supports Edward Robinson's contention that spiritual awareness is a natural human disposition. The spiritual potential of each child is independent of cultural context, but the culture can obscure or amplify this potential.

The theories of James Fowler on stages of faith have been important for many early-years' religious educators. Fowler followed the structural-developmental theories of Jean Piaget, Lawrence Kohlberg and Erik Erikson, who argued that the human mind has certain formal structures within which development occurs under the influence of the social environment. Movement from stage-to-stage is dependent on successful achievement of the tasks of the previous stage. Fowler theorised that a person's faith developed in a similar way, according to a series of fixed, sequenced stages. Faith, for Fowler, is a human universal that, though variously expressed, is concerned with each person's relationship to an ultimate environment, which many name as God. Fowler argued that a person's faith develops in six fixed, hierarchically ordered stages. Later, Fowler described in greater detail a pre-stage of faith that exists in very young children, effectively constituting seven stages in the development of faith. The early stages of development in faith are characterised by play, fairy tales, myths and stories. The young child is immersed in mystery, spontaneous expression and the great cosmic struggles between the forces of good and evil.

One insight that has emerged from studying young children's religious development is the very notion of human development itself. Many researchers have noticed how the process of human development involves, not so much a set of onward and upward steps, but rather a process of circling back to re-encounter 'the puzzles of childhood' – those experiences, questions or insights that occurred early in life and whose meaning is processed through the maturing phases of a person's life. What happens to young children, then, significantly affects the images of life and death that they carry forever.

Issues and Directions in Early Childhood Religious Education
Researchers and practitioners in early childhood Religious Education are engaged in a series of lively discussions about the ways and means of Religious Education of young children.

Story and storytelling is a significant part of the work of early childhood religious educators. In stories, young children find ways to order their own experience and construct their own reality. Stories are a way of knowing. Stories invite children to enter a world not their own. They also ground children in their heritage and encourage them – albeit at a preliminary stage that will be amplified over the course of a lifetime – to ponder questions about meaning and significance. Stories introduce young children to metaphorical language. Metaphors help humans to transcend ordinary experience. They push us to consider possibilities beyond the ones we already know. Metaphors are nurtured in religious communities (sheep and shepherds, landowners and workers, God as father etc.). They help religious people to speak an ordinary language that points to extraordinary possibilities. For young children, the ideas of people such as Sofia Cavalletti and Jerome Berryman show us some of the ways to teach parables and other stories using concrete materials and personal experience.

Catholic early-childhood religious educators take a strong interest in how young Catholics can be included in the Church's prayer and liturgical practices. As young children develop they are able to participate in the rituals and practices of religious communities. These discussions include consideration of issues such as how best to include young children in the community's Eucharistic celebrations. Should young children be removed from the assembly during the celebration to engage in their own ritual celebration, or should they participate along with the whole congregation? Some religious educators think that infants and young children should be present and participate in the whole liturgical assembly, and should not be excluded for part or all of the time. If they make some noise or become distracted then all present are reminded of what life is like sometimes. Related to these issues is the timing and placement of sacramental preparation, especially first Eucharist and Penance. These issues form the basis for ongoing discussions among religious educators.

Religious educators engage in a wide range of lively discussions concerning the educational forms most appropriate for young children and their ideas and practices are shaped by all the major theorists in early-childhood education. For religious educators working in schools, some productive dilemmas are often encountered. One professional tension is between those who favour a play-based approach to schooling for young children that allows for open exploration of materials and experiences appropriate to their stage of development, and those who argue for an approach more in line with unit or thematic studies similar to the curriculum offered to students in higher grades. Key theorists in these discussions include the Russian psychologist, Lev Vygotsky, who argued for the importance of young children's play. He believed that through play, young children develop abstract meanings that enable them to separate from objects in the world. Also influential is Jerome Bruner, the United States psychologist, who taught that even very young children could learn anything as long as the teaching is organised appropriately, and Jean Piaget, the Swiss structural-developmentalist, who disagreed and argued that children developed through fixed, sequential stages that structured how they learned and what they learned. The approach to early-years education pioneered in the Italian town of Reggio Emilia is also increasing in popularity. This approach strives to create an atmosphere of community and collaboration among the adults and young children in early childhood settings. In Reggio Emilia, children are understood as producers, not consumers. Young children are encouraged to embark on projects and investigations in real life contexts. They create material representations of their own understandings using varied media – drawing, sculpture, stories and puppets.

Some general educational discussions have a distinctively religious dimension. For example, how do Catholic schools ensure that they are not an unwitting means of indoctrination, imposing beliefs on children too young to resist? The issue of schooling in general, and Religious Education in particular, is governed by quite complex notions of rights and responsibilities, liberty and authority; as well as our conceptions of care and abandonment. The Religious Education of young children can be a helpful test case for Religious Education for all people, regardless of age. Early childhood educators working in Catholic schools need to strike a careful balance in order not to interfere with the growing abilities of the young child. Church officials have long argued for a distinction between *proposing and imposing* – the one obligatory on the part of the school; the other undesirable and an impediment to faith. The Catholic school has a responsibility to offer its particular perspective on religion, but should never impose or demand students' assent to that religious perspective. How best to achieve this balance in early-childhood Religious Education is the subject of ongoing discussion.

Further Reading

Berryman, Jerome, *Godly Play: A Way of Religious Education*, San Francisco: HarperCollins, 1991.

Cavalletti, Sofia, *The Religious Potential of the Child: Experiencing Scripture and Liturgy with Young Children*, Chicago: Liturgy Training Publications, 1992.

Grajczonek, Jan & Ryan, Maurice (eds), *Religious Education in Early Childhood: A Reader*, Brisbane, Lumino Press, 2007.

Hay, David & Nye, Rebecca, *The Spirit of the Child*, London: Jessica Kingsley Publishers, 2006.

Mercer, Joyce *Welcoming Children: A Practical Theology of Childhood*, St. Louis: Chalice Press, 2005.

CHAPTER 19

HANDS UP IN THE AIR: CREATIVE PRAYER WITH CHILDREN

Ed Hone and Roisín Coll

Introduction

Classroom and Assembly prayer play a vital role in the life of the Catholic school. Where children and teachers work together and recreate together, it is only appropriate that they pray together too. In a Catholic school context prayer is not viewed as a duty but as a natural expression of what it means to be Catholic Christians. The disciples said to Jesus *'Lord, teach us how to pray'* (Lk 11:1) and he readily taught them.

Preparing classroom prayer can be both challenging and immensely rewarding. As a teacher engaging in prayer with children you need: to believe in the value of what you are doing; time to plan and rehearse; lots of energy, enthusiasm and a good dose of imagination. The task, however, need not be daunting. The key is, as always, working *with* children, not for them. When you work in this way you engage the children so that the prayer becomes *their* prayer and their minds and hearts are raised to God. Whilst the context here is school, for creative prayer, the same principles and practice apply in all environments where people work with children in prayer.

What is Liturgy?

The word 'liturgy' comes from the Greek *leitourgos* and literally means 'the work (*ergos*) of the people (*leito*)'. When people come to worship God together this prayer is called liturgy. When we speak of liturgy in school, we are not talking about the official Liturgy of the Church (The Mass, the Divine Office, the celebration of the Sacraments) rather we mean praying together by using words, silence, signs and symbols. This kind of prayer is also referred to as 'para-liturgy', that is, unofficial collective prayer.

Liturgy is about God, and liturgy is about us. We bring our lives to God when we worship and the spiritual strength and inspiration we receive we take back into our lives. Our liturgy gives God praise and gives us life. This is true for adults and children alike. The school classroom, with its community and its routine, is a good place for liturgy. In our classroom prayer and assemblies we bring this community and routine to God. God blesses us, hears our prayer, and helps us with our daily work.

Liturgy and Community
Liturgy is the prayer of a community and really belongs in community. It is something we do together, where we open ourselves to each other and to God. In liturgy we share our hopes and fears, we pray for ourselves, each other and our world and we thank God for everything God does for us. In classroom and assembly prayer, we usually pray in the plural – 'God, hear *our* prayer', 'Lord hear *us*' rather than as individuals – 'God, hear *my* prayer', 'Lord, hear *me*'. God is at the heart of our community, so it is only right that we should pray and when we pray we are helped to live our lives more fully. The gospels tell us 'Where two or three meet in my name, I am there among them' (Mt 18:20). Our prayer together makes us more sensitive to each other's needs, more aware of our own need of God's help, more willing to face the problems of life, knowing that we are not alone. The community is with us and God is with us. If we think of the Mass, the first words we say match the first gesture we make: the Sign of the Cross. We are acknowledging that we are in God's presence. At the end of the Mass, however, the emphasis is different: 'The Mass is ended, go in peace' or 'Let us go in peace to love and serve the Lord'. The emphasis here is on going out into the world, carrying with us something of what we have received. In short, liturgy takes us from our encounter with God into our full engagement in life.

Where Liturgy Takes Place and Why it is Important in the School
Prayer and liturgical celebrations are central to the life of a Catholic school and it is recognised in the official teaching of the Church that the Catholic teacher has a responsibility to help children engage with God.

> The teacher will assist students to open their hearts in confidence to Father, Son, and Holy Spirit through personal and liturgical prayer.[1]

If there is adequate provision for prayer, it is during this time that God can communicate directly with children and they have the opportunity to respond fully in adoration and praise, in thanksgiving and in petition. In order to maximise the impact of any prayer experience for children, time should be set aside that is neither rushed nor seen to be simply an add-on to the day.

If we want to sustain a relationship with anyone, we must spend time with that person. We must try to find the way in which we can best *communicate* with each other. Likewise, with God, if we want to help children to relate to God, we need to help them to become aware that God is present in their lives. We also need to help them communicate with God: to be able to talk to God in prayer and to be able to listen to God speaking to them in the silence of their own heart (emphasis added).[2]

Traditionally, prayers are said at the beginning and end of the school day, as well as before and after lunch. However there are many other openings that provide children with liturgical and prayer experiences throughout the school week. In both the primary and secondary school, assemblies provide opportunities for children and students to participate in active and creative communication with God. The effectiveness of assemblies is inevitably reduced where the teacher or someone in senior management takes sole responsibility for writing the material and instructing the children in what to say and do. Using the *children* as the chief means of resource enables material for assemblies to be created by working together, sharing ideas and tapping into the children's own prayer experience and culture. Ultimately, children should have ownership of their prayer time. They will then be sharing their own faith with their peers in a way that will be understood and sympathetically received.

Having ownership of the liturgy is vital for two reasons. Firstly, if children are directly involved in the preparation of the prayer, then the opportunity for *catechesis* is present. The teacher can work with the children as they plan the prayer while directing, informing and explaining to them the relevance of their work. Catechesis can take place not only through the prayer itself but through its preparation. Secondly, ownership is important because it enhances the *experience* of worship. If the children have been involved in its planning and implementation, then their understanding of it, engagement with it, and response to it, will be strengthened. When children present an assembly or engage in classroom liturgy they have ownership of what they do, they are more committed to the project, more energised, and consequently communicate more effectively. All who participate in the prayer will gain more from the experience.

What Liturgy (and Preparation for Liturgy) Can Achieve
It is worth repeating that in classroom and assembly prayer, the *process* of producing liturgy is as important as the end result. There is a world of difference between the teacher giving the class a script for classroom prayer, and the children being encouraged to generate a prayer themselves. Pupil and teacher creativity is vital. However the teacher must be a realist and should be aware of what classroom and assembly prayer can achieve. It is important to consider age and ability differentiation. For example, it is impractical to think that young children could engage in meditation for long periods of time or even compose elaborate prayers. Furthermore each prayer time should have a particular aim. For example, a liturgy on the theme of friendship could have the aim of encouraging the children to be kind to others as Jesus is kind to us.

EXPLORING RELIGIOUS EDUCATION

Below are outlined some of the positive effects of creative prayer with children in the classroom:

- Classroom prayer can bring the class together, uniting teacher and children more closely
- Prayer can help those who take part to reflect more deeply on life, giving them a new understanding of something which concerns them
- Prayer can help children to give voice to their longings and hopes (and, of course, their fears and concerns)
- Prayer can instruct, painlessly catechising children whose knowledge of faith grows through engagement in liturgy
- Prayer can motivate, giving a new determination to a class, so it might then wish to actually do something practical after having been inspired in prayer
- Lest we forget, classroom prayer can entertain – it is not always solemn and worthy – God enjoys humour too!

Knowing what you want the prayer to achieve is vitally important. We all know the impracticality of engaging children in an action song, for example, and then trying to calm them down to do some serious work!

Classrooms are often such busy places that it should not be surprising to discover that silence can play an important part in classroom prayer (though it is harder to achieve in an assembly situation). Careful attention must therefore be paid to the effective creation of silence. Reflective music, simple chants (e.g. Taizé), a gently paced liturgy – all help in the *creation* of silence. Silence is shaped by what surrounds it, what comes before it and what follows it. The silence you create in the classroom may be solemn, joyful, expectant, grateful, sorrowful, even exuberant – depending on how it is created.

To Whom Do We Pray?
Consciously or not, when we pray we have some kind of image or understanding of God in our mind. God might be the judge we have to appease, the friend with whom we can be ourselves, the mother who nurtures us and makes us feel safe, the father who loves us (or of whom we are afraid). Many images of God are evident in our prayer. Classroom prayer can reinforce or challenge these images, promoting an image of God who is merciful, forgiving, understanding: a God of light, life, peace and hope. The nearness of God in Jesus can be communicated, as well as the otherness and majesty of the Father and the restless inspiration of the Holy Spirit. Trinitarian prayer will become natural to children and the image of God they form in their school prayer may well be the image that stays with them throughout the rest of their lives. The God to whom we pray is influential in the life we lead.

At the most basic level, how we think of God is shaped in the representations that we use. For instance in prayer a teacher might use traditional representations of Christ like a crucifix, a Sacred Heart image; Holman Hunt's painting of Jesus as Light of the World, the Good Shepherd, or the Infant of Prague – each containing nuanced messages about who Jesus is. In the religious art of different cultures, Jesus is represented in a variety of ways that express aspects of these cultures. For example, Eastern European icons often show Jesus as an enthroned Byzantine emperor; South American depictions of Jesus often emphasis his simplicity and closeness to the oppressed poor whom he leads to freedom.

At the next level teachers might focus on the words we use in song and in prayer – and explore with children the different images of God that they portray. The formality or informality of our approach to God is significant (and it may vary from occasion to occasion). Finally the kinds of things we say to God and ask of God are significant. If we call God 'Creator of heaven and earth' we evoke God's power and might whereas if we call God 'Father of the poor' we evoke God's care for the disadvantaged – all in a title! The teacher must be conscious in preparing liturgy with children which image of God is being evoked.

Seasons, People and the World – Keeping Classroom Prayer Real
When children come to school they bring their home concerns with them. Their busy minds are full of ideas and their concerns can range from family to pets, friends and games. In class it can be quite a challenge to help them to focus on work or on prayer. It helps their concentration when the prayer is real. By 'real' we mean if prayer emanates *from* their concerns and expresses these concerns then it is truly *their* prayer to God. For example;

> Dear God,
> Sometimes I worry about not making friends at swimming. Please help me not to worry. Sometimes I worry about my little cousin Aidan because he was in hospital for a long time after he was born.
> Please help him.
> Sometimes I worry about my Granny because she is quite old.
> Please help her.
> Please help me with all my worries.
> Thank you God.
> Amen.
> (Girl – Aged 8)

Three ways of keeping classroom and assembly prayer real are:

- praying the *seasons* of the year and of the Church
- praying for the *people* and relationships which make up their daily lives
- praying for the *world*, that is, the world beyond their own immediate experience, whether it be on another street or indeed continent.

Praying the seasons is relatively simple. It involves observing nature and bringing nature into the classroom through flowers, leaves, berries, fruits, bare branches etc. Advent, Christmas, Lent and Easter have their own rich symbolism that can be represented in the classroom, along with the colours associated with the liturgical cycle (e.g. Purple for Advent, White for Christmas etc.). The whole appearance of the classroom can be changed in a way that evokes the season and affects the tone of the prayer. When the visual appearance of the prayer space is combined with appropriate music, seasonal words and liturgical actions, the resulting prayer can be very powerful.

When praying for people, the teacher's first exercise should be a listening one. What is of significance to the children? Who are the people who are important to them? Is someone ill or has someone died? Is there a new member of the family on the way? Have there been new friendships, fallings-out, or new playground groups? Teachers need to be attentive to the people in a child's prayer. The child might open up in the reflective, prayerful environment in a way that they might not do at other times. A child might begin to cry whilst praying for someone thereby indicating a level of emotion of which the teacher should be aware. If this happens the teacher will then comfort the child without drawing undue attention and then follow up, as soon as the prayer is finished, by chatting with the child and providing appropriate support. It is healthy to balance prayers of intercession or asking for something with prayers of thanksgiving, so children do not just focus on asking God to help people in prayer, but also give thanks for the people who make up their lives.

In praying for the world, children become more aware of the needs of others and they also exercise generosity and openness by allowing themselves to be affected by the plight of people they have never met. In such a process prayer can enhance their awareness of their global citizenship. A sense of common humanity is encouraged and co-responsibility becomes their second nature. Here thanksgiving is important as well as praise to God, the Lord of all creation.

The Creative Process
So how does a teacher go about this process? How can this kind of positive, creative and also engaging liturgy come about? There are a few key principles:

1. *Involve the children from the start.* Invite children to work with you from the start when preparing classroom prayer or school assemblies. Let them know that this will be something that will involve teamwork, where ideas will be shared and worked on together. At the very beginning ensure that the liturgy will be relevant to them by including them when deciding on the theme of the prayer. Quite often this discussion is very revealing as children share the issues that currently affect them and their community.

2. *Be rooted in Scripture.* Liturgy provides the opportunity to communicate effectively with God. It is a two-way conversation so listening to God's Word as well as listening to each other should be at the heart of the prayer. Let scripture be at the centre of your Liturgy. This can be done in two ways:

    • Children can choose a theme for their prayer and then, with the help of their teacher, consider a suitable Scripture reading as the basis from which to work
    • Choose a Scripture passage from the outset and then from this, the theme and subsequent ideas will emerge.

    In choosing appropriate Scripture passages with children, the gospels are often the most suitable to work with, especially gospel narratives and stories. In working with the Old Testament, stories are the most accessible parts to include in liturgy. For example, if children choose forgiveness as a theme for their prayer, the teacher could then suggest various suitable scriptural passages from which the children could choose, such as the story of the Prodigal Son (Lk 15:11-32), the Repentant Thief (Lk 23:41-43), or the Lost Sheep (Lk 15:4-7).

3. *Respect Tradition.* Children have great ideas (which sometimes need careful monitoring!) and using them to communicate the theme can be exciting and worthwhile. However, it is also important to respect tradition and to recognise appropriate opportunities to include well-known Church prayers and hymns. It is important for children to recognise, learn and understand traditional prayers and to appreciate that inclusion of them in a liturgy, alongside more creative and imaginative ways of praying, can add to the prayer experience.

4. *Keep focused.* Have one scriptural message or theme that the prayer develops. It is sometimes helpful to have a phrase which reinforces the theme, repeated throughout the prayer and this can be done in a variety of ways (said aloud, chanted, or written on a banner etc.). For example,

working again with the theme of forgiveness, the phrase 'God forgives us, so we forgive each other' could punctuate the liturgy at appropriate points. This means that the children ministering the prayer, and all those who take part, are likely to leave the liturgy with the message clearly in mind.

5. *Appealing to the senses.* When prayer consists only of words, it easily becomes a mental exercise, engaging only the mind. Children in class or assembly are prone to losing concentration, so the more they are engaged, the longer they are likely to remain involved. Appealing to the different senses in liturgy has a long history and involves such things as candles, bells, movement, incense, visual images, bread, wine, oil, music, and rosary beads – and there is no reason this tradition cannot be built on in the school situation. Ensure that you build into each prayer-preparation session the question, 'how can we enhance this prayer by appealing to the senses?' Then watch the result! Returning to the theme of forgiveness, children might be invited to wash each other's hands, or place a pebble at the foot of a cross, symbolising offering their sins to God for forgiveness.

6. *Don't be scared.* While appropriateness is important, do not hold back. If the children are being creative in their suggestions, then try them out. God speaks to us though the work we do, and even if some of the preparatory work for the liturgy is not used, the process of involving the children and participating in such work – based on the Word of God – is significant in itself.

Conclusion

Creative prayer with children is as much about the process as the final result. Creative prayer helps children 'own' their prayer. It can draw children closer to God and to each other. It can strengthen them for everyday life while nourishing spiritual life and encouraging spiritual growth. Creative prayer challenges adults to new ways of thinking about God and approaching God. Finally and most importantly, it can form the children in a mature faith, focused on God and in touch with their real lives so that they become at the same time full citizens of this world and of the Kingdom of God.

Notes

1   Sacred Congregation for Catholic Education, *The Religious Dimension of Education in a Catholic School*, London, CTS, 1988, par. 83.

2   C. Maloney, F. O'Connell and B. O'Reilly, *Alive-O 7 Teachers' Book*, Dublin: Veritas, 2003, p. 21.

CHAPTER 20

VOICES FROM THE CATHOLIC PRIMARY SCHOOL CLASSROOM

Fiona Dineen

Practising Catholic Religious Education in an Irish primary school today is a challenging yet rewarding task. As a consequence of the economic, social and cultural development that Ireland has undergone in recent decades, the primary classroom context has changed immensely. This is particularly noticeable in the area of Religious Education, as it appears that more and more people in Ireland are disengaged from their faith. As a practising primary teacher, I witness first hand the tendency to address the child's intellectual, social and material needs while neglecting the spiritual dimension of their lives. While this tendency is evident in the wider society it also impacts significantly on the Catholic school where parents often want their children to be brought up in the Catholic faith family while struggling to practice the faith themselves. In the Catholic primary school, both parents and children are very much aware of the importance of the sacraments. In Ireland, primary school children normally receive the sacraments in Second (age 7–8) and Sixth class (age 11–12). In the course of these years of sacramental preparation, parents cooperate closely with the school in the Religious Education of their children. However, apart from these two years, there is a noticeable decline of parental involvement in the children's Religious Education. This inconsistency can sometimes create a fragmented approach towards Religious Education in the primary school and make it more difficult to establish effective home-school-parish links. While this is just one example of the many challenges faced by the contemporary primary school teacher, it does not imply that Religious Education in the Irish Catholic primary school is ineffective. Rather it suggests that the teacher can play a pivotal role in stimulating the faith development of the child.

I began my teaching career in a Catholic primary school in Limerick City. The inner city school where I teach has an enrolment of over two hundred and twenty students. The children come from a variety of social backgrounds with the majority coming from a socially disadvantaged area of the city and some from middle class homes. In recent years there has been a growing number of international children attending the school. I have always had a positive attitude towards teaching Religious Education and I did not feel daunted by it as some teachers do. This is partly due to my involvement in my parish church from a young age. I have been a member of a parish choir since my own days in primary school and I am currently responsible for organising and preparing the music for various liturgical ceremonies during the Church year. This parish involvement was advantageous as it familiarised me with the primary school programme and gave me first hand experience of different approaches to liturgies and prayer before I embarked on my teaching career.

My initial teaching post was with First Class. From the outset, the children's positive dispositions towards Religious Education surprised me. I had certain expectations that the children would be unfavourably disposed to religion, as I had no way of knowing what their prior experience of it would be. I was unsure as to whether they prayed or attended mass regularly or indeed to what extent their parents actively encouraged their faith. It concerned me that school and home might give the children contradictory messages. However I discovered quickly that these children were not indifferent or hostile to religion! If anything, they demonstrated a unique sense of spirituality and an awareness of God in their lives. They were very responsive in religion class and enjoyed talking about God. They were always conscious of keeping our classroom sacred space, or May altar, a well-decorated area of reverence. Once the summer months beckon, it is a regular occurrence in the school for the younger children to make daisy chains while on break to adorn the statue of Our Lady on the altar. This is just one small example of how the children show an awareness of God's presence around them.

Diocesan Advisor
One of the most significant events from my first year of teaching was the visit of the Diocesan Advisor. As it was my first experience of such a visit I had a sense of apprehension about the impending 'inspection'. I reviewed and revised *Alive-O* stories, songs and prayers in a frenzied manner. I was uncertain as to whether the children would remember the stories while also having some understanding of their significance. The music of the programme was a great aid in this task and it is definitely one of the strongest elements of Ireland's National Catechetical Programme.

When the Advisor finally arrived it was not the daunting ordeal I had dreaded. The doubts I had about the children's ability to recall their stories and songs was quickly dispelled. The sense of foreboding I felt about the visit was probably due to my own days in primary school where the Diocesan Examiner's (as it was then called) visit was a formal and somewhat frightening affair. After my first experience of a Diocesan Advisor's visit I realised it was not an event focused on 'inspecting' the teaching of Religious Education but rather on recognising the children's talent in the area of Religious Education as well as supporting and advising the teacher in delivering the programme and nurturing the religious ethos of the school. The children are always delighted to display and share their stories and journals with someone other than their teacher. They have a sense of pride in their work and enjoy the opportunity to talk and learn about God.

I realised that the visit of the Diocesan Advisor is not only important for the children but also for the teacher. For teachers, some kind of supportive assessment is critical in itself. Assessment is an intrinsic part of learning in all other areas of the curriculum so if Religious Education is part of the primary school curriculum it seems reasonable that it should also be assessed. I believe that Religious Education may appear to some to have a marginal or secondary status in the Irish primary school context because to date the Department of Education and Science (DES) has not prescribed any curriculum content or any form of assessment for it. In a rapidly changing society, where religion is no longer a social or personal priority for many, it is reasonable to postulate that the status of the subject area can be undermined by this lack of DES curriculum content and formal assessment. The fact that society seems less concerned about religion has in turn made an impact on teacher attitudes. Sometimes teachers feel uncomfortable about the subject and lack confidence in the area of Religious Education because religion does not play a major role in their own lives. Some teachers fear that they will not know the answers to biblical questions or questions on Church teaching that the children will ask them. In such a context the visit of the Diocesan Advisor can prioritise Religious Education while providing a support to the teacher and practical advice for the future growth of the subject area in the school. In an already crowded primary curriculum, teachers are at least aware that their work in Religious Education is vital and appreciated.

Sacramental Preparation
For the past number of years I have been preparing Second Class children for the sacraments of First Penance and First Eucharist. I enjoy this task immensely. From the beginning of Second Class everyone (children, parents and teacher) shares a sense of excitement about this special year. It involves working closely with the parents, as they are actively involved throughout the year in the preparation of the children for the sacraments. It is rewarding to receive such support from the home and it creates a positive bond between home, school and parish.

The children's enthusiasm for First Penance and especially First Eucharist comes predominantly from the home by way of parents or guardians, grandparents, older siblings and cousins. While children display some knowledge of the religious significance of the sacraments, they are sometimes preoccupied with the material and social expression of First Eucharist. Of course in some instances the focus tends to shift to the children's attire for the day, the party afterwards and of course, how much money they will make. Lessons on First Eucharist often sidetrack into conversations about dresses, suits and hair trials but the teacher can prompt the children beyond this to a deeper understanding of the sacrament.

Indeed the teacher's constant challenge is to focus on the foundational religious and spiritual significance of the Eucharist. Now the structure of the *Do This in Memory* programme in Second class is effective in progressing the children on their faith journey and changing the focus of the sacramental occasion from the monetary and material trappings to the significance of listening to the word of God, receiving Jesus in the bread of life and celebrating with the Christian family. The year begins with a meeting with parents followed by the children's enrolment ceremony, regular masses, and finally the reception of the sacraments of First Penance and First Eucharist.

In my school, a meeting takes place early in the school year where the teacher gets to know the parents. The parish priest and principal also attend this meeting. One of the fundamental aims of the meeting is to welcome parents, to highlight to them the importance of this momentous year for their child and the positive role they, as parents, can play in the faith development of their children's lives. They are told how the children are prepared for the sacraments in school and how they can work collaboratively with the school in their children's faith formation at home. To conclude the meeting each parent is given a prayer pack to use at home with his or her child. The effectiveness of this pack is evident year-after-year. It is encouraging to hear the children regularly boast of their special pack that they use at home with Mum or Dad, guardian or grandparent.

Before the children make their First Eucharist, they receive the Sacrament of Penance. This sacrament is often overshadowed by the pomp and ceremony of the First Eucharist. It is interesting to note that the children approach this sacrament with a different mindset. Some display anxiety concerning the occasion. They take the preparation seriously and at times can be quite inhibited about eventually having to acknowledge their shortcomings to the priest. On the night of First Penance there is always a serenely reverent atmosphere in the Church. One can sense the apprehension from the children and sometimes even the parents. Having made their First Penance many children comment on how much better they feel in school the following day. This 'feeling better' may be linked to any anxiety they felt regarding the occasion – having to share the times when they did not live as Jesus asked them to. However the teacher constantly emphasises that the whole ritual focuses on receiving the love and unconditional forgiveness of God and celebrating that love with their faith family.

The preparations for First Eucharist begin in earnest once the children receive the Sacrament of Penance. The preparation for the ceremony takes many weeks. I try to ensure that the ceremony changes each year to reflect the lives and talent of each particular class that I teach. It makes the celebration of the sacrament more meaningful for the children if they are intimately involved in the liturgy through displays of their artwork, selection and singing of their favourite songs, participation in liturgical dance and readings as well as witnessing their parents' involvement. All of these elements make the ceremony special for the children. They enjoy taking part and being active in the liturgy. When the children are actively involved in a liturgical ceremony, they are experiencing and gaining an understanding of a lived religion. This has a great impact on the child at a variety of levels, from the physical and cognitive to the affective, moral and spiritual. To foster the child's experience of God and others through prayer and liturgy is one of the fundamental aims of the National Catechetical Programme and so preparation for and participation in the sacraments is a valuable teaching and learning experience.

As the communion day approaches more organisational aspects tend to come to the fore. There is a flurry of activity trying to get each child to remember the formalities of where to sit, stand, and genuflect. At these times, when the organisation begins to get frenzied, I often stop, reflect and ask myself whether I am keeping sight of the true meaning of the day. I must be careful that these organisational aspects do not overshadow my task of preparing the children to welcome Jesus into their lives and to celebrate his love for them.

On the First Communion Day, there is always much hustle and bustle outside the Church. The excitement about this anticipated day is very evident. The children spend some time admiring their peers but are always anxious to begin the ceremony. They do realise that this is a momentous day and that it is not only about getting dressed up and having a big party but more importantly, about meeting Jesus in a special way for the first time. The children feel honoured to be taking part in the ceremony, especially receiving the Body of Christ.

In my experience of sacramental preparation, we often underestimate the role of significant adults in the life of the child. Children learn by example from older adults around them. The teacher obviously has an important role in the education of every child he or she teaches, but this is particularly evident in the teaching of Religious Education. The teacher tries to make links between life as experienced in home, school and parish.

The School Ethos

One way in which Religious Education can become especially meaningful to the child is if it is reinforced by the ethos or characteristic spirit of the school. The ethos of the school is of paramount importance. For instance, the Mercy Sisters founded the school in which I am currently working. At an immediate level, as soon as one steps inside the door, the symbols of the ethos are evident. There is the school name, statues, religious icons, a school uniform bearing a religious emblem and an altar bearing the colours of the liturgical year. Throughout the year, various events in the Church calendar (e.g. All Saints, All Soul's, Advent, St. Brigid's Day, St. Patrick's Day, Lent, Easter, Pentecost) are celebrated and honoured. At a deeper level the ethos is manifest in many intangible elements of school life. This includes the relationships between all who share the teaching and learning environment, the school garden and outreach programmes, as well as the school policies.

It is important that the school celebrates many events on the liturgical calendar as a school community, because it makes the children aware that faith is a living gift that spreads beyond the four walls of the classroom. Children have much to learn not just from attending these liturgies and assemblies, but from participating in them also. Primary school children enjoy a hands-on approach in all curricular areas and Religious Education is no different. While conventional ways of participating include singing, readings and prayers, it is beneficial for the teacher to be creative with liturgies by including elements such as movement to music, bible processions and dance and drama, which make liturgies more accessible and enjoyable for the children. It is vital to remember that the teacher in the Catholic school is invited to nourish and create space for their own faith life and for their own faith development. *Alive-O's* notes for the teacher addresses this need in a preliminary manner. Teachers themselves are on a faith journey and may struggle with the tasks of sacramental preparation and liturgical celebration. Increasing support and in-service is crucial for teachers in Catholic schools as they face the challenges of Religious Education in a religiously and culturally diverse society.

Conclusion

Teaching Religious Education in a Catholic school is challenging but highly rewarding. A teacher has the potential to be a very significant person in the faith formation of children. In my experience, primary school children have an open and positive disposition towards Religious Education. Teachers can do much to promote the Catholic ethos of the school in a way that is creative and relevant to the child. If a teacher has a positive attitude to faith formation and sacramental preparation in the primary school, and is open to working in tandem with parents and parish, the religious life of the child will flourish.

CHAPTER 21

THE ACT OF JUDGEMENT IN RELIGIOUS EDUCATION: LIGHT FROM NEWMAN, LONERGAN, GIUSSANI AND GROOME

Raymond Topley

The need for verification manifests itself surprisingly early on in the life of the human being. Many a parent, on reading bedtime stories to children or in telling them something interesting and new, has noticed the look of surprise and the subsequent enquiring, 'Is it true?'; 'Is it real?' This chapter invites reflection on the necessity of this act of verification and on the desirability of including it in catechetical activity and methodology from an early age. It will also contend that an approach to Religious Education which does not systematically make room for such activity of judgement is incomplete and, consequently, inadequate. In support of this assertion, 'four contributors' will be drawn into the discussion and their respective positions explored. Two of the contributors have had an explicit involvement in education, namely Luigi Giussani in Italy and Thomas Groome in North America. The contributions of the other two, John Henry Newman and Bernard Lonergan, are epistemologically foundational in nature and more educationally implicit than explicit. Each of these four figures or witnesses are dealt with individually under the headings of contextual anecdote, contribution in respect of judgement, and concluding comment.

Luigi Giussani (1922–2005)

THE RIMINI TRAIN JOURNEY

Fr Luigi Giussani is the inspirational figure who gave rise to the lay movement known as *Communion and Liberation*. In 1954, when on a train journey to Rimini, he found himself in conversation with a group of teenage boys. The encounter convinced him that they knew little or nothing about their Christian faith and this observation shocked him into action. Soon afterwards he dramatically resigned his lecturing position at the local seminary and joined the teaching staff of Berchet High School in Milan. There, over the following ten years, he developed his own distinctive approach to teaching religion, which he himself described as, 'A True Method'.[1]

CONTRIBUTION: 'A TRUE METHOD'
At the heart of Giussani's methodology is an insistence that only a form of Religious Education that is essentially critical will suffice to prepare young people to meet the ravages and challenges of a culture which would put to the test whatever religious sensibility they might have from their childhood. 'We insist,' he declares, 'an education must be critical.' There are three elements in his system.

FIRST ELEMENT: HANDING ON THE TRADITION
On the day he ascended the steps of the school for the first time, Giussani kept repeating to himself: 'I am coming here to give these young people what was given to me.'[2] What he was referring to, in this instance, was the Christian tradition and this, precisely, is what he was taking into the classroom with him. He believed it was important for the learners to be aware of their own tradition, which they then had to encounter personally through questioning and reflection.

SECOND ELEMENT: HONOURING EXPERIENCE
However, despite his belief in the centrality of the tradition, Giussani did not see it as being necessarily the starting point of his methodology. Experience was to occupy that position. In his view, the experience of those sitting before him in the classroom was all-important. To arrive at and unearth this experience, the students had to learn how to enter within themselves and locate the God-given longings of their human hearts, such as the desire for happiness, truth, justice, beauty and total meaning. This, according to Giussani, is what constitutes each individual's religious sense. What was located there would provide the yardstick or touchstone against which all hypotheses of meaning would have to be measured. And one such hypothesis of meaning was the Christian tradition itself. This, in its turn, would have to submit to being judged against and by the desires of each student's heart. In such a manner a personal appropriation of the Christian faith ensues.

THIRD ELEMENT: MAKING A JUDGEMENT
Giussani's 'True Method' now required that a judgement be made:

> From my very first day as a teacher, I've always offered these words to my class: 'I'm here to teach you a true method that you can use to judge the things I will tell you.'[3]

Here, Giussani discloses his intention of submitting to the judgement of the learners whatever was presented to them by teachers and by life in its totality.

Giussani's approach is quite a demanding one. The students are expected to test vigorously every hypothesis of meaning presented, including the Christian one. This critical participation is the essential element of the process. Reasons have to be given in support of positions taken. The whole process moves relentlessly towards the making of a judgement, a judgement as to the truth of any situation or topic discussed. Such judgements are the prelude to deciding how Christianity ought to be lived in today's world. Giussani, looking at the overall approach, concludes,

> Without these factors—tradition, a hypothesis of meaning, a life experience that offers the reasons for this hypothesis, and criticism – young people will be like fragile leaves separated from the tree.[4]

In sum then, students must take this past, look at it critically, compare it with the longings of their own hearts, and say, 'This is true,' or 'This is not true,' or 'I'm not sure'.[5] The student, according to Giussani, will say yes or no, and by so doing, will gain maturity and will grow towards adulthood. Such is the understanding of the act of judgement in his system. Positing judgement at the heart of his methodology helps explain the provocative title of his book, *The Risk of Education*. The risk in question is a twofold one. There is the risk on the part of the teacher that the hearers might reject the overall tradition and teaching. On the learner's part, there is also a risk, namely the risk involved in confronting reality, reflecting upon it, and responding to its demands. It can be seen therefore that such an education is risky for teacher and pupil, parent and child, priest and parishioner. It also holds risks for the sponsoring community, in this instance, the Christian community. Giussani sees no way around this, declaring,

> True education must be about an education in criticism. Up to about the age of ten (maybe even sooner these days) a child is allowed to say, 'Because the teacher said so, because mommy said so . . .' What one has been told must become a problem! Unless this happens, it will either be irrationally rejected or irrationally kept but will never mature.[6]

A more complete treatment of Giussani's educational approach, whereby learners are required to self-appropriate the Christian message – that is, come to see for themselves and take on board its meaning and value – is to be found in his book, *The Risk of Education*. At Georgetown University in April 2003, this volume was the subject of a conference at which the keynote speaker, Methodist Stanley Hauerwas, declared concerning some of its assertions, 'I wish I had said that.'[7] The potential effect and benefits of Giussani's insistence on the centrality of judgement may be noted in the following observation from an address delivered at a youth conference in Rimini in 2005, by Julián Carrón, who knew Fr Giussani personally:

> The first thing that struck me was how he spoke of experience. Experience was not just trying something out, but having a judgement, reaching a judgement on what I was living, and this required a criterion for judgement: my heart, the only thing able to perceive when something corresponds to my humanity.[8]

Fr Giussani, whose work was greatly admired by Pope John Paul II, died in February 2005 and his funeral homily was delivered by the then, Joseph Cardinal Ratzinger.

Bernard Lonergan (1904–1984)

While Fr Giussani was teaching youngsters in Milan in the 1950s, a Canadian priest, Fr Bernard Lonergan, 600 kilometres further south, was taking up residence as a lecturer at the Gregorian University in Rome. He, also, had a particular interest in the act of judgement and in its importance.

THE HEYTHROP LETTER

Prior to his arrival in Rome in 1961, Bernard Lonergan had spent the previous four years writing a book entitled *Insight: A Study of Human Understanding*. It is not certain whether or not either man – Lonergan and Giussani – knew about or was familiar with the work of the other. However, in the writings of both, the description of what the act of judgement entails bears a striking similarity. That, however, may have more to do with the nature of the act of judgement than with any mutual scholarly acquaintance. For Lonergan, the journey to *Insight* began in the late 1920s when he was studying at Heythrop College in England. It was from here that he wrote home to a fellow-Jesuit in Canada the following revealing lines, 'The theory of knowledge is what is going to interest me most of all.'[9] In pursuit of this goal, he posed for himself three questions, the first of which only, need occupy us here: 'What am I doing when I am knowing?'[10] The answer he eventually arrived at, in relation to this question, constitutes his cognitional theory, which also includes his understanding of the act of judgement.

CONTRIBUTION: COGNITIONAL THEORY

What Lonergan was searching for was a method for arriving at certainty regarding truth. This method he located within the operations of the human mind. His question, 'What am I doing when I am knowing' can be adjusted somewhat to 'What am I doing as I am coming to know' or, indeed,' ... as I am learning?'[11] Such a way of formulating this fundamental question has obvious attractions and implications for educators. Lonergan, in seeking an answer, began by observing the operations of his own mind and identifying within it various levels of consciousness, through which the human person passes in reaching upon and arriving at genuine human knowing. He subsequently named these, sequentially, as the Experiential Level, the Intellectual Level, and the Rational or Reasonable Level. Later, in his other great work, *Method in Theology* (1972); he added a fourth layer that he termed the Responsible or Moral Level.

According to Lonergan, to be truly authentic at each respective level, the human subject has to adhere rigorously to a particular imperative known as 'a transcendental imperative.' The first of these requires that the person be attentive to the data at Level One, then be intelligent in seeking understanding and insight at Level Two and, finally at Level Three, be reasonable in checking one's understanding against the data given, arriving thereby at a judgement. The fourth level entailing deliberation, choosing, and actual implementation of decision, ensured that the adjudged truth of a situation would, in turn, eventually find expression in the creation, construction and accomplishment of the good.

In the present discussion it is the act of judgement at Level Three that claims our attention. To appreciate what Lonergan means by the act of judgement it is necessary to see it in the context of his overall structure, particularly in relation to the two previous steps. Presented with a problem at Level One, the human subject goes in search of a solution that may, hopefully, manifest itself eventually as an insight. However, as Lonergan himself colourfully notes, 'insights are a dime a dozen.'[12] There has to be a checking process to establish the accuracy and veracity of the solution. This is achieved by measuring the proposed solution or insight, namely one's understanding of the situation or issue, against the data presented initially, as well as against the data of life generally. Human subjects, claims Lonergan, 'pass judgement on the correctness of their understanding.'[13] For good measure, he adds,

> The combination of the operations of sense (Level One) and of understanding (Level Two) does not suffice for human knowing. There must be added judging (Level Three). To omit judgement is quite literally silly: it is only by judgement that there emerges a distinction between fact and fiction, logic and sophistry, philosophy and myth, history and legend.[14]

Lonergan's Authentic Human Subject

The similarity with Giussani's position on judgement may be noted in Lonergan's observation that reflection at this level 'marshals the evidence and weighs it either to judge or else to doubt and so renew enquiry.'[15] Lonergan's subject is bidden to ask the question, 'Is this true?' or, 'Is this really so?' Commenting on the

Lonerganian approach, Hugo Meynell notes that the cultivation and fostering of its four transcendental imperatives – Be attentive, Be intelligent, Be reasonable, Be responsible – 'is what makes education education, as opposed to the mere imparting of uncriticised dogma and moral attitudes by an older to a younger generation.'[16] This uncanningly parallels Giussani's observation, already referred to, concerning the ten-year-old child who can no longer find refuge in the excuse, 'because the teacher said so.' Ten-year-olds, also, need to look into their hearts and engage in the critical act in respect of their received religious tradition.

Finally, for Lonergan, the judging activity of Level Three is the essential stepping stone to Level Four where the subject tackles the question of values and acts in accordance with conscience in responding to life's specific challenges and situations.

Before moving on to the next contributor it may be of interest to note that, while Giussani and Lonergan are at one regarding the necessity of the act of judgement in the development of the human subject, there is a discernable difference in terms of the context in which such judgement is exercised. The former favours its exercise within a companionship or communal setting,[17] as occurs in practice in the *Communion and Liberation* movement, with which his person is closely associated. Lonergan's subject, however, is more of a spiritual loner–not unlike an Ignatian retreatant – bravely waging a personal battle in pursuit of human and religious authenticity.

Thomas Groome
Bernard Lonergan spent most of the final decade of his life at Boston College where he was attached to the theology department. During that time, over at the College's Institute of Religious Education and Pastoral Ministry, a young Irish theologian, Tom Groome, was making his own mark, with an innovative approach to Religious Education. His is the next voice we hear in support of the primacy of judgement in the process of Religious Education.

THE CARLOW TEACHING PLACEMENT
In the opening pages of his 1980 work, *Christian Religious Education*, Groome tells the story of his introduction to the task of Religious Education.

> In September 1966, I walked into a 'religion' class for the first time as teacher. The setting was a Catholic boys' high school. On that Monday morning, I had my own first 'great awakening' as a religious educator. By the end of my third lecture I knew only one thing with certainty – I was using the wrong method.[18]

Arising out of this humbling experience, Groome developed a distinctive approach to the task of Religious Education. Asked by one of the Carlow teaching staff, 'What are you doing in this class?' which, incidentally, has interesting parallels with Lonergan's question, 'What am I doing when I am knowing?' Groome defensively, but revealingly, responded, 'Well, I'm not shoving religion down their throats any more.' This reply, however, was but the first step in the formulation of a more intellectually grounded and comprehensively systematic answer to the penetrating question of that perceptive teacher. Groome's fully worked out proposal came to be known as 'Shared Christian Praxis'.

CONTRIBUTION: SHARED CHRISTIAN PRAXIS

Like Lonergan and Giussani before him, Groome prioritises the act of judgement which, for him, is arrived at in the following fashion. The students are asked to articulate their own story and vision in respect of a particular topic. For instance, they might be asked to name for themselves their current practice in relation to a topic such as honesty, or bullying, or a religious activity such as Sunday church attendance. They then have to identify the reasons undergirding their practice, before endeavouring to predict the probable future direction of their lives, in respect of the particular issue, should they persist in their present practice. Following on from this, a presentation of the ideal or wider Christian Story and Vision regarding the topic in question is made to the whole group.

When this Movement Three is completed there are two things on the table, as it were. Firstly there is each participant's personal story regarding the issue under consideration. Secondly there is the wider Story as held by the community itself. Movement Four consists in placing these two in dialogue. It is here, in Groome's system, that judgement enters the frame. In Shared Christian Praxis it is a double-judgement that is called for in the course of each participant's experience encountering the Community's Experience. The participants are invited to judge their own practice in light of the Community's Story and Praxis. However, they are also invited to judge the wider Story in light of their own experience and point out where the Community's Story might be lacking, either in theory or in practice. The participants therefore, in and through the process, pass judgement both on the wider story and on themselves and do so with the intent of appropriating the Christian faith to their lives.

Returning to the example suggested above, participants in Shared Christian Praxis might be asked, for instance, a question along the following lines, 'Is it a good thing that people attend church at all?' Whatever answer is forthcoming needs to be justified and supported by reasons, which the participants are invited to articulate. They are then asked to measure their own church-going practice against the Community's norm or ideal and to make a judgement as to where they are at in respect of the accepted tradition. The fifth Movement in Shared Praxis consists in deciding upon personal action following on from the reflective exercise.

GROOME'S COMMUNITY OF CONVERSATION

Groome's approach was novel when it first appeared over a quarter of a century ago. It has stood the test of time. In respect of the concerns of this article, particularly, it may be noted that it serves well the activity of judging. Moreover it incorporates judgement within a system that is both theoretically coherent and educationally practical. In addition, shared praxis is precisely that, 'shared,' by which is meant that it occurs ideally within 'a community of conversation' a phrase used repeatedly by Groome to describe the ideal pedagogical setting for his approach. Learners learn from learners as together they explore the meaning of the Christian message for their own lives. Participants in Shared Christian Praxis are precisely that – participants. There is no other valid way, besides that of personal involvement, of engaging in the educational event as it is structured in this system. Each learner is confronted and challenged by the process. Regarding Movement Four, which requires the making of a judgement, Groome notes, 'This may be the most challenging of the movements of shared praxis to do well'.[19] A similar observation might justifiably be made regarding Lonergan's Level Three judging activity and, indeed, of Giussani's suggested judgement event in that the activity of judging, in all of these approaches, demands supportive reasoning and articulation. This, in turn, can expose the personal presuppositions and biases out of which one operates, even when such disclosure is to none other than oneself.

The early Groome, seemingly, did not 'know' Lonergan, at least not to the extent of allowing for a discernable Lonerganian influence on the initial expression of the praxis model. A cursory perusal, for instance, of the index to Groome's 1980 book, *Christian Religious Education*, reveals this to be so. Lonergan is merely mentioned in two footnotes, neither of which, in relation to the question of judgement, is of any great significance. However, by 1998 when Groome re-articulated and re-presented his praxis material under the title, *Sharing Faith: The Way of Shared Praxis*, he drew much more extensively on Lonergan particularly in relation to judgement and the work of Movement Four, which he admits, 'encourages judgement in the Lonerganian sense'.[20]

Similar to Giussani, Groome notes the risk involved in a pedagogy that engages the judging faculty of the learners. He refers to a question often put to him on the lecture and workshop circuit, 'What if the participants make choices contrary to what we hope they will choose?'[21] By way of response to this concern, he finds comfort and encouragement in the gospel account of Jesus' encounter with the

rich young man (Lk 18:18-25) and in the Galilean's comments to his disciples (Jn 6:67) following the discourse on the bread of life. In both episodes, Jesus respects fully the freedom of the human subject to
say, 'No!'

> Throughout the Bible the call of Yahweh and the call to discipleship always carry with them the right of refusal. That is the risk God takes in giving us free will. Our risk as Christian religious educators can be no less.[22]

John Henry Newman (1801–1890)

All three of the preceding contributors have deep roots in the work, writings and witness of John Henry Newman. Groome, in both of his major writings on praxis, acknowledges his dependence on Newman for assistance regarding the development of doctrine particularly, while Lonergan once confessed,

> My fundamental mentor and guide has been John Henry Newman's *Grammar of Assent*. I read that in my third year of philosophy about five times and found solutions for my problems.[23]

At the Georgetown Conference on the educational philosophy of Giussani, Katherine Tillmann, a Newman scholar from the University of Notre Dame, pointed up certain parallels between the work of the Italian and the work of the Englishman.

The Boat to Marseilles

In his early thirties, Newman visited Italy and joined up with some friends. Sometime later, on his own, he made his way to Sicily where, in fact, he became quite ill. When he eventually began his return journey to England via Marseilles his boat was becalmed in the Straits of Bonifacio. This enforced week of reflection provided the occasion for the composition of the wonderfully searching and haunting sentiments of *Lead Kindly Light*, in which Newman gave expression to a sense of being led by something or someone other than himself.

> I was not ever thus, nor prayed that Thou
> Shouldst lead me on,
> I loved to choose and see my path, but now
> Lead Thou me on.

This prayer-poem captures well the essence of Newman's responsiveness to the truth of a situation once the particular truth suggested itself to him. There were times when such responsiveness made enormous demands upon him both personally and professionally. Fifty years later, in *An Essay in Aid of a Grammar of Assent*, he undertook the task of analysing such workings of the human mind. In so doing he concentrated in particular on the question of how one interacts with truth and arrives at a correct judgement – something that had been so much part of his own life's journey from the beginning of his religious awakening at around the age of fifteen.

Contribution: The Illative Sense

It is in *A Grammar of Assent* that Newman extensively uses and elaborates upon the term, the 'Illative Sense,' which he noted was 'a solemn word for an ordinary thing'[24] and nothing more than 'right judgement.'[25] What provided him with the starting point for his cognitional investigations was the ordinary human experience of how people arrive at certainty in the course of their everyday lives. According to Newman, reasoning, for most people in their daily circumstances, occurs as a fairly simple and straightforward operation. The person moves from inference to assent, in one single simple movement, as it were, without adverting consciously to the medium linking the two in the reasoning activity occurring in the mind. Newman labels such commonplace cognitional experience 'instinctive' because it operates as a spontaneous impulse. However, in order for it to meet the conditions of the Illative Sense, it has to be of a higher order. The intervening medium has to be adverted to.

> The Illative Sense, that is the reasoning faculty … has its function in the beginning, middle, and end of all verbal discussion and inquiry, and in every step of the process. It is a rule to itself, and appeals to no judgement beyond its own; and attends upon the whole course of thought from antecedents to consequents.[26]

Acting agents can thus declare confidently by the end of the process, that they know what they know is true and they know that they know it is true. It can be seen therefore that Newman reserves the term, Illative Sense, for the perfection of the reasoning process whereby the subject has well and truly reached a judgement after exhaustive mental activity ensuring that all the conditions for truth laid down by the person's own mind and conscience have been met. Assent, his term for judgement, can then be given to the proposition definitively and unconditionally.

The value of going beyond the instinctive, by means of adverting to the medium, is twofold. First of all it enables individuals to carry out their own personal mental investigations and so establish a firmer basis for their conviction that they are right. Secondly, by analysing for themselves the veracity of their own procedures and the conclusions arrived at, they are in a better position to discourse and share their findings and beliefs, if necessary, appropriate, and desirable with others. It is for these two reasons especially that the issue of the Illative Sense is of importance for education.

Inference is no more than the conditional acceptance of a proposition whereas assent is the unconditional acceptance. Assent or judgement, therefore, is of a much higher order and is a task worthy, indeed, of education in general and of Religious Education in particular. The correct use of these two 'instruments' – inference and assent – is necessary to achieve the advancement of human nature both in and for oneself and for the whole human family. Such advancement and progress, which is facilitated by the acquisition of knowledge with the help of the Illative Sense, is regarded by Newman as 'a sacred duty'.[27] The progress in question, however, is anything but mechanical as it is dependent on 'the personal efforts of each individual.'[28]

NEWMAN'S PRIMACY OF ASSENT
Newman's investigations are foundational and require serious thought and reflection. In his system, however, one element remains constant, namely the centrality of assent in the overall process of knowing. In addition, because the Illative Sense is formed and matured by practice and experience, it is a fitting component for any educational agenda.[29] The eminently practical nature of this faculty, which Newman also terms 'the authoritative oracle,' is indicated in the observation that it manifests itself as:

> A capacity sufficient for the occasion, deciding what ought to be done here and now, by this given person, under these given circumstances. It decides nothing hypothetical, it does not determine what a man should do ten years hence, or what another should do at this time. Its present act is for the present, not for the distant or the future.[30]

In this may be detected an echo of another line of his Mediterranean poem, 'I do not ask to see the distant scene – one step enough for me.' In other words, assent focuses on the particular circumstances of the individual at the time and does not deal in vague generalities. It is specific, requiring an appropriate moral or religious response to whatever calls and challenges life presents to the person at a particular time.[31]

Points of Convergence and Divergence
In bringing this discussion to a conclusion, it is necessary to return to the substantive question and offer an opinion as to whether or not it is a good thing to encourage and include the act of judgement in Christian Religious Education. To assist in answering this question it may be of benefit to note those points of

convergence and, indeed, of divergence between the four chosen contributors to this conversation.

Regarding convergence, it can be stated that each one clearly manifests:

- a respect for the Christian tradition
- a recognition of the need to take seriously the experience of learners
- an assigning of a definite role to reason
- a clear unanimity as to the pivotal and central place occupied by judgement in the process.

Divergences may be noted in respect of the starting-points chosen by each of the pedagogical approaches in question and to the accompanying sequencing of operations. Yet a difference of approach may also be detected regarding the environment or setting of the respective approaches. Groome lays emphasis on the fact that his approach is best applied within a community of conversation or dialogue; the Spirit operating in and through the various participants. Though not stated as explicitly nor in the same kind of language by Giussani, the fact is that the ideal setting for his approach is that which is exemplified in the communal meetings of *Communion and Liberation*. Such an incarnation of *communio*, in fact, goes further than Groome in its emphasis on some degree of common life and worship as against an approach heavily dependent upon conversation and discussion in the main. While Newman and Lonergan, in one way or another, were also involved in education, their respective approaches do not lay any emphasis upon a communal setting. Their human subject can be the lone individual. An attempt is made in the following table to categorise the particularities of each of the four approaches under consideration.

Table: Comparative Analysis of the Approaches in respect of Judgement

C = Certainty; C–D = Christian Discipleship

Approach	What is being Judged	Measure/Yardstick	Portal	Goal
Giussani	Human experience including the Christian tradition	The heart's desires	> C	C–D
Lonergan	The subject's understanding	The data of life	> C	C–D
Groome	The subject's lifestyle	The Christian ideal	> C	C–D
Newman	Spontaneous intuitions	Evidence & experience	> C	C–D

In each approach, the goal of Christian Religious Education is presumed to be the same, namely the exercise and achievement of Christian Discipleship (C-D). Additionally, in each case, the goal is preceded by a portal or gateway, which is certainty (C) in respect of the truth. In order to launch a life of commitment, one first needs conviction. It is the function of the act of judgement to establish the necessary truth which, in turn, provides the human subject with the certainty that is the prerequisite for personal commitment and the adoption of a corresponding lifestyle.

From an epistemological point of view, also, there is something of inestimable value here. Passing through the portal of certainty to the goal and experience of Christian living, enables access to further vistas and horizons of knowing, namely knowing arising from being and from doing. In other words, 'walking the walk' of Christian discipleship becomes, itself, a source of Christian knowing. A form of catechesis, which fails to promote this because of its neglect of higher forms of questioning – entailing judgement and decision – amounts to little more than a catechetical cul-de-sac. Judgement needs to be an essential part of Christian Religious Education and from a much earlier age than, is the case, apparently, at present. This assertion, in turn, raises the question of readiness for exposure to such a form of Religious Education. Groome has no doubts as to when the process should begin:

> From about the age of twelve on a person can begin to reflect critically in a qualitatively improved way. However, developmentally a person is capable of engaging in reflective knowing before that stage. From an educational perspective, that reflective dimension of knowing must be promoted and encouraged at the earlier stages of cognitive development if the person is to have the likelihood of full critical reflection later on. Critical reflection needs to be encouraged from the beginnings of intentional education.[32]

In this assertion, he would have the support of the other members of this prestigious quartet as well as that of a sizeable proportion of developmental psychologists!

Notes

1   Luigi Giussani, *The Risk of Education: Discovering our Ultimate Destiny*, New York: Crossroad Publishing, 2001, p. 10.

2   Chris Morgan, *Communion and Liberation*, London: CTS, 2002, p. 6.

3   Giussani, *The Risk of Education*, p. 11.

4   Ibid.

5   Ibid., p. 9.

6   Ibid., p. 10.

7   Michelle Riconscente, 'Yes, It is Worth the Risk: An Experience Offered', in *Traces*, Vol. 5, No. 5, 2003, p. 20.

8   Julián Carrón, 'The Winning Attraction,' *Traces*, Vol. 7, No. 5, 2005, p. 46.

9   See Mark and Elizabeth Morelli, *The Lonergan Reader*, London: University of Toronto Press, 1997, p. 5.

10   Bernard Lonergan, *Method in Theology*, London: Darton, Longman & Todd, 1972, Chapter 1: pp. 3–25.

11   See Tom Daly, 'Learning Levels', in *Australian Lonergan Workshop*, William Danagher (ed.), New York: University Press, 1993, p. 233. Daly argues that Lonergan's opening question of his famous triad of questions is more concerned with 'coming to know' than with 'knowing' and, hence, with 'learning'.

12   Lonergan, *Method in Theology*.

13   Bernard Lonergan, 'Cognitional Structure', in *Collection: Papers by Bernard Lonergan*, F.C. Crowe and R.M. Doran (eds), *Collected Works of Bernard Lonergan*, Vol. 4, Toronto: University of Toronto Press, 1988, p. 211.

14   Lonergan, 'Cognitional Structure', pp. 206–7. Parenthesis added.

15   Ibid., p. 207.

16   Hugo Meynell, 'On the Aims of Education', *Proceedings of the Philosophy of Education Society of Great Britain*, Vol. X, July 1976, p. 81.

17   Giussani, *The Risk of Education*, p. 10: 'With the help of another person – for a person without companionship is too subject to the storms of his heart ... – the student will say yes or no.'

18   Thomas H. Groome, *Christian Religious Education: Sharing our Story and Vision*, London: Harper and Row, 1980, Preface, p. xi.

19   Groome, *Sharing Faith: The Way of Shared Praxis*, Eugene OR: Wipf and Stock Publ., 1998, p. 250.

20   Ibid., p. 251.

21   Groome, *Christian Religious Education*, p. 223.

22   Ibid.

23   Richard M. Liddy, *Transforming Light: Intellectual Conversion in the Early Lonergan,* Collegeville: The Liturgical Press, 1993, p. 16.

24   See Liddy, *Transforming Light*, p. 26.

25   John Henry Newman, *An Essay in Aid of a Grammar of Assent*, I. T. Kerr (ed.), Oxford: Clarendon, 1985, p. 221.

26   Ibid., p. 233.

27   Ibid., p. 226.

28   Ibid., p. 225.

29   Ibid., p. 229.

30   Ibid., pp. 228–229. See also the following which emphasises the particularity of assent over against inference: 'The course of inference is ever more or less obscure, while assent is ever distinct and definite', p. 226.

31   See *Grammar of Assent*, where the particularity of assent over against inference is noted: 'The course of inference is ever more or less obscure, while assent is ever distinct and definite.' Ibid., p. 226.

32   Groome, *Christian Religious Education*, p. 237.

Further Reading

Carrón, Julián, 'The Winning Attraction', *Traces*, Vol. 7, No. 5, 2005, pp. 46–49.

Daly, Tom, 'Learning Levels', in *Australian Lonergan Workshop*, William Danagher (ed.), New York: University Press, 1993, pp. 233–248.

Giussani, Luigi, *The Religious Sense*, Montreal: McGill–Queens, 1997.

—— *The Risk of Education: Discovering our Ultimate Destiny*, New York: Crossroad Publishing, 2001.

Groome, Thomas H., *Sharing Faith: The Way of Shared Praxis*, Eugene OR: Wipf and Stock Publishing, 1998.

—— *Christian Religious Education: Sharing our Story and Vision*, London: Harper and Row, 1980.

Liddy, Richard M., *Transforming Light: Intellectual Conversion in the Early Lonergan*, Collegeville: The Liturgical Press, 1993.

Lonergan, Bernard, *Method in Theology*, London: DLT, 1972, (Chapter 1).

—— 'Cognitional Structure'. In Frederick E. Crowe and Robert M. Doran (eds), *Collection: Papers by Bernard Lonergan, Collected Works of Bernard Lonergan*, Vol. 4, pp. 205–221. Toronto: University of Toronto, Press, 1988.

Meynell, Hugo, 'On the Aims of Education', *Proceedings of the Philosophy of Education Society of Great Britain*, X, July 1976, pp. 79–97.

Newman, John Henry, *An Essay in Aid of a Grammar of Assent*, I. T. Kerr (ed.), Oxford: Clarendon, 1985 (1870).

CHAPTER 22

EDUCATING FAITHFUL CHRISTIANS
IN A DISSENTING WORLD

Thomas H. Groome

God knows, it's not easy to be a catechist today; there seems to have been times when it *was* easier. Who has not heard grandparent stories of 'the time when . . .' and fill in the blanks: 'when what father or sister said was the law,' or 'when everyone accepted the teachings of the Church.' I sometimes wonder if our foreparents in the faith really were so submissive or did they just keep their dissent to themselves. Indeed, I often heard my father, a local politician and farmer in Co. Kildare, grumble under his breath about 'those priests,' but my mother would scold him not to speak that way in front of the children. At least on the face of it, catechesis would seem to have been easier in those days. In 'post-modern' Ireland, however, 'those days' are gone for sure.

No one as yet has defined precisely what this social phenomenon of postmodernity amounts to, or provided a philosophy of postmodernism, though cultural commentators assure us that both are all-pervasive. However, a friend of mine tells of calling her children to supper recently and instead of 'in a minute, Mom,' she heard back, 'Mom, your call is important to us, and if you hold that supper, the first available child will be with you shortly.' Now, that's postmodernity. Or, on a cold March day I entered the lobby of an old Dublin hotel and approached a glowing turf fire to warm myself. Alas; it was artificial; now that's postmodernity writ large.

Whatever it is, every description notes a proclivity in postmodern consciousness for dissent from 'authorities' of every kind. It reflects a deepened prejudice against tradition and great suspicion of meta-narratives – any claim to possess the fullness of truth for everyone, everywhere, and all the time. On the face of it, such attitudes pose a real challenge for Catholic religious educators.

We are called by our faith and Church to teach the Bible and Christian tradition as God's primordial and normative revelation, and to nurture people in faithful discipleship to Jesus Christ as *'the* way, truth, and life' (Jn 14:6). Indeed, our

Church often positions itself as a bulwark against postmodernism, roundly opposing its alleged 'dictatorship of relativism.' On the other hand, this postmodern era might also offer new possibilities for life-giving catechesis.

Might its skepticism challenge us anew to catechize with deeper conviction that God's Good News in Jesus Christ is of 'liberating salvation,' to represent Christian discipleship as the most truthful and meaningful way to live human lives, our best hope for true happiness? This time requires faith education that fosters deep personal conviction; that encourages people to embrace Christian faith because they 'see for themselves' the truth of its claims, the wisdom of its ethics, the sacramental power of its rituals. Surely when people 'make the Faith their own' rather than accepting on the weight of tradition or submitting on the height of authority, they are more likely to live it faithfully, to have it permeate their whole 'being' – who they are and how they live.

I believe we have such an opportunity; yet it would be naïve to underrate the challenge to impart a Religious Education that is effective in this dissenting postmodern world and also deeply faithful to Catholic Christian faith. For we must always educate people in the 'whole story' of Catholic Christian faith with its vision of God's Reign, and yet do so, as Aquinas would advise, 'according to the mode of the receiver.'

Guidance from Contemporary Catholic Consciousness
I note six features of contemporary Catholic consciousness that can be assets to 'educating faithful Christians in a dissenting world.'

First, not every belief, ethic, or ritual practice is equally constitutive of Catholic faith. *The Catechism of the Catholic Church*, echoing Vatican II's *Decree on Ecumenism* (*UR*), reiterated a number of times that our faith reflects 'a hierarchy of truths, since they vary in their relation to the foundation of the Christian faith' (no. 90; see also no. 234). Here is a very important point for catechesis; not every aspect of our faith tradition should be represented as of equal importance.

Second, every expression of Christian faith must be open to future developments. As Vatican II's *Dei Verbum* stated so forcefully,

> The tradition which comes from the Apostles develops in the Church with the help of the Holy Spirit. For there is growth in the realities and the words handed down. For as the centuries succeed one another, the Church constantly moves forward toward the fullness of divine truth until the words of God reach their complete fulfillment in her.[1]

So, it is not as if we possess the fullness of divine truth as a static entity; as Jesus advised, we must be like scribes learned in the Reign of God who can draw from the 'storeroom both the new and the old' (Mt 13: 52).

Third, the Church's praxis throughout history can reflect distortions from Gospel faith and the traces of past errors can be difficult to erase. It is a great legacy of the papacy of Pope John Paul II that he constantly recognised and called the Church to repent – one biographer counted up to 100 times – for all those times in history when Christians ... indulged in ways of thinking and acting which were truly forms of counter witness and scandal.'[2] Rather than canonising all Christian tradition, we must approach it with the same critical historical scholarship as we do the Bible.

Fourth, Scripture and tradition are media of God's revelation rather than immediate divine communications to be taken literally. Catholics should not be 'fundamentalist' about either Scripture or tradition. As *Dei Verbum* stated succinctly, these 'words of God' are 'expressed in human language.' Since they are 'like human discourse,'[3] we must be forever interpreting and reinterpreting these symbols of our faith, attentive to ever-changing historical circumstances and emerging issues; enabling Christianity to be the fountain of living water that Jesus promised in his conversation with the Samaritan woman (Jn 4:4-15).

Fifth, it is a Catholic truism that we must interpret our faith within the community of the Church and be guided by its teaching magisterium. Indeed, we must also remember the long Catholic tradition that the Church's official magisterium should both guide *and* consult the scholarship of its scholars who are trained in the exegesis of its sacred texts and traditions. Likewise, it should reflect the sense of the faithful – *sensus fidelium* – honouring the spiritual wisdom that the Holy Spirit makes known to all the baptised. For 'In one Spirit we were all baptised into one body ... and were all given to drink of the same Spirit' (I Cor 12:13).

Parenthetically, catechist educators must transcend the stereotype of 'answer person' entitled to 'tell' other people how to live their discipleship to Jesus. Better to see ourselves as fulfilling a dual priestly and prophetic function, lending people access with persuasion to the wisdom of Christian faith and challenging them to live it faithfully. Then, we must remember that discipleship is by invitation rather than heavy hand. Here Jesus is our best model. On a number of occasions he invited disciples to make a free choice, to follow or not, the most famous being his question to the Twelve, 'Do you want to leave me too?' (Jn 6:67; Mk 10:17-25).

Last but not least, we must remember that freedom of conscience is a doctrine of Catholic faith. Of course, we need to have an 'informed conscience' that discerns in dialogue with the faith community – the Church. Yet, Vatican II summarised a long tradition, going back to the earliest centuries, when it described conscience as 'the most secret core and sanctuary' of the person, where we are 'alone with God whose voice echoes in (our) depths'; and again, 'The gospel has a sacred reverence for the dignity of conscience and its freedom of choice.'⁴ For Catholic Christians, conscience is ever the last court of appeal.

Such guidance and nuances notwithstanding, it remains a great challenge to do faithful catechesis amidst a culture of dissent. Since that hillside in Galilee with the little community gathered around the Risen Christ, this Church and its catechists have had 'full authority' to 'go and make disciples' and 'to teach' all that Jesus had commanded (Mt 28:16-20). Like him, too, we are to 'teach with authority' (Mk 1:22). Indeed, we must never 'pervert the gospel of Jesus Christ'; even if an angel from heaven were to direct otherwise, we must be faithful to the one we have received (Gal 1:6-9).

A Shared Christian Praxis Approach
For many years I've been working to promote a 'shared Christian praxis approach' to catechesis and Religious Education. Originally much influenced by the conscientising, emancipatory, and praxis-based pedagogy of Paulo Freire, over the years, and from its employ across a great variety of contexts and cultures, age levels and time frames, this approach has developed and matured in its own right. I highlight it here because it now seems ideally suited to effect faithful catechesis in a dissenting world.

At core, a shared Christian praxis approach honours God's revealing presence and saving grace in the ordinary and everyday of people's lives and likewise the revelation and spiritual wisdom mediated by the Bible and Christian tradition. Its intent is to enable people to integrate their 'life' and 'Christian faith' into 'lived Christian faith,' using a pedagogy that *brings life to the Faith and brings the Faith to life*.

That catechesis must teach Christian faith is patently obvious but why attend to and actively engage people's lives as well? Clearly there is a whole underlying theology here of both revelation and sacramentality, of how God continues to reveal God's will and mediate God's grace through the ordinary and everyday of life, as well as through Scripture/tradition and the seven great sacraments. However, the pedagogical rationale for engaging people's lives in order to teach for Christian discipleship is stated forcefully by the *General Directory for Catechesis* – placing a shared Christian praxis approach squarely within the present mind of the Church regarding catechetical methodology.

By way of pedagogy, the *Directory* calls for 'a correct … correlation and interaction between profound human experiences and the revealed message' (no. 153). For it is by 'correlating faith and life' (no. 207) that 'catechesis … bridges the gap between belief and life, between the Christian message and the cultural context' (no. 205). Christian religious educators must not only teach the faith tradition but also engage people's lives in the world because 'experience is a necessary medium for exploring and assimilating the truths which constitute the objective content of Revelation' (no. 152). Thus, effective catechesis should present every aspect of the faith tradition 'to refer clearly to the fundamental experiences of people's lives' (no. 133). Catechists should engage participants' own lives in the world as integral to the catechetical curriculum because 'one must start with praxis to be able to arrive at praxis' (no. 245).[5]

Let me now review briefly what I have explained at length elsewhere:[6] the core components and the pedagogical movements of a *shared Christian praxis approach*.

An Approach: I deliberately refer to shared praxis as an *approach* to catechetical education rather than a method; in fact, many different methods can be used within its overarching commitments. 'Bringing life to faith and faith to life' suggests a heuristic framework for how a religious educator might craft an intentional teaching/learning event. As people embrace and practice its commitments and dynamics, however, it becomes their general style that can be affected in many varied ways and circumstances.

I've been able to honour its commitments and movements within a five-minute conversation and have spread them over a month in an undergraduate theology course. I have used it in formal teaching settings from kindergarten to doctoral seminars, in adult Bible study and faith-sharing groups, in youth ministry events and retreat weekends, and in airplane conversations with strangers along the way. I've employed it most often to catechise for Christian discipleship but also in non-confessional contexts exploring the spiritual wisdom of other religious traditions.

Praxis: Since Paulo Freire resurrected 'praxis' in educational discourse, there has been debate about what precisely the term means. Indeed, much educational literature still favours the term 'experience' instead and I often refer simply to 'life' – as in 'learning from life.' However, praxis has a more agential meaning than experience. Praxis is reflective activity in which one is an initiator or agent, whereas experience connotes something that one undergoes. John Dewey struggled to transcend this passive connotation of 'experience' throughout his writings, never with complete success.

I understand and use praxis to mean purposeful human activity, what we do reflectively and imaginatively or how we reflect upon and intend what we are doing. As such it attempts to hold theory and practice in a dialectical unity while imagining the outcome and consequences. So, praxis embraces reflective, active and creative activity. A praxis way of knowing is intentional *reflection* upon what one is *doing* or what is going on in order to imagine consequences and create new possibilities.

The *active* dimension of a praxis way of knowing engages any and all bodily, mental and volitional activities, and likewise pays attention to whatever is being done in people's 'life-world'. It can engage what people know, how they feel, what they do or what is going on in the historical reality of their social/cultural context. The *reflective* aspect of praxis entails the whole human capacity for knowing, engaging reason, memory, and imagination, to intentionally learn from and for life in the world. It entails critical reflection not as a negative exercise but as a positive act of discernment (from the Greek, *krinein*) that looks inward through self-reflection and outward at the public world through social analysis. The *creative* aspect recognises the likely consequences of present praxis, imagines what might be or should be, and acts to bring about the desired end.

Christian: Christian religious educators are under mandate to teach with integrity the fullness of Christian revelation that is mediated through Scripture and tradition. Not only must we teach the constitutive truths, values, and practices of Christian faith but also make explicit its meaning and demands for the lives of disciples today. Favouring a narrative language pattern for good catechetical reasons,[7] I find it helpful to highlight both the 'Story' and 'Vision' of Christian faith. I use these terms as metaphors to symbolise the whole historical reality of Christian revelation and the demands/promises that it makes upon the lives of its adherents and communities. Together this Story and Vision constitute the spiritual wisdom of Christian faith for lives today and how we are to live for God's reign as disciples of Jesus – doing of God's will 'on earth as in heaven.'

Shared: A *shared* praxis approach entails creating a community of conversation among participants, encouraging them to actively engage in the teaching-learning dynamic. It calls them into partnership with each other, to learn together. The exchanges among participants should entail all the give and take, listening and sharing, agreement and disagreement, cherishing one's own truth while being open to the truth of others, that is the mark of good conversation. Shared in the title also reflects the intent to help people bring 'life' and 'faith' together, to integrate Christian faith into daily life as 'lived faith'. This amounts to people appropriating its spiritual wisdom as their own, coming to see for themselves and embrace its truth and meaning for their lives.

In summary, a shared Christian praxis approach to Religious Education/catechesis involves creating a community of conversation and active participation in which people reflect together critically on their own historical agency in time and place, and on their socio-cultural realities; have access together to the spiritual wisdom of Christian Story and Vision; and are encouraged to appropriate this wisdom with the intent of renewed praxis of Christian faith toward the coming of God's Reign.

Pedagogical Movements of a Shared Christian Praxis Approach
The movements of a shared praxis approach should be much more symphonic than sequential; it should not be practiced as a lock-step process. This being said, the dynamic of 'bringing life to faith, and faith to life' suggests a pattern of pedagogical moves that fulfil the foundational commitments of this approach. I outline its dynamics as a focusing activity and five subsequent movements.

The *Focusing Activity*: Here the educator's intent is twofold:

- to engage people as active participants in the teaching-learning event
- to focus a curriculum topic as something of real interest to the lives and/or faith of participants.

Thus, it should dispose people to participate actively by turning them to look at their own lives in the world, and begin to engage them with a generative theme, symbol or text – something of real import to their present praxis of life or faith or both.

Movement One (M1): Expressing the Theme as in Present Praxis: The educator's intent here is to encourage participants to express themselves around the generative theme, symbol, or text from the perspective of their present praxis. They can express what they do themselves or what they see others doing, their own feelings or thoughts or life-centred interpretations, or their perception of what is going on around them in their socio-cultural context. The key is that people 'pay attention' to the focus and name what emerges as their own encounter with the theme, symbol or text – how they see it, engage it, interpret it, or whatever. Their expressions can be spoken, written, drawn, constructed or mediated by any means of human communication.

Movement Two (M2): Reflecting on the Theme of Life/Faith: The intent here is to encourage people to reflect critically on what they expressed in Movement One. As noted, critical reflection can engage reason, memory, imagination or a combination of them; such reflection can be both personal and social. Reason questions or questioning activities can ask why things are the way they are; what causes them to be this way; what their meaning might be; why participants' own perceptions or interpretations are as they are; and so on. Memory questions or questioning activities might ask participants about the origins of their present praxis, their own recall or past experiences regarding it, to uncover how the social history is shaping their expressions and to recognise how their own biography or social location influence how they respond to the theme, symbol, or text, and so on. Imagination type questions or activities invite people to imagine beyond present praxis for its likely consequences, its possibilities and its desired outcomes.

Movement Three (M3): Christian Story and Vision: Here the pedagogical task is to teach clearly the Christian Story and Vision around the particular theme, symbol or text, and to do so with integrity and persuasion. Though this will often entail a doctrinal review, it is more important that people have persuasive access to the spiritual wisdom of Christian faith around the particular life/faith focus. Likewise, it is important to intentionally raise up the Vision out of the Story, what Christian faith teaches and means for lives now around the topic and how best to respond.

Movement Four (M4): Appropriating the Wisdom of Christian Faith to Life: M4 begins the dynamic of moving back to life again with renewed Christian commitment (M5). The pedagogy here encourages people to come to see for themselves what the wisdom of Christian faith might mean for their everyday lives, to personally appropriate this wisdom and to 'take it to heart' in who they are and how they live. So the educator might inquire how participants are feeling, or what they are coming to recognise for themselves, what they agree with or disagree with or might add to what has been presented in M3, and so on.

Movement Five: Making Decisions for Christian Faith: Here the intent is to give participants an opportunity to choose how to respond to the spiritual wisdom of Christian faith. Decisions can be cognitive, affective, or behavioural – what people believe, how they might worship or relate with God in prayer, or the ethics and values by which to live their lives. The imperative is that all decisions be 'real,' influencing how participants live their Christian faith and grow in identity as disciples of Jesus Christ.

Though I lay out these movements sequentially, let me reiterate that they have great flexibility and many possible combinations. I have often combined the focusing activity with M1, and M1 with M2; I've borrowed from M3 – briefly – as a focusing activity to engage people's interests; I've often shared from M3 as the conversation of M1 and M2 unfold; I've done M3 and then some M4 to return to M3 again before going back to M4 and eventually on to M5; I've combined M4 and M5 only to return again to M3 for more access to the wisdom of the faith tradition. And many times the decisions made in M5 have constituted the focusing activity for the next gathering of an ongoing community of conversation.

More important than the movements are their underpinning commitments. The focusing act reflects commitment to *engage* participants in the teaching/learning dynamic and with something generative for their lives. M1 reflects commitment to have people *pay attention* to their own lives in the world and *to express* their present praxis. M2 reflects commitment to *critical reflection*, encouraging people to think for themselves, personally and socially, to question and probe, to reason, remember and imagine around the life/faith theme, symbol or text from the perspective of their present praxis. M3 reflects the commitment to give people *access* to the Story and Vision of Christian faith, enabling participants to encounter its spiritual wisdom for their lives. M4 reflects commitment to *appropriation*, encouraging participants to integrate their lives and Christian faith, to make its spiritual wisdom their own. M5 reflects commitment to invite people to *decision*, choosing a lived faith response to the spiritual wisdom they have encountered.

These commitments to *participation* and *conversation*, to engaging and attending, to *expressing* and *reflecting*, to *accessing* and *appropriating*, and to decision-making should run throughout the process. In other words, engagement does not end with the focusing activity but must be maintained throughout; likewise expression is not limited to M1, nor reflection to M2, nor decision-making to M5, and so on. Rather, the religious educator should promote these activities throughout the whole event.

For Our Question Here
By way of 'educating faithful Christians in a dissenting world,' I make explicit the following points. Overall, a shared Christian praxis approach is set within a community of conversation and shared faith, reflecting the broader community of the Church. The dialectics of conversation – the shared faith of the group – provides a buffer against unduly individualised discernment and whimsical decision-making; all is tested within a community of discourse. Then, its dynamics invite people to active participation, encouraging them to be agents of their faith rather than dependents; in this regard it seems more likely, by God's grace, to encourage faith development toward Christian maturity.

Then, its focusing act and opening movements honour people's own wisdom from life and God's presence in their lives. However, the pedagogy here also encourages critical reflection, personal and social, inviting people to 'think twice' about their actions and reflections rather than settling for personal bias or blithely accepting the influences of their social and cultural contexts.

Movement Three gives access to the 'whole Story' of Christian faith and its Vision for people's lives now, doing so with integrity; it should never compromise anything that is constitutive of Christian faith. However, the fact that Christian Story/Vision is mediated into the context of people's lives (their own stories and visions), highlighting its spiritual wisdom for life, enables the religious educator to present Christian faith in a persuasive way and yet without indoctrination – in a mode respectful of but also appealing to participants.

Movements Four and Five encourage people's own discernment and decision-making but assure that both are well-informed by the constitutive truths of Christian faith. If people are intent on dissenting they will do so anyhow, regardless of the pedagogy. Shared praxis certainly does not encourage dissent but that people's honest thoughts and feelings be brought to explicit discourse in the teaching/learning community. There they can be addressed and tested in ways more likely to lead to lived faith as disciples of Jesus. No approach can promise more.

Notes

1   'Dogmatic Constitution on Divine Revelation', in Walter M. Abbott (ed.), *The Documents of Vatican II*, New York: America Press, 1966, p. 116.

2   Pope John Paul II, *On the Coming of the Third Millennium*, Washington, DC: USCCB, 1994, no. 32.

3   'Dogmatic Constitution on Divine Revelation', in Abbott, *Documents*, p. 121.

4   'Church in Modern World', nos. 16 and 41, Abbott, *Documents*, pp. 213 and 240.

5   Congregation for the Clergy, *General Directory for Catechesis*, USCCB: Washington, DC, 1998. It is fascinating that the Directory refers to this pedagogy which integrates 'life' and 'faith' as 'the pedagogy of God' (no. 139) and likewise of Christ (no.140).

6   My most complete statement of a shared praxis approach is in *Sharing Faith: A Comprehensive Approach to Religious Education and Pastoral Ministry*, San Francisco, CA: HarperSanFrancisco, 1991; now published by Wipf and Stock Publishers, Eugene, Oregon, USA, 97401. See especially Chapters 4–10.

7   See ibid., pp. 138–142 for my rationale to favour a narrative paradigm for Christian Religious Education.

CHAPTER 23

BEYOND SHEEP AND GOATS: FROM JUDGEMENT TO ASSESSMENT IN RELIGIOUS EDUCATION

Anne Looney

Introduction

Two stories – one old, one new – provide the background for this introduction to some of the issues associated with assessment in and of Religious Education in schools. The new one comes from a newspaper article about an examination paper in Religious Education – the Junior Certificate examination in Ireland in 2008. Under a headline that ran *'The meaning of life is a test for students of all faiths and none'*, a teacher was interviewed about the examination paper taken the previous day. Noting that Religious Education was now one of the most popular Junior Certificate subjects, the piece drew on the views of a teacher of the subject; 'I have plenty of different religions in my class and they all enjoy it … it's a core subject in our school, but students can opt out if they want to. Very few do'. Commenting on the examination paper itself, she continued by observing that 'it's an onerous task to set a paper that allows students of all belief systems to be included'.[1]

The second, older, story is also about assessment (and is not conducted by the State Examinations Commission in the Republic of Ireland!) but is told in the gospel of Matthew, by the Son of Man, in all his glory.[2] The assessment task here, the sorting of the sheep and the goats, may have power as a story, but as an evaluation of performance it is deeply flawed. If the story is analysed, it is clear that those assessed had no idea of the assessment criteria, and were not aware that in their interactions with the hungry, the lonely and the imprisoned they were being assessed in what turned out to be an extremely high-stakes test! Their failure leads to their eternal damnation, just as those who score highly – the upright – gain admission to eternal life. As a test, it is poorly designed and executed. As a tale of judgement its power is undeniable, and its influence on thinking about tests and religion is deeply felt by those who plan for, design and deliberate on assessment in Religious Education.

In a school context, assessment of Religious Education shares the challenges of assessment across the curriculum. However it also has some particular challenges

– the power of that judgement story, the nature of the 'stakes' in religious belief, and the complexities of the idea of 'success' in religion to name a few. This introduction to assessment in Religious Education seeks to escape the clutches of that powerful judgement metaphor to begin to form a workable understanding of assessment in Religious Education. In moving beyond the metaphor of sheep and goats, the discussion will focus on some of the core principles in assessment and consider them from the particular perspective of Religious Education.

The focus of this discussion is on Religious Education in Catholic schools. The broader catechetical mission of the Church is shared across three sites – the home, the parish community and the school. While this discussion confines itself to assessment in schools, and to the school curriculum, catechesis in homes and parishes is not without its own 'assessment dimension'. Consider sacramental celebrations for example, and the place of questions, answers and declarations of understanding in the words and rituals. The 'testing' is of intention, against community norms and expectations, and the 'results' are generally as predictable as the questions. Despite the highly ritualised context, the underlying idea of a 'test' for admission to the community, or for progression to greater inclusion, or to a particular status within the community, is a powerful one, and one that further complicates the task of those working to construct workable theories of assessment within Religious Education.

The school context offers its own complexities however, and it is on these that this discussion will focus.

Assessment as an Educational and Public Project

In the contemporary field of education, research into and publication on assessment has been one of the most popular projects for academics and policy-makers. This popularity has several sources. Developments in cognitive psychology, the influence of Lev Vygotsky (1896–1934), and a greater focus on learning as a social process, have all fuelled increasing interest in assessment from within the education academy. Developments in theories of learning, cognition and motivation have all informed new theorising in educational assessment and excitement about the potential of these new theories for teaching and learning in classrooms.

However, interest in assessment is not confined to those working as education professionals or practitioners. A greater focus on accountability for public services, a concern for equity in educational outcomes, and an interest in measurement, scales and comparisons in many spheres of public life – have all served to excite the interest of policy-makers, the media and the general public in assessment, especially as it relates to schools, and to the generation of results expressed in numbers and grades. In a world fascinated by number, comparisons and data, the generation of such outputs from *social* processes as well as more instrumental ones has become increasingly important. Consider the popularity of polls and surveys in the media, of instant SMS or text polls on radio shows for example. Think about how statistics are used in debates about the quality of healthcare. Advances in data-handling and processing means that the hitherto unmeasurable has become more accessible to measurement, and to the generation of a score or rating.

Schools are not impervious to these trends. As sites of public spending and social selection, various means to measure the 'effectiveness' of schools are much sought after. Debates about school league tables continue and despite a legislative ban on the generation of these, the publication each year of rank orders of schools by the national media, based on entry to higher education, is the subject of considerable public interest!

Within assessment debates there is a certain polarisiation between the *educational* aspects of assessment and those more *public* dimensions. At one level, this seems something of a false dichotomy, particularly given the role of education as a public project and its value as a public good. However, for those working within education, the tensions between these two sets of purposes are deeply felt. Just how deeply, probably depends on the educational setting. For early childhood education and for a great deal of primary education in the Republic of Ireland, educational assessment dominates both policy and practice. The Framework for Early Learning discusses assessment of children under six, but makes it clear that the purpose of assessment is to support all those who work with a child, and the child's own development.[3] In post-primary education, the focus shifts towards the more public purposes of assessment, in the state examinations, and in the senior cycle of post-primary school, the backwash from the public purposes into the educational purposes can almost result in the latter being washed way. In the context of this tension, the first core principle of assessment should be self-evident. It is vital to be clear about the purposes of assessment. Or, to use the imagery of the gospel story, surprise neither sheep nor goat!

A Question of Purpose
One of the most recent articulations of the educational dimensions of assessment in an Irish context has been the National Council for Curriculum and Assessment's (NCCA) publication of *Assessment in the Primary School Curriculum, Guidelines for Schools* (2007).[4] The guidelines provide a very useful definition of assessment in their opening pages.

> Assessment is the process of gathering, recording, interpeting, using and reporting information about a child's progress and achievement in developing knowledge, skills and attitudes.

This description appears relatively straightforward. However, the story of the examination paper and the gospel story of judgement, highlight the radically divergent purposes for which the process of gathering, recording and reporting information is used.

The discussion of the tension between the educational and public dimensions of assessment point to even more potential purposes for an assessment process. Purpose is important because assessment is a social process. Students and teachers approach assessment differently depending on the purpose of the assessment. While assessment is generally classified as either *formative* (for the purpose of giving feedback during learning) or *summative* (for the purpose of providing information on achievement after learning), discussions of purpose rarely fall neatly under these headings. Similarly, it is tempting to categorise assessment by 'type' and to discuss formative and summative as categories. To do so is to miss the important point that when it comes to assessment, what something appears to be, may not always be what it actually is. Purpose makes a difference.

For example, think about a final year university examination, and a spelling test in third class. Clearly, both tests serve two very different purposes. Both serve to gather information on progress and achievement – that purpose they have in common. One test will also determine the progress of the learner into the next phase of education, while the other will provide important feedback to the learner and the teacher on spelling challenges and the next steps required to support the learner in developing good spelling habits. The third class student may well prepare for the test by rehearsing some spellings at home on the night before the test. The university student, at least in theory, will prepare for many weeks for the final year examination. It seems that the examination is summative assessment, while the spelling test is formative in purpose.

Yet all is not as it seems. What if the third class teacher decides that this spelling test will be the basis on which she will allocate children to a particular level in a reading programme? Or as the basis for access to some extrinsic reward – extra play time or more computer time? Or if she decides to simply score the test to create a mark for a school report and offer no feedback on spelling strengths and weaknesses. The test remains the same, the purpose has shifted. What if the university has a modular degree programme and the purpose of the final examination is to validate all work previously submitted? When considering clarity of purpose, it is important to be wary of hasty judgements.

Consequently, when planning for assessment it is important to be clear about purposes, and to sustain the purpose through the assessment. Learners should know why the assessment is taking place, what is being assessed, and, importantly, the criteria for success. They should also know how and to whom the results will be reported.

For learners to know this, teachers must be clear in setting the task and in contextualising that task. Those who interacted with the poor, the homeless and the lonely in the gospel story have some cause for complaint – they did not know this interaction was an assessment task, nor did they know the criteria for success. In the examination paper, the test was praised because it did what it set out to do – assess young people of all faiths and none.

Assessment in Religious Education

Planning for assessment in Religious Education requires absolute clarity of purpose. Why are students being assessed? What is being assessed? What are the criteria for success? What about reporting? The national report card templates for primary schools in Ireland all include Religious Education as a heading for reporting to parents on children's learning.[5] Of note is that these templates were developed with teachers and schools who clearly felt that reporting progress in Religious Education was an important part of the official recording and reporting process.

The purpose of the assessment process, questions and answers being sought and given should underpin the planning process and needs to be shared with students, parents and others in the school community. If assessment is about gathering information concerning knowledge, skills and attitudes, then everyone should be clear about what knowledge, what skills and what attitudes are being assessed in a given task or test. There should also be clarity about how the information gathered in the test will be used. While these are questions that form part of the planning process for teachers, the answers to these questions need to be shared with the students *before* the assessment takes place. This planning for clarity of purpose applies across the curriculum, but it is easy to see why it is particularly relevant in Religious Education. If learners are drawing on a range of experiences of religion, if they approach Religious Education class from different perspectives, then clarity around assessment purposes becomes particularly important. The teacher should communicate the purpose of the assessment to the learners so that all are clear on it. If Religious Education in school is part of a wider catechetical mission – in a Catholic school for example – the shared understanding of purposes across the different catechetical sites of home, school and parish, are important. More than any other subject area, I would argue, assessment in the Religious Education classroom needs to be reflected upon and talked about with and by learners of all ages.

Some writers on Religious Education draw clear distinctions between the assessment of attitudes and the assessment of knowledge and skills in Religious Education. Writing in an Australian context, Marie McDonald describes assessment in Religious Education as the systematic collection and interpretation of information about the knowledge and skills related to the content of what is being studied – in the Australian case, the content of Catholic faith. She does not exclude attitudes, but claims that these can only be assessed by student through self-assessment and therefore are not the subject of the same information and reporting processes as knowledge and skills.[6] Her dual approach is probably more useful in considering attitudes associated with faith development and broader catechetical goals. It would be difficult to collect information and report on 'holiness' for example, and it would of course depend on the aims and purposes of a school's Religious Education course. Nonetheless it would be a mistake to exclude attitudes from the assessment process as a matter of principle. Reticence in approaching the assessment of attitudes in Religious Education is understandable, given that 'holiness' factor, but other curricular areas are less reticent. The assessment of appreciation, of critical discernment, of respect for difference, of a spirit of enquiry – all are undertaken as a matter of course across a range of curriculum subjects.

Some attitudes are easier to assess than others. Assessing something like a student's spirit of inquiry can be done using case studies and questions that require a student to take multiple perspectives, or consider a range of options. The NCCA guidelines for primary schools offer some good suggestions for questions that challenge students in this way.[7] Yet what about more complex attitudes such as a student's sense of justice or fair play? This too can be assessed using a case study, or scenario to discuss. However this can only be done if the student has been learning about justice and fair play, and is clear that the assessment task seeks to assess his/her sense of justice following those lessons. Equally, the criteria for demonstrating a sense of justice needs to be discussed before the assessment event. How student performance in this context is to be scored or rated is challenging. Self-assessment, or peer assessment against the criteria offers some possibility. Clearly, a label of just/unjust is not appropriate – but labelling of any kind should be avoided in assessment. Which brings us to the second core principle– good assessment is focused on learning and feedback.

A Matter of Learning and Feedback

Take a look at the teacher comments on the written work of any school student, or reflect on your own school experience. Research shows that these comments often bear little relationship to the assessment purpose. Comments about neatness and volume abound followed by generic labelling about the good-ness (good, very good, really good!) of the work, or the effort, or even the personal attributes of the student – *excellent student*, or the wistful *tries hard!* Listen to the spoken feedback provided by teachers, or if you are a teacher, tune in to your own comments … good-ness pervades, with classroom discourse dominated by good answers, good girls, good boys, good efforts, and good work. While this positive feedback is of some value, its focus on the learner and not on the learning means that its value is limited, and, over time, can actually work to undermine student motivation. As feedback, it gives little clue to the learner about how they can do better, or what the next steps might be.

Ten years ago, the Assessment Reform Group in the UK published *Assessment for Learning; Beyond the Black Box* in which they suggested that better feedback was the key to better learning.[8] Much has been written about what has come to be known as *assessment for learning* since that time, but the principles of good feedback, and the focus on learning have proven useful for teachers in classrooms with students of all ages. The NCCA guidelines on assessment in primary schools offer an extensive exploration of assessment for learning approaches in classrooms and some interesting examples of teacher assessment practice.

If an assessment task or question has as its purpose the assessment of a particular piece of knowledge, or a particular skill or attitude, then that knowledge, skill or attitude should be the focus of the feedback – not the neatness of the work, nor the amount written, nor the style of the drawing, nor the loudness of the oral answer. Equally, the feedback should include a 'feed-forward' dimension – an idea of next steps, or of what to be done to improve performance next time. In the Religious Education classroom, such distinctions between the learner (who may or may not have personal religious belief) and the learning is important and needs to be carefully flagged in feedback. This dialogue between teacher and learner about learning is important for two reasons. Firstly, it affords the teacher and learner an insight into the learning process, and secondly, it signals that the process of learning is a shared responsibility, with the learner taking an active rather than a passive role. Learning is an active verb! In this context, the gospel story is a better case than the examination paper. Those being judged at least had the opportunity to query the process, and to ask further questions. Examinations, particularly formal written tests, are one-way processes where there is no opportunity for dialogue or engagement. As such, while they may be effective at assessing the outcomes of learning, they offer little insight into the learning process.

Religious Education – whether associated with a particular faith tradition or not – values dialogue. Religion as a phenomenon is inevitably relational – whether that relationship is between the human and the divine, between believers and other believers or between believers and non-believers. As a project, Religious

Education should reflect this essential quality, just as art education must reflect the artistic and creative processes. For this reason, assessment-for-learning approaches with their focus on discussion and engagement, learner responsibility and on clarity of purpose, are particularly relevant for the Religious Education classroom. They are also important for the wider catechetical mission – actively engaged learners in school have a better chance of being active learners outside school. Those who have been assessed in silence rather than in dialogue have little enthusiasm for engagement in learning beyond school. The process of catechesis – which literally means 'echoing' has little hope of success if learners are silent, passive and unquestioning. Assessment should make learners, before it measures them. That is what happened to those who were condemned for eternity. They did not just fail the test. They missed out on the learning. Most of those who sit examinations in Religious Education in Ireland, and elsewhere, pass the test. We continue to reflect on what they have learned in the process.

Notes

1   *The Irish Times*, 13 June 2008, p. 6.

2   Matthew 25:31.

3   Available on www.ncca.ie/early childhood (accessed 10.08.08).

4   *Assessment in the Primary School Curriculum, Guidelines for Schools*, NCCA, 2007, p. 7.

5   Available on www.ncca.ie (accessed 10.08.08).

6   Marie McDonald, 'Assessing Knowledge and Evaluating Faith: Dual Approaches to Determining Outcomes of Religious Education', in *Word in Life*, Vol. 43, No. 2, 1995.

7   NCCA, p. 87.

8   *Assessment for Learning: Beyond the Black Box*, Cambridge: University of Cambridge School of Education, 1999.

SECTION 5

MINISTERING IN A CATHOLIC SCHOOL

CHAPTER 24

THE ROLE OF RELIGION IN THE CURRICULUM OF A CATHOLIC SCHOOL

Andrew G. McGrady

A Vision of Religion in the Curriculum of the Catholic School

On the one hand defining the role of religion in the curriculum of the Catholic school is a simple task; on the other hand it is an increasingly complex task (we will talk more about this later). We shall therefore begin by addressing the 'ideal'. In terms of the vision, the core motivation for the establishment of Catholic schools flows from a distinctive religious understanding of the integrating role of faith in full human development and the role of religion in communal and societal living. It is the Catholic ethos of Catholic schools that differentiates them from other State or what we may call 'common' schools. It is usually the case that parents make a deliberate choice to enrol their children in a Catholic school and teachers, when seeking employment in such schools, are aware of their ethos. The Church sees the establishment of schools as a vital part of its work of evangelisation, inculturation and the on-going catechesis and sacramental preparation of Catholic pupils who have been baptised as infants. An important point of reference for the Church's understanding of the Catholic school is the statement of the Second Vatican Council:

> The Catholic School pursues cultural goals and the natural development of youth to the same degree as any other kind of school. What makes the Catholic school distinctive is its attempt to generate a community climate in the school that is permeated by the Gospel spirit of freedom and love. It tries to guide the adolescents in such a way that personality development goes hand in hand with the development of the 'new creature' that each one has become through baptism. It tries to relate all of human culture to the good news of salvation so that the light of faith will illumine everything that the students will gradually come to learn about the world, about life and about the human person (*GE*, 8).

There have been a number of follow-up documents from the Church concerning Catholic schools and the role of religion in its curriculum. One of the most important is the *Religious Dimension of Education in the Catholic School (RDECS)* issued by the Congregation for Catholic Education in 1988. Paragraph one of this document notes that what makes the Catholic School distinctive is its religious dimension and that this is expressed in its educational climate, the personal development of each student, the relationship established between culture and the gospel and the illumination of all knowledge in the light of faith.

A distinctive understanding of the human person underpins a Catholic vision of education and the work of Catholic schools in the area of Religious Education. This can be simply expressed by asking the question – *'who* are we educating the pupil to be as a person?' This is a deeper question than the ones which are normally asked, such as *'what* are we educating the pupil to know and understand?', or what are we educating the pupil to be able to *do?'* While these questions are important they do not go far enough. The Catholic school educates the pupil for full development as a human person and the religious, spiritual and the moral constitute the very heart of such an education rather than being something additional or tangential.

Catholic tradition has always emphasised that parents are the primary educators and that the role of the school is to work in partnership with them. In particular, the Church highlights that the faith development of the child is primarily the task of the family. In providing for the religious dimension of the school curriculum therefore the Catholic school cannot work in isolation. More than in any other area of the curriculum the school must offer Religious Education in a real partnership with parents and families. Of equal importance is the insistence of the Church that Religious Education is part of the dialogue between religious faith and culture, be that the culture or cultures of the pupil and the culture and cultures of the local and global society in which the pupil lives. Religious Education therefore also involves a partnership with the pupils who are invited to become aware of the culture in which they live, critically reflect on that culture and become active agents for cultural transformation. They are supported in this by the culture of the school itself which should provide, as a clear alternative, an experience of a nurturing culture based upon gospel values.

The Catholic school is usually linked in a concrete way to the wider Catholic community either by being a diocesan or parish school, part of a network of schools under the trusteeship of a religious order, or having representatives appointed by the Church on its Board of management or governance. Thus the Catholic school has an essential 'ecclesial dimension' which influences every aspect of its life as an 'educating community'. This is well expressed in paragraph forty-four of *RDECS* which states: 'just as the Church is present in the school, so the school is present in the Church'. Paragraph 101 of this document also draws attention to the fact that 'while school authorities are the ones primarily responsible for the educational and cultural activities of the school, the local Church should also be involved in appropriate ways; the educational goals should be the result of dialogue with this ecclesial community'. Thus a Catholic school is deeply embedded in the work of the wider Catholic community of which it is a part.

In its documentation on Catholic schools the Church uses this phrase 'educating community' in preference to the phrase 'learning community' or 'teaching and learning community'. The phrase 'educating community' highlights the fact that in its work the school is a contemporary, localised manifestation of an educational project with which the Church has engaged for many centuries and in the major cultures and countries of the world. As an 'educating community' the Catholic school is the heir to a rich educational heritage and tradition. It is part of a network of schools across time and geographical location and its 'catholicity' means that it is an 'educating community' within an 'educating community'.

When the above foundational ideas are applied to the curriculum offered by the school we can identify a number of ways, 'formal' and 'informal', 'taught' and 'lived', in which the identity of the school as a Catholic school finds expression in its curriculum.

Religion in the Formal Curriculum of the Catholic School
In terms of the formal curriculum the Catholic identity of the school is expressed in its approach to the 'taught subjects' provided. Of particular importance is of course the provision of Religious Education as a classroom subject taught in a manner which includes an appreciation of the ongoing faith formation and sacramental catechesis of Catholic pupils (this is often referred to as the 'religious instruction' or 'catechetical' element of Religious Education). Whatever else Religious Education aims to achieve, central to Religious Education in a Catholic school is the invitation to the Catholic pupil to deepen her or his understanding of, appreciation of, and commitment to the Catholic faith and the accompanying of the pupil on this journey of faith development. The Irish Catholic Bishops' Conference sees the general aim of Religious Education as 'to awaken people to faith and to help them throughout their lives to deepen and strengthen that faith.'[1]

A distinction is commonly drawn in the general literature on Religious Education between 'educating *about* religion', educating *from* religion' and 'educating *for* religion'. 'Educating *about* religion' adopts a phenomenological or sociological approach to the study of the religious traditions of humankind. The school remains respectful, but neutral, towards the faith of the individual pupil seeing the task of faith development as being the work of the home or the local religious community. Even in those countries, such as France, in which there is no Religious Education proved in public schools, there is a growing realisation that the study of religion as a cultural phenomenon is an important part of the education of the pupil as an active citizen who is tolerant towards religious difference in increasingly pluralist and multi-religious Western societies. In particular, the school can counter the rise of religious fundamentalism, especially when this underpins religiously motivated violence, by promoting inter-cultural dialogue about religion. This can occur across the school curriculum. 'Educating *from* religion' seeks to overcome the detached stance to religious faith that often arises in practice from phenomenological or sociological approaches. This second approach sees the religious traditions of humankind as a gift offered to the spiritual and moral imagination of every pupil to enhance his or her religious literacy. However, once again, the school does not invite the pupil to make a commitment to a particular religious faith but to draw upon the broad religious heritage present within society. 'Educating *for* religion' is deemed by many working in Religious Education outside of the Catholic school context to be inappropriate for the work of the school since it invites the pupil to deeper involvement within the life of a particular religious community.

While the above distinctions between educating 'about', 'from' and 'for' religion may have some usefulness for Religious Education in the State school context, they are of little use in the context of the Catholic school which must synthesize all three aspects in its approach to Religious Education. There is a danger that the compartmentalisation expressed in these distinctions creates a false tension for both teachers and pupils. The synthesis between these aspects of Religious Education must occur in the individual pupil and flows from the nature of 'religious knowing'. Religious knowing is not simply the accumulation of knowledge 'about religion' or 'from religions'. It is not simply an affair of the mind. Rather religious knowing is 'heart-felt' knowing expressed best through the language of the heart – interaction with symbols, analogical and metaphorical thought and story. Just as good food can only be appreciated by being tasted, so too religious faith can only be appreciated by 'being religious'. Religious knowing (notice the use of the verb rather than the noun) calls for conversion to fullness of life on the part of each individual, a conversion reflected in the quality of the relationship between the individual and himself or herself, with other people, with the whole community of life on the earth, and with the ultimate Other whom Jesus has revealed as the Divine Father of all. Religious knowing provides a language with which to articulate such mystery. It has a strong affective and behavioural component being more like learning to dance than learning geometry or algebra. Just as the dancer learns to dance by practicing dancing, or the pianist learns to play the piano by practicing the piano, or the athlete learns to run by rigorous training, so too the religious person learns to know religiously by practising religion and by faith-based person-to-person encounter and sharing. And just as the best dance is danced with others, and the playing of one musical instrument contributes to the more enthralling sound of the orchestra, so too there is an essential communal aspect to religious practice. Religion is not just an individual preference, it is best lived as part of a people of God, a community of faith, the Church. Thus the Catholic school is a place in which religious practice is in evidence and in which pupils are encouraged to practice religion. The academic study of religion is of course important, but this flows from 'faith seeking understanding' and from a philosophy which sees the human person as free, rational and relational. To be effective such Religious Education requires the commitment of teachers who are themselves journeying in faith. Thus while 'common' schools may provide Religious Education or 'religious studies' as part of their curriculum it is the 'religious instruction / catechetical' and 'religious practice' elements that distinguishes the Religious Education provided by the Catholic school.

At primary level in the Irish context the majority of national schools are Catholic schools under the patronage of the local bishop and in some cases also under the trusteeship of a religious congregation or order. The characteristic spirit (or ethos) of all Catholic primary schools is defined in the Schedule attached to the *Deed of Variation for Catholic Primary Schools* (agreed between the Irish National Teachers Organisation, the Catholic Primary School Management Association, the bishops, the National Parents' Council, the Department of Education and the Minister for Education and Science). This includes the statement that 'the Catholic school provides Religious education for the pupils in accordance with the doctrines, practices and tradition of the Roman Catholic Church and promotes the formation of the pupils in the Catholic Faith'.[2] In such Catholic primary schools, the various subjects of the curriculum are taught to each year group of pupils by a single class teacher. There is no specialist teacher of Religious Education. In Catholic and Church of Ireland schools the class teacher therefore teaches the Patron's Religious Education programme. The class teacher in a Catholic school must be the holder of a recognised *Certificate in Religious Education* or *Certificate in Religious Studies* from an approved Catholic Institute of Education. *The Rules for National Schools* (especially nos. 54, 68 and 69) also refer to religious instruction. Sacramental preparation provides the structure for the Catholic Religious Education programme (presently the *Alive-O* series) used in primary schools. A new Catholic syllabus for use in Catholic primary schools is currently under preparation (2008). Once this is in place it is probable that a number of new programmes will emerge. Finally, it should be noted that not only do parents have a right to withdraw their child from the religious instruction provided by the school (and the timetabling of Religious Education in the primary school should allow for this) but they also have the right to request that arrangements be made for the instruction of such children in their own faith by a person nominated by the parents.

At post-primary level new State Syllabuses for Religious Education during the junior and senior cycles of post-primary schooling have recently been provided on an optional basis. These syllabuses provide for a Religious Education programme which is open to pupils of all religious faiths and none. It is important to note that they are taught in a manner which reflects the 'characteristic spirit' or ethos of the particular school. Although these syllabuses are State syllabuses they are not 'secular' or 'detached' and they do not espouse a 'religious studies' approach. Instead they offer the religious traditions of humankind as a resource to the individual pupil in the search for meaning and values (they are closest to a 'learning *from* religion' approach). Their construction is a major achievement and they have given Religious Education in the Republic of Ireland an academic profile that it did not enjoy previously. The up-take of the new syllabuses is greatest at the Junior Certificate level. However, the Catholic school must ensure that the basic assumption of the syllabuses is followed, namely that they are taught in a manner which reflects the 'characteristic spirit' of the Catholic school. While the syllabuses are clear that Religious Education contributes to the search for meaning and values, implementing the syllabuses in a Catholic school is part of a wider curriculum process that contributes to the pupils' search for meaning, values and faith. There is a danger that the State syllabuses, if poorly taught, will lead to pupils simply having information about a range of other religions and having little understanding, appreciation of or commitment to their own religion. *The Guidelines for the Faith Formation and Development of Catholic Students* published by the Irish Catholic Bishops' Conference in 1999 are an important point of reference for Catholic schools in providing for the Religious Education of junior cycle pupils. Senior cycle Religious Education also provides a challenge. Transition year provides an ideal opportunity for an approach to Religious Education which revisits the sacraments (often not addressed since primary school) and invites pupils to make a real commitment to the Catholic faith and to work closely with local parish communities in a range of liturgical and action for justice initiatives. The need for a non-examination approach to senior cycle Religious Education (for the majority of pupils who do not follow the State syllabus for leaving certificate Religious Education) is also being creatively addressed by the provision of new programmes such as *The Inner Place* (Gunning, 2006).

The influence of a religious vision on the curriculum of the Catholic school however extends beyond the teaching of Religious Education as a particular curriculum subject and is intended to find expression in the teaching of all subjects. A religious faith commitment is not just an isolated part of human life but integrates all aspects of what it means to be a fully human person. Religious belief enters into sustained dialogue with every aspect of human culture and life. Within the formal curriculum this dialogue is often referred to as the 'integrated curriculum' which seeks to develop a sense of the sacred in all the subjects taught in the Catholic school. The light of faith is to illuminate all knowledge and growing knowledge is to be accompanied with a deepening of wisdom and insight.

Religion in the 'Informal', 'Lived' Curriculum of the Catholic School

The work of the Catholic school in the area of religion and faith also finds expression outside of the formal curriculum in the lived and living experience of the school as educating community. While such an experience obviously differs from that provided by a parish, since it occurs in an educational context, it remains an experience of a community founded on Catholic faith, values and practice.

The 'lived-curriculum' sustained by the school includes the invitation to pupils and staff to participate in the liturgical life of the school through the regular celebration of the Eucharist and other sacraments either in a school oratory or in the local parish church. Such celebrations should provide an experience of the rythmn of the liturgical year. Prayer should also form a normal part of the daily life of the school. Retreats should be provided for both staff and pupils. The work of the School Chaplain (either full-time or part-time) should be actively supported and resourced by the leadership of the school. The experience of a living educating community also finds expression in the invitation to pupils to actively engage with the work of justice at local, national and global levels. Such initiatives develop a sense of altruism, empathy and solidarity on the part of pupils and staff. It is particularly beneficial if such activities are linked to the work of the wider parish or diocesan community or carried out in partnership with members of other Christian denominations or faiths. The symbolic environment of the school should creatively and imaginatively enhance this 'lived-curriculum'. Resonant religious images, both traditional and contemporary, provide a strong abiding statement of the school's Catholic ethos. It should be as 'normal' for the Catholic school to have an oratory or dedicated 'prayer space' as it is to have a dedicated laboratory for ICT or facilities for sport.

The lived experience of the school should witness to the possibility and challenge of living a virtuous life based upon core gospel values such as love, freedom, forgiveness, self-sacrifice, commitment, hospitality and peace. Central to the Catholic vision of the formation of the human person is the nurturing of character. Character is strengthened not just by the academic exploration of values and narratives in the classroom but by the cut and thrust of every human interaction in the lived experience of the school as a community, within a local community, within a national community, within a global community. It is here that real choices are presented and personal decisions made, that fundamental options are lived, that conscience is formed, that the call to discipleship is answered, that the face of God is revealed in the face of the other.

The Complexity of Defining the Role of Religion in the Catholic School

The practical implementation of the above ideal requires pastoral sensitivity. This vision is of course based upon a notional situation that assumes the Catholic school is supported by committed and practising Catholic pupils, parents and teachers, intimately tied to a local parish or religious order, adequately resourced and funded and free to fully define its curriculum. Such is never fully the case and the Catholic school always adapts to the circumstances in which it finds itself. There is no single model of a Catholic school. The vision of the school, and the way in which it integrates religion into its taught and lived curriculum, will always vary. This is the concrete challenge and the ever-present invitation.

Parental choice is an increasingly important factor to be taken into consideration. In some countries such as the UK, Northern Ireland, Australia, New Zealand, Belgium and the USA, parents have a real choice between schooling systems and can select between a private Catholic school sector and a secular, or multi-religious State schooling sector. In the Republic of Ireland, in which most schools are either denominationally owned or managed and fully State funded, there is effectively no State schooling system at present and parental choice is largely between Catholic schools themselves. The Catholic school is regarded as the local school and many parents select it for reasons other than the place assigned to religion in the curriculum. Parents effectively choose what they consider to be the best school, usually Catholic, for their children. Even when there is a real choice between a Catholic school and a State schooling sector, parents may select a Catholic school because of the academic education it provides or because at post-primary level, it may be single sex, or, in areas of socio-economic disadvantage, because of the way in which the Catholic school through its commitment to the development of its pupils, enhances upward social and economic mobility. Further, parents who are not Catholic often choose a Catholic school because it is a faith-school which promotes values and presents an alternative to a purely secular education. This is often the case for Muslim parents worldwide who select a Catholic school as a faith-school in the absence of a Muslim school being available. As a result there are many Catholic schools, both internationally and within countries such as the Republic of Ireland in which Catholics form a majority within the population overall, in which a significant number of pupils are non-Catholic. Conversely, in many countries there are many Catholic pupils enrolled in State schools.

It is also the case that many parents, teachers and pupils are only nominally or socio-culturally Catholic and exhibit low levels of personal religious practice and religious literacy or are alienated from the institutional Church. With growing secularism in the West, religious literacy and religious culture are declining in many homes and the school can no longer take it for granted that pupils will receive the 'basics' of the Catholic faith from the home or from involvement in their local parish.

It is clear that the manner in which the Catholic school defines the role of religion within its own curriculum differs from place to place. The vision must be negotiated. The inevitable tensions that arise between the ideal and the real can be somewhat reduced if the school communicates clearly with all involved (prospective and existing parents, pupils, teachers) the way in which it is approaching the teaching of religion within its formal and informal, taught and lived, curriculum. In primary schools this can be assisted by the further specification of the standard *Schedule* of a Catholic school by the production of an *Ethos Statement* (also known as 'mission statement' or 'vision statement'). Guidelines for the drawing up of such a statement have recently been completed by the Catholic Primary School Management Association. The process involved is that of creating a shared, ongoing dialogue between the core values of the Catholic school and the school's daily practices which endeavour to embody these values. The statement must be drawn up in consultation with the Patron and Trustees, the Board of Management, the school principal and staff, the parents and the students. The approach to Religious Education is a vital part of the *Ethos Statement*. A similar process should be followed at post-primary level. A helpful document, *Towards a Policy on Religious Education in Post-Primary Schools*, was published by the Irish Catholic Bishops' Conference in 2003.

Conclusion: Some Key Principles
The negotiation between the 'ideal' and the 'real' concerning the approach to religion in the curriculum of the Catholic School must of course be based upon a number of key principles. These can now be summarised as follows:

1. The Catholic school should assign a place of honour to the religious, spiritual and moral aspects of its formal and informal curriculum. It should not be fearful of doing this in a confident and distinctively Catholic way.

2. The Catholic school must work in close partnership with the home and the local Catholic community in providing for a coordinated approach to religious development in which the distinctive contribution of each partner is respected.

3. The Catholic school should sensitively, but insistently, offer an invitation to faith and accompany the pupil as he or she responds to the gift of faith. In an increasingly secularised society the invitation to faith does not presume faith, but neither is faith to be ignored.

4. Priority should be given to helping the Catholic pupil to understand and appreciate his or her own Catholic religious tradition. This involves providing inspiration through the witness of others who are committed to the Catholic faith, and providing a positive experience of Church in the context of an educating community. When supporting the faith development of Catholic pupils in the contemporary Irish context particular attention should be paid to developing a sense of Catholic religious identity, awakening the religious imagination through prayer, symbolic engagement, worship and a creative engagement with biblical tradition, providing a firm foundation for religious literacy (with a particular concern for an appreciation of the culture and tradition of Catholicism and doctrinal awareness), awakening moral consciousness, developing personal responsibility and promoting virtue, and finally developing awareness of, and affiliation to the Catholic community.

5. The School should be a place of hospitality for faith in all its diversity. The experience of faith is the key learning and teaching resource for Religious Education. Thus, while Catholic pupils should always be the first to be welcomed within the community of the Catholic school, pupils who are committed to other mainstream Christian faiths or who are committed to other major faith traditions in a non-fundamentalist way, should also be welcomed. The Catholic school as an educating community is enriched by diversity of commitment of faith; its work is undermined by those who do not value its vision of full human development and who reject the integrating role of the religious, spiritual and moral in such development arguing instead for individualism, materialism and radical secularism.

6. The Catholic school should provide a quality Religious Education and regularly audit the effectiveness of this in both the formal and informal aspects of its curriculum.

7. To facilitate the above, and build consensus among the Board of Management, school leadership, staff, parents and pupils, the Catholic school should develop either a clear *Ethos Statement* or *Policy of Religious Education* which flows from the characteristic spirit of the school as a Catholic school. This should be drawn-up in dialogue with all interested

parties and reviewed on a regular basis as the socio-cultural, ethnic and religious environment in which the school finds itself changes.

8. Staff development is an essential aspect of the effectiveness of the Religious Education provided by the school. In particular this should accompany staff members on their own personal faith journey, provide a deeper understanding of the content and methodology of the Religious Education programme in use in the school and resource teachers of all subjects to facilitate the dialogue between faith and culture and faith and life in the subjects that they teach.

9. The taught curriculum in religion in the Catholic School should be supported in the broader life of the school by the work of a School Chaplain who should be responsible, among other things, for the accompaniment of individual pupils and staff on their faith journey and championing the ecclesial dimension of the life of the school in partnership with the local parish community and the home.

To conclude, the Catholic school should have a clear vision of the outcomes that it intends from its Religious Education curriculum, both 'formal' and 'informal', 'taught' and 'lived'. One way of doing this is to ask the question – 'how would we describe the religiously educated graduate of our school'? In general terms such a pupil is a person who has a life-giving relationship with God, with his or her own 'inner self', and with others, who is aware of the strengths and limitations of the culture in which he or she lives. The graduate journeying towards fullness of humanity with a confidence that he or she is loved and with the ability to cope with religious and moral failure, who has been strengthened in a religious faith that has been personally freely chosen, has a clear religious identity and is aware of, appreciative of and committed to a religious community. Finally, the individual can link personal religious faith to the work of justice, commitment to human rights, civic responsibilities, and empathy and solidarity with all. In short, such a person is 'confidently and responsibly religious' in today's pluralist and multi-cultural Ireland.

Notes

1   Religious Education Syllabus, 1982, p. 4, repeated, Irish Catholic Bishops Conference, 1993, p. 3.

2   CPSMA, 2000, p. 16.

Further Reading

Catholic Bishops of Northern Ireland, *Building Peace, Shaping the Future*, Armagh: the author, 2001.

Catholic Bishops of Northern Ireland, *Proclaiming the Mission: The Distinctive Philosophy and Values of Catholic Education*, Armagh: the author, 2001.

Catholic Primary School Managers' Association, *Management Board Members' Handbook*, Dublin: the author, 2000.

Congregation for Catholic Education, *The Religious Dimension of Education in a Catholic School: Guidelines for Reflection and Renewal*, Rome: the Vatican, 1988. Available on line at http://www.vatican.va/roman_curia/congregations/ccatheduc/documents/rc_con_ccatheduc_doc_19880407_catholic-school_en.html.

Drumm, Michael and Gunning, Tom, *A Sacramental People*, Volume I: Initiation, Dublin: Columba Press, 1999.

Gunning, Tom, *The Inner Place: Senior Cycle Religious Education*, A Curriculum Framework for Senior Cycle, Dublin: Veritas, 2006.

Irish Catholic Bishops' Conference, *Guidelines for the Faith Formation and Development of Catholic Students*, Dublin: Veritas, 1999.

Irish Catholic Bishops' Conference, *Towards a Policy on Religious Education in Post-Primary Schools*, Dublin: Veritas.

Northern Ireland Commission for Catholic Education, *Catholic Education – the Vision, Resource Manual*, Belfast: the author, 2006.

CHAPTER 25

MANAGING THE CATHOLIC SCHOOL

Joseph McCann

What Are We Talking About?

Running a school is a daunting task. To keep a school ticking over daily, ensuring that teachers are content, classes are taught, parents satisfied and students happy, is a challenge. Getting to Friday sometimes seems achievement enough. Might not adding a goal (like 'Catholic') be expecting too much? Firstly, a goal does not add anything new. Our actions have direction even if we do not know it. It makes sense to appreciate what we are doing. It ensures that we know where we are going. Secondly, we define what we mean by 'managing a Catholic school'. The word 'Catholic' will be discussed later, but there are three words for 'manage'. It is important to distinguish them: school *management*, staff *leadership* and educational *administration*.

The first word is *management*. It comes from the Latin for 'hand' and it means 'to control'. Good management handles resources, tools, money, time, space and people competently. Nothing breaks down. Things are in place. Books are available. Rooms are cleaned. Bells are rung, bills paid, doors opened. Members of staff and students do their jobs.

The second word is *leadership* from the old English word meaning 'to guide'. It suggests followers. This word points to the relationship between leader and led. It is a 'people' word. Management is more a 'thing' word. The leader influences, instructs, escorts and directs followers. The leader embarks on fresh starts. The leader takes the organisation in new directions. Leadership is often contrasted with management: implying that it is a nobler and more worthy exercise than the daily grind of bureaucratic paper pushing ...

However, this is not so. Listen to complaints about leaders and managers. Sometimes, indeed, the gripe is about 'lack of leadership', when the organisation has lost its sense of purpose. Yet, very often, complaints concern more mundane matters: routine communication, failure to follow-up consistently, or simple confusion in arrangements. Leaders come unstuck because of failure in management, rather than the other way about. The devil, as they say, is in the detail. It has to be worked out on the ground. That is management. Both words – management and leadership – describe complementary aspects of the same activity.

The third word is *administration*, from a Latin word signifying 'a servant'. Hence, its meaning is to render aid or give support. The administrator looks to see what help or assistance the service brings. It is not good enough for the organisation to be well-arranged, or the personnel well-motivated, if the effect is not really beneficial for others. Thus, the administrator looks outside the organisation to assess where it fits into the whole scheme of things.

Educational administrators, for instance, enquire about the place of education and schools in relation to the state, to the Church, to the community, the family, and for that matter, to industry, leisure, career, and retirement, to life and eternity. So the attribute 'Catholic' or 'Christian', or indeed, any attribute of a religious, philosophical or ideological character for the school, is quite properly discussed as the task of administration.

How Do We Do It?
The manager, leader and administrator who runs a Catholic School requires a range of habits, that is, customary and almost automatic ways of thinking, feeling, and acting. This range comprises five kinds of habit:

- Knowing: your information
- Understanding: your grasp of relationships
- Attitudes: your deeply held feelings
- Skills: what you are able to do
- Behaviour: what, in practice, you do.

The acquiring of these customary ways of living (thinking, feeling, acting) takes much more time than reading an article, or attending a course of lectures, or even achieving an academic award. Just like the habits of teaching, or of playing a musical instrument, or of speaking a language, acquiring the habits of management, leadership and administration is the project of a lifetime.

Specific managerial, leadership and administrative habits fall into three areas. Let us illustrate these with the job of school principal. The first is the *technical* area, in the case of schools at the classroom level. The principal needs to know, understand, like, have a capability and a track record in teaching. So much is obvious. The staff of a school that discovers that their recently appointed principal is not a competent teacher will not be confident about their new regime.

The second area is the *human*, dealing with people. Again, the principal requires the knowledge, the understanding, the feel for, the ability and the reputation for getting on with people and groups, and any failure in this area is damaging. A brilliant teacher may shine in the classroom, but prove quite inadequate when in the staff-room, or the corridor and school yard, and be shown up disastrously while speaking to parents or the community.

The third is the *strategic* area. This will not so easily be recognised inside the classroom, or maybe, in the school. A principal should be a person who has an eye for Catholic education as a whole. This entails that the school principal possesses a facility for analysis and planning; appreciates, and indeed enjoys, issues of policy and governance; is adept in legal, financial, procedural and philosophical matters, and has some successful experience of them.

It may seem that the three areas (technical, human and strategic) parallel the three aspects of managing (management, leadership and administration). This would suggest that a teacher or department head, for example, needs management and technical abilities, the principal needs leadership and human abilities, while the board member or trustee requires administration and strategic abilities.

This is true, to some extent. The aspects of managing and levels of administration may be aligned with the areas of knowledge, understanding, attitudes, skills and behaviour, but only in part. It is always a matter of 'less and more' rather than separate kinds of capabilities at each level of the organisation. Management, leadership and administrative awareness will be called for wherever someone is responsible for organising others to achieve the purpose of an educational system at whatever level they work. So we will use the terms interchangeably, but with some sense of the distinct contribution of each to the challenge of running a Catholic school.

What Are We Doing?
A newly appointed principal or board chairperson can be confused. The complexity of the organisation, from students to teachers, to ancillary personnel, to parents, to the Department of Education, to trustees or sponsors, to the public, to past pupils, to the media, to business interests, can be bewildering. The leader may not see a way to intervene. Then, many managers, leaders and administrators confine themselves to running the school in the way in which it has been run. This makes for uninspired management, timid leadership and undiscerning administration. A helpful template to analyse a school (or indeed, any) organisation – and so see what is going on – identifies four perspectives: *Structure, People, Politics and Culture*. Each of these approaches affords the manager-leader-administrator with a handy point of view from which to see what is happening in the organisation, judge how it is doing, and determine where to change it.

The first perspective is *Structure*. Examining organisational structure is like taking an X-ray of the organisation in order to trace its skeleton. The organisational structure holds the enterprise together. It reveals how the different parts of the organisation are connected, and how each relates to the main business. Each organisation has tasks that it is meant to accomplish. These tasks should directly dictate the roles and functions of the various parts of the organisation. So, for example, the tasks of a school may, generally, be defined as the education of students in academic subjects such as english, mathematics, history and so on, and the pastoral care of individuals as they progress through the school.

In a primary or elementary school, the class teacher is responsible for instruction in all of the subjects to the same pupil group throughout the school year. As the group of children stays together for most of the time, the class teacher is also responsible for their pastoral care. In a secondary school, by contrast, separate teachers deal with different subjects, so that an individual student might have ten or eleven different teachers during a school week. Therefore, the school might organise the pastoral task of the school separately with a structure that cuts across subject departments; for instance, a system of class tutors, or year heads, or some other mechanism.

The second perspective is *People*. From this point of view, organisations are collections of different individuals, each unique in talent, energy, education, age, culture, motivation, disposition, ambition, and so on. Consideration of the 'people' side of an organisation introduces the human implications of decisions, procedures and policies. Here is an example. People join organisations because they have signed contracts. The organisation promises to give them a salary for their work. There is a *quid pro quo* – a 'something for something' exchange. It often happens that managers interpret the agreement between the organisation and the staff member in money and benefit terms alone. Yet people also want other things from organisations: sociability, friendships, a sense of achievement, the esteem of colleagues, recognition from superiors, the opportunity to exercise their professional qualifications, a feeling of contributing to a cause that is really worthwhile. This has been called the 'psychological contract'. In exchange for these rewards, they will expend great efforts in time, energy, ingenuity, and spirit, as the phrase goes, 'beyond the call of duty'.

It is possible for management to so organise their work that the staff members can gain some of those non-monetary rewards. One can imagine the enthusiasm such an approach would release. That is only one example that emerges from an examination of the people perspective.

The third is the *Politics* perspective. Every organisation possesses limited resources. There are only twenty-four hours in the day, so many days in the week.

Buildings, no matter how big, have limited numbers of rooms. Budgets are always too small. Departments could always use another person. And so on. This means that everyone competes for resources – this is the foundation of organisation politics.

Political analysis begins from the different interests in the school: the older staff, the younger staff, the ancillary staff, the year heads, the teachers of various subjects, the senior students, the parents, and so on. Each group wants some or other resource: more time, more space, more money, more people, more attention and profile etc. Effective management assesses the interests represented inside the organisation. This means trying to identify their diverse standpoints, discern which of them would be possible allies; that is, who can be relied upon to support rather than oppose. Only after such an assessment can a management initiative be successful. Otherwise, promising ideas and imaginative innovations will be lost in the fog of politics.

The last organisational perspective is the *Culture* one. This may appear to be more a matter for national characteristics, ethnic differences and tribal peculiarities than for relatively small groups like schools or other organisations. Twenty years or so ago, though, anthropologists noticed that individual organisations generate their own cultures, and management has since taken corporate cultures into account. Each school will have its own language or jargon, its own stories of the past, its own heroes and heroines, its customs and rituals, its ambitions, its 'habits of the heart' expressed in school flag, coat-of-arms, motto, colour and song. Culture has been described as 'the way we do things around here', and it embodies values and virtues, motives and emotions, desires and aspirations, history and destiny.

Culture excites people in certain ways. Culture is what people take for granted. When management wants to affirm or challenge a value, it does well to pay close attention to the culture in which it is working. When assumptions are hidden, structural change, personnel intervention and political bargaining will be to little avail. This kind of problem can be solved only through an astute grasp of culture and an apt use of symbol.

Why Are We Doing It?
Mention of values and meaning introduces the question of ethos. Ethos is defined as the 'characteristic spirit of an organisation'. Just as human beings have character, so an organisation has ethos. A human being acts from a sense of value, a personal meaning, an awareness of the over-all direction and purpose of living. So too, a school management should be conscious of its characteristic spirit, because the 'why' will influence the 'how' and even, the 'what' of what it does. A

Catholic school has a particular ethos: a 'why' that through history has shaped the 'what' and 'how' of Christian education. Christians believe that God created everything on heaven and earth, that knowledge is good, and that human beings have a calling in the world. Christianity encourages young people to be curious, to love learning, to value the truth, to develop their talents, to help the poor and needy, and to co-operate with others in making a more just and more humane world.

Early Christian thinkers adopted the motto of the pagan writer Terence, 'Nothing human is alien to me', and applied it to the task of education. Of all the major world religions, Christianity, and particularly, the Catholic tradition, has invested the most in education, including education in the secular subjects. It has insisted that true knowledge of God is available through the study of God's works, the world and the people in it. This tradition is a rich source of inspiration for Catholic school leaders.

The Christian ethos has been analysed into typical activities, in order to apply it to life. This comes from one of the earliest descriptions of the Christian church in the New Testament *Acts of the Apostles:*

> They devoted themselves to the apostles' teaching and fellowship, to the breaking of bread and the prayers ... All who believed were together and had all things in common; they would sell their possessions and goods and distribute the proceeds to all, as any had need. Day-by-day, as they spent much time together in the temple, they broke bread at home and ate their food with glad and generous hearts, praising God and having the goodwill of all the people. And day-by-day the Lord added to their number those who were being saved. (Acts 2:42-47)

These verses suggest four responses or modes of presence of the characteristic Christian spirit: *Evangelisation, Liturgy, Service* and *Community.*

The first typically Christian response is *Evangelisation,* that is, telling others the good news of Jesus Christ. In a school context, it is Catechesis (the explanation of Christian teaching to Christians) or Pre-Catechesis (the preparation for Christian teaching to those seeking to be Christian), or Religious Education (teaching Christianity – and other religious ideas – to Christians and to those who are not committed Christians).

The second Christian response is *Liturgy,* that is, the worship of God in praise, thanksgiving, contrition and petition. The prayer and formal ceremonies of the Church are always part of the life of the Catholic school. Religious symbols and rituals, such as informal prayer in classrooms, pictures and statues, processions and decorations, all have their role. School is a symbolic spot, and the corridor walls, bulletin boards, and even, the classroom windows reveal much of the spirit of the place.

The third Christian response is *Service*, the exercise of charity and justice as Christians work to make a better world. A school is primarily intended for the formation of young people. Social justice based on Christian principles is a part of the school's teaching and formation. Catholic teachers aim to sensitise their students to poverty, arouse their indignation at injustice, and alert them to the responsibility of those privileged with an education to use their knowledge and talent to improve society, rather than profit from it.

The fourth and final Christian response is *Community*, the easiest to understand and teach. 'They know we are Christians by our love', the hymn says, and the work of God is recognised by the communion among God's people. This is a real challenge for the Catholic school to put into practice, as schools are typically hierarchical and paternal organisations. Yet it is an activity of Christian life that Catholic teachers and students alike endorse as really valuable, socially beneficial, and authentically Christian. In memory, everyone is very grateful if their experience of school life has been truly a community one.

Who Is Doing It?
A final consideration is the *Person* of the manager of a Catholic school. Different philosophies of the leader (as organiser or modeller or practitioner or problem-solver or animator) have in common that the leader's influence is one-way, from leader to follower. Catholic philosophy, however, sees leadership as a service, exercised for the benefit of others, and not for the convenience of oneself or, even, one's colleagues. This means that the leader must be prepared to change the self. Robert Greenleaf was a chief executive of Bethlehem Steel. When he retired, he served as consultant for educational institutions and religious organisations. He formed the conviction that the main leadership problem today is that the leaders were running organisations, not being servants. Only when administrators, leaders and managers personally embody the spirit and ethos of genuine service, will they earn the trust and confidence of subordinates, clients and wider society. Consequently, Robert Greenleaf developed the concept of 'Servant Leadership'.

The leader and manager must be open to personal change and transformation. Management is not a matter of a leader influencing an organisation. It is a two-way process. Just as a teacher who does not learn from the students will not be a very good teacher, so a leader, who is not transformed by the challenge of leading, will not be a good leader. The leader must be vulnerable, and even wounded, before becoming credible. The lesson, to use a school word, is clear for school managers, leaders and administrators. How the leader deals with the internal – as well as the external –struggle will define success.

Further Reading

Adair, John, *The Inspirational Leader: How to Motivate, Encourage and Achieve Success*, London: Kogan Page, 2005.

Bolman, Lee G. and Deal, Terrence E., *Reframing Organisations: Artistry, Choice and Leadership* (3rd ed.), San Francisco: Jossey-Bass, 2003.

Canavan, Noel and Monahan, Luke (eds), *School Culture and Ethos: Releasing the Potential*, Dublin: Marino Institute of Education, 2000.

Feheney, J. Matthew (ed.), *From Ideal to Action: The Inner Nature of a Catholic School Today*, Dublin: Veritas Publications, 1998.

Furlong, Catherine and Monahan, Luke (eds), *School Culture and Ethos: Cracking the Code*, Dublin: Marino Institute of Education, 2000.

Greenleaf, Robert K. *Servant Leadership: A Journey into the Nature of Legitimate Power and Greatness*, New York: Paulist Press, 1977.

Handy, Charles, *Understanding Organisations* (4th ed), London: Penguin Books, 1993.

Kouzes, James M. and Posner, Barry Z., *The Leadership Challenge* (3rd ed.), San Francisco: Jossey-Bass, 2003.

McCann, Joseph, 'Improving our aim: Catholic school ethos today' in Ned Prendergast and Luke Monahan (eds), *Reimagining the Catholic School*, Dublin: Veritas Publications, 2003, pp. 157–167.

CHAPTER 26

SACRAMENTS OF INITIATION:
HOW WE COME TO BELONG!

Maeve Mahon

Every religious tradition has its rites of initiation, some much more elaborate than others, but all with the same purpose. These rites provide a means of entry, a way of becoming a member, of belonging, to a faith community. In the Catholic tradition the rite of initiation is a sacramental one and at present it has three distinct yet intrinsically linked stages or movements. These stages consist of Baptism, Confirmation and First Eucharist. In the Western European context, in particular in Ireland and the United Kingdom, the vast majority of people initiated into the Church are children and so this chapter will concentrate on the process with which we are most familiar, that is, baptism of infants, followed by the celebration of First Eucharist at age eight and Confirmation at age eleven or twelve. This process is relatively straightforward. Children are baptised at the request of parents with very little preparation being required by parishes. The preparation for Confirmation and First Eucharist is still mainly school-based and age related. The main purpose of this chapter is: to explore briefly the history of the sacraments of initiation; to outline present practice in a manner that takes account of the many anomalies that may arise and finally to suggest a way forward that offers an opportunity for children, parents and parish team members to be more actively involved.

While infant baptism followed by the celebration of First Eucharist and Confirmation is the norm in Ireland and the United Kingdom, it is important to note that the Rite of Christian Initiation of Adults (RCIA) has become an increasingly important part of parish life as more and more adults decide that they want to belong to the Church. This rite has tremendous potential to enrich, enhance and renew the life of a parish community and deserves further debate and study. However for the purposes of this chapter we will focus on the initiation of children and in particular the sacraments of Confirmation and First Eucharist.

One of the first things that we noticed is that this order of celebration differs from that outlined above. The reasons for this are many and complex. We will begin by attempting to outline briefly how we have come to this point in the story of Christian initiation. If we are clear where we have come from, it is always easier to move forward.

The Story So Far
After the death and resurrection of Jesus those who believed in what he had said and done quickly began to gather together, to tell stories about Jesus, to share all that they had with each other and perhaps most significantly, to do what he had done at the last supper. These early Christians soon discovered that they needed to find ways to welcome other people into their community. They developed a rite of initiation with three key elements, each of which is directly linked to events in the life of Jesus.

The first part of the rite was baptism with water. This baptism has definite resonances of Jesus' baptism by John (Lk 3:21-22; Mt 3:13-17; Mk 1:9-11). Jesus' baptism by John was radically different to all others conducted by him since it was during it that Jesus was confirmed to be the Son of God. The second part of the rite was a confirmation of the baptism by an anointing with oil. For the early Christians this anointing was seen to indicate the presence of the Holy Spirit who was gifted to the apostles at Pentecost. The final part of the rite was an invitation to the table to share in the Bread of Life and in a powerful echo of what happened at the Last Supper to 'do this in memory of me'.

It took a long time for these early rites of initiation to become what we now know as the *sacraments of initiation* or Baptism, Confirmation and Eucharist. For four centuries the three sacraments were always celebrated together at the Easter Vigil and the local bishop presided. This ritual was very different from our present experience. Baptism was usually by total immersion. The catechumen, the one preparing for initiation, undressed and walked into the baptism pool. They were then plunged three times into the water in the name of the Father, Son and Holy Spirit, by the deacon or deaconess. The catechumen then walked out of the pool on the other side and was wrapped in a new white garment. This was a very visible sign of leaving behind the old way of life and beginning again in Christ Jesus. Wearing the new white garment, clothed in their garment of salvation, they were taken to the local bishop who then anointed them with perfumed oil. This oil was rubbed into their hair and was a pungent reminder of the new way of life they had chosen. Finally they came to the table to share in the Eucharist with the rest of the community.

Over a number of centuries significant changes took place. Infant baptism became the norm under the influence of the teaching of Saint Augustine (354–430 CE) on original sin. Baptism was therefore less about conversion and more about the need to be forgiven. In a time of high infant mortality it became necessary for babies to be baptised almost immediately after birth and so the connection with the Easter Vigil came to an end. In this situation it became the custom for priests to baptise and for the bishop to confirm. The bishop could not be present at every Baptism and so Confirmation became a separate celebration. For many years Eucharist was still linked to baptism and even babies were given the Bread of Life or in later years a taste from the chalice. In the Eastern Orthodox Church this practice continues today. In the Roman Catholic Church this practice continued until the thirteenth century however after the Fourth Council of Lateran (1215) it was largely discontinued and First Communion was received at fourteen or fifteen years of age. By this time the Bishop had usually visited the parish and confirmed the children and so the original order of Baptism, Confirmation and Eucharist remained unchanged.

Almost a hundred years ago, in 1910, Pope Pius X in a decree called *Quam Singulari*[1] changed the order in which the sacraments are celebrated. He pointed out that children were ready to begin receiving the Bread of Life when they attained the age of reason, which was then deemed to be seven. He also acknowledged the lifelong nature of learning, which meant that children were not required to understand their faith fully before they could celebrate the sacrament for the first time. In an extremely enlightened approach he suggested that if they could recognise the difference between the Bread of the Eucharist and ordinary bread they were ready. This decree also had the effect of ensuring that First Confession was celebrated prior to First Holy Communion and that Confirmation was celebrated later, somewhere between the ages of eleven and eighteen. Since Vatican II (1962–1965) there have been some successful attempts to restore the original order of celebration in dioceses across the world. This has not yet happened in Ireland.

Present Practice in the Irish Context
Now that we have outlined, albeit very simply, the journey so far, we must take stock of present practice. At the beginning of the twenty first century one of the main challenges facing those involved in Catholic Religious Education is how best to prepare children and young adults for the sacraments. It might be comforting to note that this challenge is not peculiar to Ireland but it must be stated that this island has its own inimitable peculiarities in the area of sacramental preparation and these certainly shape the experience of preparation and celebration for people today. The most significant of these peculiarities is the almost completely school-based nature of the preparation and indeed the

celebration. Coupled with this is the fact that the vast majority of Irish primary schools are Catholic and yet the growing Irish population is becoming more and more secular in its outlook and practices. Ireland also has a small but increasing number of children from the other faith traditions enrolling in Catholic schools and the challenge to be welcoming and inclusive while still maintaining a Catholic ethos is most keenly felt at times of sacramental preparation. The intriguing paradox of parents who no longer consider themselves as members of the Church but who wish to have their children baptised, confirmed and brought to First Eucharist is another factor in the increasingly challenging environment in which teachers prepare to celebrate these sacraments. Finally we must acknowledge the isolation being experienced by teachers in the classroom. It is clear from recent surveys that teachers are more than willing to teach religion but that they are finding the work of sacramental preparation very difficult as they struggle with what they perceive to be a lack of support from home and parish.[2]

The schoo-based nature of sacramental preparation made a lot of sense in Ireland thirty or forty years ago when there was a strong sense of belonging to both parish and Church. Belief in God and the practice of faith ran as a deep undercurrent to daily living. Our lives were punctuated by the faith we professed. Expressions of this faith were manifest in regular attendance at Mass, blessing ourselves as we passed the church and graveyard and saying prayers at home. Home, school and Church operated synchronously and what was taught in one place was generally supported and re-inforced in the others. So when it came to preparing for sacraments it was only natural that the teacher would undertake the work of helping the children to learn what they needed to know. However this work made sense and became real for the child when they saw the adults in their lives practicing their faith each day in their lives at home and in the Church. The faith they were learning about in school became real in the lived experience of home and parish.

It is clear to anyone living in Ireland today that this homogenous grouping of home, school and parish no longer exists. In 1999 Martin Kennedy was commissioned to research the National Catechetical programme in Ireland.[3] In the report that followed he coined the phrase 'islands apart' in an attempt to articulate children's experience of religion and Religious Education. He found that children inhabited three different and distinct islands of home, school and parish. He further opined that for a large majority of children the island of school was the only place of positive religious experience. The island of home was generally positive towards and supportive of Christian values but had little room for offering children experiences of their faith. The island of parish was often associated only with the activities or clubs engaged in by the children. The findings of this research supported the belief that the growing secularisation of

Irish society is having a profound effect on children's religious experiences and nowhere is this more evident than at times of sacramental preparation.

The lack of connection between home, school and parish as outlined above needs to be addressed as we move forward and seek to find new ways of preparing children for sacraments. The abdication of the work of sacramental preparation to the teacher in the classroom is clearly not the best model that we can offer. Teachers do a wonderful job in preparing children for sacraments and we are very fortunate that they continue to be willing to undertake this work despite the increasingly difficult environment in which they operate. The sacraments of initiation that we celebrate with these children are essentially about how we come to belong to a community of faith. Like all the other sacraments they are not magic and do not work automatically. Sacraments require an active faith, a desire to respond in that same faith. Sacraments also offer us opportunities to deepen our faith. How then can we realistically expect a teacher to prepare children who have never been to Mass, who have no experience of prayer or any other form of religious activity outside the classroom, to celebrate these sacraments?

The school-based preparation of children creates a context where preparation for sacramental celebration depends on being in a particular class in a school system and takes absolutely no account of faith experience and commitment. In fact if we are honest, the rationale for changing the celebration of First Eucharist from First to Second Class was to accommodate those families who were not attending mass and who had no commitment to Church. It was easier for teachers to prepare children who were a year older. Indeed in many instances much of the teacher's work of sacramental preparation consists of teaching children when to sit and stand and how to behave in the Church environment. This is necessary because many of the children have never visited a Church prior to coming to school. However moving the celebration from First to Second class took no account of families who are faithful members of the Church and whose children are more than ready to celebrate the sacrament at seven years of age. These children are, in fact excluded from the table for a year longer than they need to be simply because the rest of their peer group are not ready. The inclusion of a shorter Rite of Confirmation in the National Catechetical Programme (*Alive-O* 7 and 8) indicates that in some parishes there is a need for a separate Rite of Confirmation that is celebrated outside of Mass. This shorter rite is a perfectly legitimate form of celebration and may deserve to be considered as an option for more parishes in the future. However, it raises the question as to why such a departure from the norm has recently occurred in some parishes with very little apparent reflection or conversation as to its appropriateness as a response to the difficulties experienced in the celebration of the sacrament. These difficulties are well known and consist mainly of noisy, irreverent congregations who are unfamiliar with the church environment and the celebration of the Eucharist. The celebration of a shorter form of the rite may, on the surface, appear to offer a solution to these concerns yet it does not address the critical underlying issue of the celebration of sacraments in isolation from a lived faith experience. This attitude to the sacraments is perhaps best summed up in the apocryphal tale about the child who was missing from church on her First Communion day. When the teacher finally contacted the parent she was told that they had been delayed at the hairdresser and had decided to skip the church and go straight to the hotel where they were having a meal. This may or may not be an urban myth but the sad truth is that it is all too easy to believe.

A Way Forward

So how do we address these attitudes to the sacraments of Confirmation and First Eucharist? At the moment I suggest that the best model for us seems to be one which creates a context within which we can begin to prepare to celebrate sacraments in a more inclusive way. In order to do this we need to shift some of the emphasis away from the school and the teacher as we challenge and encourage parents and parishes to become more actively involved in the process. This means that we are still asking teachers to help children understand and know about their faith. They do this through the Religious Education programmes designed for use in the classroom. The difference lies in the involvement of parents and parish team members who are invited, encouraged and challenged to participate in the preparation through a parish-based pre-sacramental programme. In designing any such programme I believe that the following four principles may be useful:

- The sacramental preparation of children is the responsibility of the home, school and parish working together in partnership.
- The work of sacramental preparation begins long before the day of the sacramental celebration.
- The celebration of First Eucharist and Confirmation are sacred and important moments on a long journey of faith development. They must not be seen as an end in themselves.
- The sacramental preparation of our children must always be seen as one element of the broader task of whole community catechesis.

Do This in Memory[4] is one such programme designed on the above principles. It is a parish-based preparation programme for First Eucharist that has been in use in Ireland for the past four years. The programme was originally developed in Kildare and Leighlin and Ossory and offers a model of co-operation between home, school and parish that may be useful as we begin to find new ways to prepare for sacraments. The Sunday mass is the main focus of a programme that is continued at home through the use of various resources. The commitment to come to Mass once a month is a key element because it offers the opportunity to model the importance of participation in the life of the community into which the child is being initiated. Parents are also invited to promise to pray with their child at home, to read the gospel with them and to engage in many different activities that will make the promises they made at Baptism real in their lives.

After four years some data is now available that runs contrary to the perceived wisdom that religion was not a generative issue for parents. In fact the vast majority are delighted to be asked to make such a commitment. For some it is an opportunity to reconnect with the Church perhaps for the first time since their child's baptism. For those who have continued to come to Mass and be involved in their community it offers some help in the challenge of handing on the faith in a culture that gives very little recognition to this task. There is a small percentage that resist the invitation to become involved and yet continue to want their child to be present on the day of First Eucharist. How we respond to this group is perhaps the most challenging question for the future.

Situating the programme in the Sunday Mass highlights the role of the community in handing on the faith and encourages those present to be more actively involved in the process of welcoming new members to the community. There is direction given on the importance of making the church and indeed the mass itself as child-friendly and welcoming as possible. This does not mean that we have jobs for every child in the group but rather that we make every effort to remember that there are children present when we gather to celebrate. The readings are chosen from the Children's Lectionary and so are in simpler language. The homily is directed to the children and therefore may be listened to more closely by the adults. Children are involved in presenting the gifts of bread and wine.

The programme begins in September and hopefully this signals the need for reflection on the importance of the decision to present a child for the sacrament. It also begins to address the growing belief that we are simply preparing for a one-day event. The emphasis of the programme suggests that we are preparing for much more than that, in fact we are preparing children for their twenty-first and one hundred and first communion and beyond. This also allows us to raise the question of why a parent would present a child for the sacrament if they have no intention of bringing them to share in the Bread of Life for many Sundays to come. Anecdotal evidence also shows that teachers find their job easier because the children are more familiar with the church and with the prayers of the mass.

Conclusion

Any pre-sacramental programme is only a small step in beginning to address the challenges that face us as we prepare to celebrate sacraments with children. There are those who believe that it is time to bring in rules and regulations and make it more difficult to celebrate sacraments. Yet there is also a perception that we have overdone the rules and regulations and that now we need to think more creatively while still holding onto our integrity. Can we begin with an invitation that was also offered by Jesus to 'come and see'? This invitation might be extended at least a year in advance of the celebration and posted with the question 'Come and see what the parish has to offer you and your child as you prepare to celebrate the sacraments.' Be clear, unequivocal and unapologetic about the programme of preparation and the level of commitment expected. Invite parents and children to make a choice to opt in to the process and see where this leads. This is not quite an open door policy, but it is leaving the door open and we must do this because we have already baptised the vast majority of these children. They are already members of the Church. We have a responsibility to help these children and their parents continue their faith journey and to experience a true sense of belonging to the community of faith in their local parish. There is of course an underlying presumption in that invitation, that we have something to offer and therein lies the biggest challenge to the parish community. We need to create environments of welcome, offer hospitality and provide liturgies that are truly celebrations of God's love for us. When we invite people in we want them to stay and when they choose to walk away we have to ask ourselves 'why?'

This chapter has endeavoured to chart the journey that has led us to this point in our sacramental story. It has outlined the present situation in the Irish context and suggested a model for preparation that is a first step in making our sacramental celebrations more about the sacred and less about the secular. It is clear that we are beginning, albeit slowly, to face up to the challenges that sacramental preparation and celebration offer in our rapidly changing culture. Over the past four years I have been privileged to speak about these challenges at diocesan and parish gatherings all over Ireland and I sense a mood for change. The gatherings in question consisted of different combinations of the interested parties: priests only, parents only and the most interesting and life giving of all, those to which all three partners were invited, parents, teachers, priests and parish team members. At these gatherings many hard questions were posed. However one of the comments made over and over again was that when offered the opportunity to get involved both parents and parish stepped up to the plate and accepted the challenge with a heart and a half. Talents for leadership and ministry were uncovered when the invitation was offered and accepted. The communities were enhanced by those who came. Some even stayed after the celebrations were over.

Notes

1   *Quam Singulari*, Decree of the Sacred Congregation of the Discipline of the Sacraments on First Communion, Pope Pius X , 1910.

2   *Teaching Religion in the Primary School: Issues and Challenges*, Dublin: INTO, 2004.

3   Martin Kennedy, *Islands Apart*, Dublin: Veritas, 2000.

4   Maeve Mahon and Martin Delaney, *Do This in Memory*, Dublin: Veritas, 2004.

Further Reading

Drumm, Michael and Gunning,Tom, *A Sacramental People*, Volume I: Initiation, Dublin: Columba Press, 1999.

Guzie, Tad, *The Book of Sacramental Basics*, New York: Paulist Press, 1981.

Sheridan, John Paul, *Promises to Keep: Parents and Confirmation*, Dublin: Veritas, 2004.

Turner, Paul, *Confirmation: The Baby in Solomon's Court*, revised, Chicago/Mundelein, Illinois: Hillenbrand Books, 1993, 2006.